London's Olympic Legacy

Gillian Evans

London's Olympic Legacy

The Inside Track

palgrave
macmillan

Gillian Evans
Department of Social Anthropology
University of Manchester
Manchester, United Kingdom

ISBN 978-0-230-31390-3   ISBN 978-1-137-29073-1   (eBook)
DOI 10.1057/978-1-137-29073-1

Library of Congress Control Number: 2016949488

© The Editor(s) (if applicable) and The Author(s) 2016
The author(s) has/have asserted their right(s) to be identified as the author(s) of this work in accordance with the Copyright, Designs and Patents Act 1988.
This work is subject to copyright. All rights are solely and exclusively licensed by the Publisher, whether the whole or part of the material is concerned, specifically the rights of translation, reprinting, reuse of illustrations, recitation, broadcasting, reproduction on microfilms or in any other physical way, and transmission or information storage and retrieval, electronic adaptation, computer software, or by similar or dissimilar methodology now known or hereafter developed.
The use of general descriptive names, registered names, trademarks, service marks, etc. in this publication does not imply, even in the absence of a specific statement, that such names are exempt from the relevant protective laws and regulations and therefore free for general use.
The publisher, the authors and the editors are safe to assume that the advice and information in this book are believed to be true and accurate at the date of publication. Neither the publisher nor the authors or the editors give a warranty, express or implied, with respect to the material contained herein or for any errors or omissions that may have been made.

Printed on acid-free paper

This Palgrave Macmillan imprint is published by Springer Nature
The registered company is Macmillan Publishers Ltd. London

For my daughters—valiant warriors well-versed in the ways of the world—they bring me honour.

Preface

On the eve of the 2016 Olympic Games, in Rio, this is a book about London's Olympic legacy. I have written it, because I believe that London will become the planning-for-legacy test case city, against which all future Olympic cities will be judged. London has done better than any other host city to plan legacy uses for its Olympic Park, and sporting venues, both in advance of the Games, and in the few years immediately after. However, London still has lessons to learn, even while it also has lessons to teach the world, and especially other future host cities, about how to plan better for Olympic legacy.

Mine is a story about the drama at the heart of London's legacy planning operation between 2008 and 2012, a drama that centres on the fight for the political prestige of the Olympic legacy, and the struggle of a few determined individuals to take seriously and to honour the promises made in the Olympic bid to transform the heart of East London for the benefit of everyone who lives there. The heartening thing was to witness, inside the Olympic Park Legacy Company, the practical power of a vaguely left-wing political idealism inspired by, or in tune with, the promises of Ken Livingstone's Olympic bid, and Tessa Jowell's framing of the legacy challenge.

From the privileged perspective of a researcher on the inside of the planning operation, I capture here, a sense of the unfolding drama as attempts were made in London to harness the juggernaut of Olympic development, and its commercial imperative, to the broader cause of meaningful post-industrial urban regeneration and transformation in the Olympic host boroughs of East London.

The book is very purposefully written for a public audience, because the public deserves to know what happened with their money, what went well, and why, what failed, and for what reason, and who some of the champions of legacy were, and still are. I want the general public to be able to follow me on what is a difficult journey into the heart of a complicated situation, so my language is plain. At the end of each chapter, I include a list of ten suggested readings for those who wish to find out more, and some of those books, or articles, will lead the interested reader further into the considerable body of academic work that now exists about London 2012, and which is also a legacy of the Games.

I make no attempt to be exhaustive in my treatment of the Olympic legacy; there are many themes and issues that I do not cover at all. My focus is very specifically on the life and death of the Olympic Park Legacy Company, which came into existence in 2009, and met its end just before the Games in 2012. I speak here of unsung heroes behind the scenes, and the battle they fought, to hold fast to a set of principles they believed in, even when it often looked like all hope was lost. I describe too some of the scandals and controversies, and I shine a light under the carpet where one or two things have been swept. I do this not to be sensational, but to allow for reflection on how things were done, and what could have been done better. I show how there was nothing straightforward about the attempts to plan for, and deliver an Olympic legacy from the 2012 Games, and despite outward appearances, the whole thing was an experiment, from start to finish, in how to do something that had never in the world been done before.

There is no need for any future host city to reinvent this wheel, and part of the legacy ought to be that host cities learn from each other about how to ensure that the multi-billion pound spectacle of the Olympic Games yields more than the flow of international capital accumulation to cities competing for world-class status through 4 weeks of fabulous sport. There is the potential, instead, for the development of a new model of twenty-first-century urban transformation in which dispossession, disrespect, and violence towards those people living in relative poverty is rendered globally unacceptable, and replaced by the attempt to solve the problems of urban marginality through an unfailing commitment to regeneration properly conceived.

My hope is that this book will provoke members of the public, policy-makers, academics, students, other host cities, and people who were part of London's Games and legacy-planning operations, to want to add their own perspectives about London's continuously emerging Olympic legacy. I have created a website for this purpose, so that an ongoing archive can be produced and enlivened by the contesting voices whose multitude it was impossible for me to capture. I encourage you to contribute.

www.gillianevans.co.uk

Gillian Evans
Manchester, UK

Acknowledgements

This book has been a long time coming. To a certain extent, I got lost in the labyrinth I describe here, and it has seemed a surreal eternity, trying to find my way out.

For their endless patience, I want to first thank my editor at Palgrave Macmillan, Harriet Barker, and her assistant Amelia Derkatsch. For its constant support, and the inspiration of that intellectual and collegiate environment, I wish to express my gratitude to the Department of Social Anthropology at Manchester. This research was funded by an RCUK Fellowship, which was hosted at the Centre for Research on Socio-Cultural Change (CRESC) at the University of Manchester. I am grateful to CRESC Directors, Professor Penny Harvey, and Professor Mike Savage, without whom this project would have been impossible.

David Ryner, thank you for long walks, engaging conversation, and for giving me a way in. For their openness to my project and for their tolerance of my presence, I am indebted to the Olympic Park Legacy Company, and all who worked there between 2008 and 2012. I am especially grateful to Tom Russell, Richard Brown, and my boss at OPLC, Emma Wheelhouse (now Frost), whose support for my project, along with the rest of the Comms. Team, was tireless. Thank you to Paul Brickell for teaching me about urban planning as a problem-solving process, and to Adam Williams at EDAW (AECOM UK) for taking a chance and allowing me to witness something of the master-planning process.

To the many organisations and people of East London who opened their offices and homes, and took time to talk to me, I am most grateful. And, finally, deepest thanks to Sola, and to all my family and friends, for keeping the faith and waiting for me to emerge on the other side of this undertaking.

Contents

Part I	The Old World	1
1	Enter the Labyrinth	3
2	A Herculean Effort	19
3	Future-Scaping	51
4	Fighting to Be Heard	75
Part II	The New World	101
5	Odyssey Becalmed	103
6	The Doldrums	129
7	Unruly Suitors	151

8	An Interminable Saga	181
Afterword: Summer 2015		207
Bibliography		221
Index		227

Acronyms

BNP	British National Party
BOA	British Olympic Association
CPO	Compulsory Purchase Order
CSR	Comprehensive Spending Review
DCLG	Department of Communities and Local Government
DCMS	Department of Culture Media and Sport
DLR	Docklands Light Railway
ECDST	Economic, Culture, Development, Sport, and Tourism Committee
ELBA	East London Business Association
EMT	Executive Management Team
EP	English Partnerships
EU	European Union
GLA	Greater London Authority
GOE	Government Olympic Executive
HCA	Homes and Communities Agency
IAAF	International Association of Athletics Federations
ICA	Institute of Contemporary Arts
IOC	International Olympic Committee
KCAP	Kees Christiaanse Architects and Planners
LCS	Legacy Communities Scheme
LDA	London Development Agency
LETF	Local Area Training Framework

LLDC	London Legacy Development Corporation
LLV	Lower Lea Valley
LLVRS	Lower Lea Valley Regeneration Strategy
LOCOG	London Organising Committee of the Olympic Games
LSC	Learning and Skills Council
LTGDC	London Thames Gateway Development Corporation
LVRPA	Lea Valley Regional Park Authority
MAA	Multi-Area Agreement
MDC	Mayoral Development Corporation
MOL	Metropolitan Open Land
NEM	New East Manchester
OAPDF	Opportunity Area Planning Development Framework
ODA	Olympic Delivery Authority
OPRSG	Olympic Park Regeneration Steering Group
PCT	Primary Care Trust
RDA	Regional Development Authority
RSL	Registered Social Landlord
SPAD	Special Adviser
SPV	Special Purpose Vehicle
SRB	Single Regeneration Budget
SRF	Strategic Regeneration Framework
TAG	Teviot Action Group
TELCO	The East London Communities Organisation
TfL	Transport for London
UDC	Urban Development Corporation
UEL	University of East London
URC	Urban Regeneration Company

Part I

The Old World

1

Enter the Labyrinth

© The Author(s) 2016
G. Evans, *London's Olympic Legacy*,
DOI 10.1057/978-1-137-29073-1_1

When London won the right to host the 2012 Olympic and Paralympic Games we promised to create a sustainable legacy for London and the UK. We are committed to ensuring that this legacy—the imprint that the 2012 Games make on the UK—begins to take shape now and lasts until well after 2012.

Staging the Games has meant different things for different host cities—for Barcelona the driving force was regeneration, for Sydney it was about putting itself on the map as a global destination, for Athens it was about redefining itself as a modern European city.

Our ambition for 2012 is different again. We will not only regenerate one of the most deprived areas in the UK but we will also seek to spread the magic of 2012 outside the Olympic Park so that all communities in the UK feel the benefits of hosting the London Games. If everyone joins in and takes part, we can make the following happen:

1. Make the UK a world-leading sporting nation
2. Transform the heart of East London
3. Inspire a generation of young people to take part in local volunteering, cultural, and physical activity
4. Make the Olympic Park a blueprint for sustainable living
5. Demonstrate the UK is a creative, inclusive, and welcoming place to live in, visit, and for business

These are ambitious aims. Government alone cannot deliver them… This document is therefore a call to action—we have five years to make these commitments a reality, but only your imagination, commitment, and involvement can make it happen.
　　　　　　　　　　　Tessa Jowell, Olympics Minister, June 2007
　　　　　　　　　　　　　　　　Our Promise for 2012[1]

---

[1] Public sector information licensed under the Open Government Licence v3.0 (https://www.nationalarchives.gov.uk/doc/open-government-licence/version/3/) https://www.gov.uk/government/uploads/system/uploads/attachment_data/file/77718/Ourpromise2012Forword.pdf Accessed 5th May 2015)

For the Blairites, Canary Wharf was the high temple of aspiration where you could arrive with nothing, and leave with everything. The trick for them was to open up the channels that could allow that to happen for anyone who aspired. Going there and praising it was to purge yourself of Old Labour: redemption.

David Ryner,
Assistant to the Special Adviser of Tessa Jowell, Olympics Minister

November 2008

Canary Wharf, 21st floor: the Barclays Building. Double-sided banks of computer workstations form the digital production lines of the tripartite London 2012 Olympic planning operation. Here are LOCOG,[2] ODA,[3] and the Legacy Directorate of the Mayor of London's Development Agency (LDA).

One hundred metres below in the vast, light-filled marble foyer of the Barclays headquarters, hip-hugging pencil skirts and stiletto heels clamour for attention as women-who-mean-business cut a swathe through a stream of men in sharp suits. Among people who still believe they are going up in the world, I wonder what I might wear to work. It is the autumn of 2008, and, in bad taste, I long to embody what seems most exotic—the swagger of women-in-banking-in-four-inch-heels, whilst only a few skyscrapers away Lehman Brothers comes tumbling down.

Here, in the Legacy Directorate, the women are smart-casual, prepared to be colourful; they dress down The Wharf's more formal mode of attire, and I follow suit. These are public sector professionals, who break with bureaucracy in the powerhouse of private enterprise and hope for urban development as usual even though a financial crisis is a shock wave in their world. At first, this seems like a strange marriage: Olympic planning wedded to high finance at Canary Wharf, but the Games cost £2 billion to stage and, of course, Barclays is in bed with sport.

Surprisingly softly spoken, of gentle demeanour, and somewhat embarrassed about the heights from which he surveys his domain, which lies to the east, as far as the eye can see—from the towering offices at Canary Wharf to the valley of the River Lea—almost at the limit of London, Tom Russell, Group Director of the Legacy Directorate, worries, at our first meeting, that the perspective, from on high, is somewhat 'colonial'. He knows full well that the local population is not enamoured of Canary Wharf, and he is anxious to bring the legacy operation down to earth,

---

[2] London Organising Committee of the Olympic Games. LOCOG's task is to raise £2 billion in private sponsorship to pay for the staging of the Games.
[3] Olympic Delivery Authority. The task of the ODA is to construct the Olympic Park, the sporting venues, and associated infrastructure.

to take it to the East End where he feels it belongs. Tom emphasises that unless the people who are to be affected by it feel a sense of 'ownership', the project of urban regeneration will fail.

Equally as surprised as I am by the encounter between us, Tom gracefully plays the game of pretending that a range of strategic manoeuvres, and contingent circumstances, do not underlie the possibility of our meeting. My requests for research access have already, twice, been rejected lower down the managerial hierarchy, but I have been stubborn, and refused to take no for an answer. Against all the odds, and third time lucky, here I am: foot in the door, trying to reassure Tom that I am a manageable risk. Neither of us declares it, but each knows full well that London 2012, and its legacy, are highly politically sensitive projects. The Games are a huge gamble, and the legacy stakes are high; billions of pounds of public money are in the combined pot, and reputations of senior political figures hang in the balance. After a few weeks of sporting spectacle, no matter how successful, London simply cannot afford to be left with a mountain of debt, a white elephant for a stadium, and a set of sporting ruins to add to its urban landscape.

Tom is polite. He does not mention that were it not for the whisper of support for my research from the office of Tessa Jowell, Minister for the Olympics, this meeting would not be taking place. Tom spares me from having to explain the connection, but David Ryner, an assistant to the Olympic Minister's Special Adviser (SPAD), is a fan of my work, and a 'friend in high places'. Our conversations about his lifelong interest in politics and my research about working-class London have left a caffeine trail through the parks, and gallery cafes of central London, and grown a friendship out of the sociological imagination.

Introducing me to the concept of 'legacy' over a cappuccino at the Institute of Contemporary Arts (ICA), David tests my concentration with labyrinthine drawings of connections between vested interests and describes a complex world condensed in a surplus of acronyms. He refers to the Olympic legacy as 'the holy grail of Olympic politics', something elusive, and never before seen; I am confused, but intrigued, and David is amused. He wonders what sense an anthropologist might make of it all.

Whitehall and Westminster

Inspired, but always exhausted, David complains of late nights and ridiculously early mornings. These are dedicated to digesting books, reports, and other documents so that, in turn, more documents can be produced in a never-ending supply of up-to-the-minute ministerial briefings. Concisely expressing the who-is-who and what-is-what in a constantly changing and potentially hazardous political terrain, the briefing papers are part of the stuff of government, a kind of sculpting material, if you like, which creates structure, form, and a degree of stability in an unpredictable and ruthlessly competitive environment. The papers prepare Tessa, or TJ, as she is affectionately described by those closest to her, to tackle forthcoming speaking engagements, committee meetings, and appointments, and to stand a chance, therefore, of sustaining her position in the Cabinet at Whitehall where she is currently not a voting member and only 'attending' when her responsibility is on the agenda.

David explains that since 2007, when Gordon Brown replaced Tony Blair as Labour leader and Prime Minister, Tessa has already been demoted twice. This is no surprise, since Tessa is renowned for having been an ultra-Blairite, but with Gordon Brown now at the head of the Cabinet table at Whitehall, and control over the Olympic budget spread across government departments (and ring-fenced), it is going to be a long climb back for Tessa. Because of this, her political instinct and charismatic competence must appear effortless; it is vital that Tessa is seen to act with certainty, and to speak with confidence and diplomacy about the issues she is accountable for.

Hoping for constancy, if not political advancement, Tessa relies on her SPAD, and the small team of civil servants in her private office, to help her to adapt to the constant change of events in and outside of Whitehall, and Westminster, and to maintain equilibrium in her immediate environment. Up to speed, one step ahead, on top of the game, Tessa's team must keep her 'on message', supplied with the right 'lines' at the right times, speaking the right words to the right people. This is either to court media attention, so that Tessa can accrue status, and prestige unto herself, or to keep the press and its constant critical scrutiny at bay. And, the Diary Keeper must do her duty: David describes her as the sentinel who guards Tessa's power and influence; she juggles appointments, keeps time-wasters at bay, and ranks those who would be in conversation with Tessa.

Giving me a taste of what it is at Whitehall to thrive on behind-the-scenes machinations and ruthless competition not just with rival political parties, but also with politician-colleagues and other government departments, such as the Department of Communities and Local Government (DCLG), led by fellow 'Blair-Babe', Hazel Blears, David intimates at the intrigue through which any minister's closest team maintains a delicate balancing act; like medieval courtiers (or, in their own minds, the career operatives akin to US political drama, West Wing), SPADs must toe the party line, be seen to be collectively, even fiercely, loyal—in this case to the Labour Party, and within it, to some extent, to its deposed Blairite faction—and, at the same time, they must advance the minister's individual political career, supporting Tessa in her efforts to cultivate relations with key allies. Her fortunes are those of her team too, which, David explains wearily, keeps those closest to Tessa labouring tirelessly, like devoted workers, for a queen bee.

David describes how dependent Tessa is on being fed the right information at the right time. She, like all ministers, worries about not being able to keep her own finger on the pulse and relies completely on a trusted team to keep her in the know about 'what is happening now' and to maintain a meaningful boundary between herself and clusters of non-partisan civil servants lower down the hierarchy who comprise, for example, the Government Olympic Executive (GOE) housed at the Department of Culture, Media and Sport (DCMS) where Tessa was once Secretary of State. All information that is fed up the chain of command is filtered, and the dreadful, somewhat paranoid job of double-checking everything wears David and the SPAD down. Nevertheless, they are relentless in their determination to decipher what Tessa needs to be informed about. At any moment her political reputation could be jeopardised, which means no stone can be left unturned. Whatever Tessa decides to do or say reflects not just on the reputation of the projects she is responsible for overseeing, but also on the collective government of the UK, which makes for a tense, but thrilling atmosphere, a heady mix of power and political passion. And still, David stresses, Tessa is not satisfied: like all ministers (and perhaps members of inner courts everywhere), she dreams of being more in touch with the reality that exists beyond Whitehall and Westminster, external to the busily prepared briefing papers that interpret the 'outside world' for her.

Distant from, but desperate to gauge the overall public mood, ministers yearn to know more about how their policies are received and what their standing is, as personalities, in a media-driven world. Externally, popularity equates with political influence—adding up to more votes for the party and the chance of staying in power, or gaining national decision-making powers—and internally, it leads to a greater likelihood of personal promotion and the perpetual promise of a place as a voting member at the Cabinet table. David explains how the quest for popularity and political relevance leads to a determination in Tessa to find ways to gauge the ongoing reaction of East Enders to the London 2012 project. She is adamant that this development should not, like Canary Wharf, become 'an oasis of wealth in a sea of deprivation'; this has to be, Tessa insists, a project that is 'being done with and not to' the people of the East End of London. The problem, though, which David and I are all too aware of, is the long history, in the UK, of less-than-successful attempts to transform the fate of post-industrial urban neighbourhoods suffering from chronic decline. And, worse than this, there is the lesson to be learned from development projects the world over, which, no matter how well meaning, most often fail miserably to achieve their goal of improving the lives of people living in relative poverty, whilst succeeding, nevertheless, to secure the middle-class mortgages of those who manage the proliferating structures of bureaucracy that projects like these tend to reliably produce.

The Holy Grail of Olympic Politics

The more David helps me to understand about how things work inside the world of central government, and how precarious the task is of trying to build political influence, the more I come to appreciate how putting her name to the London Olympics, and their legacy, has been a huge political gamble for Tessa. Hence the metaphor of 'holy grail'—heroically, Tessa has committed herself to a seemingly impossible quest and started down a treacherous path, littered with pitfalls. Needing to resurrect her political fortunes, she had no choice but to strike out boldly, hoping to inspire confidence in her mission and win allies to her cause. The trouble, however, is that everyone in Whitehall knows the uncomfortable truth, which is not just that the unthinkable has happened—the failure of the financial markets, and everything that implies in terms of the withdrawal of private investment, and the beginning of an era of extreme caution about credit—but also that the recent sporting and cultural history, in London, of Labour's support for recent mega projects tells a tale of doom and disaster that cost Tessa's predecessor his career. The Games too have a problem-prone backstory, and every post-Games analysis of Olympic legacy tells a tale discouraging enough to dampen the enthusiasm of even the most ardent sporting fanatics.

Tessa's rhetoric about the Olympic legacy raises a rallying cry to London, and the nation, to which cynics in the press are expected to respond raucously, as if politics were no more than a Punch and Judy show, but from inside Whitehall itself, it is obvious too that the odds are stacked against Tessa. It is going to be an uphill struggle for her to convince other ministers, politicians, and even her own civil servants, never mind the British public, that an Olympic legacy is a realisable ambition. One senior civil servant spells it out for David, emphasising that 'the overwhelming majority of civil servants live in the suburbs, are conservative with a small c and would not be seen dead in East London'. It is hard to imagine them being optimistic about, or fully 'on board' with the legacy direction of travel Tessa has so wholeheartedly committed herself to.

Although Tessa is in denial about the growing list of reasons not to feel optimistic about Olympic legacy, David admires her for her idealistic insistence that London 2012 must not be just another story about the futility of top-down government intervention. Not just because her own popularity depends on their success, but because Tessa believes in what ought to be the transformational potential of The Games, she desperately wants people living local to the emerging Olympic Park, in East London, to be amenable to the Olympics, and for the event to deliver a long-term positive difference. This is true even though all the evidence about the gains from previous Games suggests that the Olympics makes a minimal social or economic difference to the populations living locally to their staging and indeed is often more likely to be destructive, for example, in terms of the disruption caused by population displacement.

Undeterred, Tessa hopes against hope that a successful Olympic Games and a meaningful legacy might provide part of the solution not just to the seemingly intractable problems of poverty in East London, but also to the problems of the Labour Party, as it begins to work out what it might mean to stay in power. Post-financial crisis, David and I discuss how after more than a decade in government, and just over a year into Gordon Brown's leadership, the question that currently vexes the Labour Party, at the end of 2008, as it begins to turn its attention to the next General Election, is whether or not Gordon Brown's bailout of the banking system can be turned from a liability into political capital for the party.

Here is a Labour government working out how to hold the centre ground and to go on courting the middle-class without further alienating its traditional working-class voters. Despite its best efforts at fiscal fixing, the financial crisis has thrown into stark relief the folly of New Labour's refusal to turn back the tide of Margaret Thatcher's Conservative legacy of an abandoned industrial and manufacturing economy, deregulation of the financial markets (a sector of the economy that is now going into global recession, causing private investors to flee from high-risk public projects, like the Olympic Games), and a wholesale switch to the knowledge and service economy. This has left many of those urban, predominantly working-class populations for whom industry, and manufacture, was once life's blood, floundering and struggling to adapt to a future whose promise is yet to be realised. Feeling abandoned, or taken for granted by New Labour, these are the people whose problems now define the post-industrial condition of Britain and whose great lament about Labour explains the phenomenal rise, in this first decade of the twenty-first century, of the far-right British National Party (BNP). Such are the economic and political challenges of the current moment whose contours define the cultural landscape and provide a less-than-beautiful backdrop against which will unfold the glittering spectacle of London's Olympic Games.

Meanwhile, in an attempt to regain power, the Conservatives, in the person of David Cameron, are ramping up the rhetoric. Keen to stake their claim to the centre ground, they are presenting themselves as 'One Nation' Tories—'Caring Conservatives'—concerned not just about preserving the profits of big business, and shoring up the privileged position of the establishment and the country's elites, but also about developing policy solutions for the problems of poverty and disadvantage.

Because the civil servants are impartial, they are, David explains, largely indifferent about the prospect of a change of government. It matters to them only insofar as it would be harder for them to serve a Conservative minister who might be leading on a downgraded Olympic agenda. For the SPADs, in contrast, the very thought of conceding power to the Conservatives fills them with dread. David describes how it makes them determined to find even more time and energy in the effort to rally to the cause. And so, at the end of 2008, with a brand-new Conservative mayor already ascendant, this year, over Britain's capital city, the drama of London's Olympic legacy unfolds on a stage set by an eternal war between mortal enemies. If Labour loses a General Election before 2012, it hands over to its rivals, like booty to pirates, all the potential prestige to be gained from groundbreaking projects, like the Olympics, initiated under a Labour watch.

London Government

The first sign of a change in the political tide, and the reason for new confidence in the Conservative Party nationally, has been the election of Boris Johnson as the Mayor of London this year. David stresses the importance of the political articulation between central and regional governments, in this case London government, which has become more complicated this year because the Olympics is a London project, but it has central government backing and oversight. This means that with Labour in power nationally, and a Conservative politician leading over London, the tussle is likely to intensify over which party, and which leading personality, will be able to lay claim, should things go well, to the political prize of the Games, their London legacy, and after that, to London itself.

As early as 2002, Ken Livingstone, London's first, and controversial, elected mayor had thrown his weight behind the idea for an Olympic Games in East London. He was backed from the beginning by his right-hand man, Neale Coleman, who David describes as a 'fixer', a description I associate with gangster movies featuring characters like Harvey Keitel, in *Pulp Fiction*—the fixer is the guy who knows how to get things done, stay out of sight, clean up the mess, and, in this case, lend to his boss an enviable understanding of the mechanics of how London works as a city. Livingstone had championed the Olympics at a critical time when it needed high-level political advocates, and it was necessary to win support, and finance, from Westminster for the development of a credible bid. It is hard to imagine how excruciating it must have been for Livingstone to lose the mayoral election and to be forced to hand over control of the capital city, and the political credit that goes with its projects, to a new Conservative mayor.

In the 1980s, when he was socialist leader of the Labour-dominated Greater London Council (GLC), Livingstone had refused to lie down and quietly take the Conservative assault on public spending. At the height of Margaret Thatcher's powers, Livingstone was notorious for provoking the Conservative prime minister. She responded mercilessly, abolishing the GLC in 1986, and thus depriving Livingstone of the seat of his power and influence. London then suffered a 14-year hiatus during which time the city suffered an overall lack of strategic direction. This persisted until the beginning of the millennium when 3 years after their landslide victory in the General Election of 1997, the New Labour government created the Greater London Authority (GLA), and the first office was established of an elected mayor of London.

Livingstone had been elected London's first mayor in the year 2000, standing, in defiance of New Labour, as an independent candidate. He quickly responded to advice from urban academics that the spatial trajectory of the city's demographic and economic growth should be to the east and put up no resistance when the idea was brought to him (by a team led by the dedicated London councillor Richard Sumray), to bid for an Olympic Games located in East London. The proposals chimed with the mayor's plans, and clarified and focused strategic thinking about the development of London as a whole.

Livingstone retained his leadership of London in the mayoral election of 2004, and in July 2005, the success of London's Olympic bid was announced in Singapore. Livingstone was ecstatic, not because of the sporting possibilities, but because winning the Games for London meant securing billions of pounds of funding from government for the regeneration of East London. Three years of planning for the Games and their legacy have followed, a planning operation that has given the mayor's LDA a special Olympic purpose.

Equally as unconventional as Livingstone, and with a talent for making himself conspicuous, Boris Johnson—a consummate self-publicist and a popular political clown—charmed the people of London, and to Livingstone's great regret, and with a lament rising from the Labour Party internally, took the Conservatives into power over London with the largest personal mandate in British political history. Johnson immediately made good on his electoral strategy, which campaigned on a ticket of 'transparency', and made Livingstone's LDA the political football of a fierce contest for power. Amid much talk of 'openness', disclosure about public sector costs, and decision-making for London, Johnson fulfilled his election promise to clean out the top tier of London governance and put the LDA under a microscope. He immediately ordered a forensic audit that was symbolic of the destruction of the reign of influence of his infamous predecessor whose allegiance, to what David Ryner describes as an 'old-school style of ethnic politics' at the GLA, spelled the end for Livingstone as he went down defending to the very last, his much-maligned Director of Equalities, Lee Jasper.

A Way-In

Determined to find my own way in to the LDA's Olympic Legacy Directorate to study the evolution of London's Olympic legacy from the inside out, I had pinned my hopes on Boris Johnson's new 'culture of openness', and suggested to gatekeepers, after my straightforward request for research access was refused flat out, that keeping me 'in-house' might be advantageous; I could tell both sides of a complex story, on the one hand explaining the perspective of politicians and urban change-makers (those leaders and regeneration professionals tasked with the responsibility to plan and deliver on the Olympic bid's promise to make the Games the means to bring about physical and socio-economic transformation in East London), and on the other, I could try to give voice to the East End, which is to be most affected by that change. Being on the inside, I insisted, would allow me to invest in a long-term, gradual analysis of the development of legacy, properly understood, rather than frequently sharing a one-sided and inevitably partial outsider's account with my contacts in the broadsheet press, who are only too happy to be cynical about the Olympics, and to court controversy.

This kind of hard-talk worked to the extent that curiosity about me was aroused at the Legacy Directorate. A very quick Google search probably generated enough information to prepare a cautionary briefing paper. In 2006, when it was still a taboo, under New Labour, to talk about social class in Britain, I had published my research about the post-industrial Docklands of Southeast London. The book had generated a national debate about the position of the white working classes in the UK and caused quite a furore. Was I the kind of social scientist the LDA could afford to allow behind the scenes? And anyway, should I not, as an anthropologist, be 'out there', studying 'cultures' and 'communities', instead of preoccupying myself with politicians, urban planners, and regeneration professionals? I imagine the perception was that I might pose a greater risk, uncontained, out there 'in the wild', doing my own thing, saying whatever I liked. Having caused just enough confusion, and concern, to get my foot in the door, I waited, while the decision to exclude me permanently was passed further up the hierarchy.

It was at this decisive moment, when it was beginning to look like all hope for my research was lost, that David Ryner invited me to speak about my research with Tessa's SPAD. Potentially prepared to listen to anyone who could help Tessa to understand how the development of Olympic legacy was, or should be unfolding outside of the endlessly manipulated narrative that was being fed to her at all levels, the SPAD was constantly on the lookout for fresh thinking on the subject. The invitation to come in and talk about my research proposal was a godsend. Immediately, I called the Legacy Directorate to let them know about the invite for me to talk to Tessa's private office about my work. I emphasised how much I would like to be able to report to Tessa on the status of my proposal to conduct research, not just in the East End but also inside the Legacy Directorate itself. And hey presto, within hours, I received an email advising me of an appointment to come in and talk about my research ideas to Tom Russell, Chief Executive and Group Director of the legacy operation.

Thus, I come to find myself, in November 2008, in Tom Russell's office on the 21st floor of the Barclays Building at Canary Wharf, playing the game of politics, wondering what to wear to work, and feeling the effects of a nascent network of connections that can be made to matter. I reassure Tom that I am genuine in my desire to tell a balanced story, and determined to reveal the human face of urban regeneration. Convinced, or rather, cajoled, and curious to know what lessons could be learned from having an academic, and especially an anthropologist, on board, Tom sanctions my future presence in the Legacy Directorate and invites me to scrutinise the work he directs. Lifting his hands in an open gesture, he issues the imperative: 'Tell us about ourselves!'

Suggested Reading

Evans, G. (2012). Materializing the vision of a 2012 London Olympics. In V. Girginov (Ed.), *The Routledge 2012 Olympics special issue*. New York: Routledge.
Evans, G. (2006). *Educational failure and working class white children in Britain*. Basingstoke, Hampshire: Palgrave Macmillan.
Horne, J., & Whannel, G. (2012). *Understanding the Olympics*. New York: Routledge.
Kavetsos, G., & Szymanski, S. (2011). National well-being and international sports events. *Journal of Economic Psychology, 2010*(31), 158–171.
Mangan, J., & Dyreson, M. (Eds.). (2013). *Olympic legacies intended and unintended: Political, cultural, economic, and educational*. New York: Routledge.
Poynter, G., & MacRury, I. (Eds.). (2009). *Olympic cities: 2012 and the remaking of London*. Surrey: Ashgate.
Poynter, G., Viehoff, V., & Li, Y. (Eds.). (2015). *The London Olympics and urban development: The mega-event city*. Surrey: Ashgate.
Ryan-Collins, J., & Sander-Jackson, P. (2008). *Fools gold: How the 2012 Olympics is selling East London short, and a 10 point plan for more positive local legacy*. London: New Economics Foundation.
Scott, J. (1999). *Seeing like a state: How certain schemes to improve the human condition have failed*. New Haven: Yale University Press.
Tallon, A. (2010). *Urban regeneration in the UK*. New York: Routledge.

2

A Herculean Effort

© The Author(s) 2016
G. Evans, *London's Olympic Legacy*,
DOI 10.1057/978-1-137-29073-1_2

Regeneration is like pushing an enormous boulder up a mountain: it takes hundreds, if not thousands, of people to lend their shoulders to the weight, and at any moment, the boulder might fall back down, and then, the effort must begin all over again.
Tom Russell, Chief Executive and Group Director of
the Legacy Directorate, LDA.
November 2008

Tom Russell has a reputation as a man who can deliver, and London is determined, against all the odds, not to fall short on its Olympic legacy promises. He was poached by the LDA from Manchester and took up his post as head of London's legacy team in December 2007. At a time when there had been fears, behind the scenes at the LDA, that existing strategy for legacy planning was not focused or commercially minded enough, and, in fact, all the signs were that the LDA was at risk of failing miserably to pull together a coherent legacy strategy, Tom had been persuaded to head south, stabilise the situation, and galvanise efforts to move forward what he described as 'the most exciting regeneration project in Europe'.

In Manchester, Tom had successfully overseen the conversion, to viable legacy uses, of the sporting venues built to host the 2002 Commonwealth Games. Most famous among the tenants of the new sporting facilities in Manchester was Premier League football club, Manchester City. Their first game in the converted athletics stadium was played in 2003, just 1 year after the end of the Commonwealth Games. Such a rapid realisation of legacy was a remarkable achievement. This was not without controversy, but it avoided what everyone feared, which was an un-used, costly to maintain, white-elephant-of-a-stadium built with £112 million of taxpayers' money.

The Manchester Model

Manchester had been first, in the UK, to come up with the idea of an urban mega-event legacy and had proved that it could lead the way in sports-led urban regeneration. So, when Tom Russell was appointed to a leading role at the LDA, it became obvious that with respect to Manchester, London was simply trying to follow suit.

Apart from securing tenants for the sporting venues, Tom was responsible in East Manchester for commissioning and putting into motion a strategic vision for the overall physical, social, and economic transformation of over 2500 acres of run-down post-industrial city. The scale of the challenge was unprecedented: this was an area almost twenty times the size of Manchester city centre. The idea was for a Strategic Regeneration

Framework (SRF) that could provide coherent guidance about core principles of development and key objectives for the social and economic, and not just physical (built environment and infrastructure) regeneration of the whole area. The SRF was to be the means for the coordination of key work, and funding streams, to do with integrated spatial planning, housing market renewal, stimulation of employment, and improvements in education and public spaces in a mainly housing-led regeneration strategy designed to transform derelict industrial land to new uses.

The SRF set out ambitious plans for the development of individual neighbourhoods, each of which was to have its own new identity, but which were to be transformed one by one, like a patchwork quilt, in relation to both specific local neighbourhood histories/geographies and integration into a vision for the rebranded whole called New East Manchester. Intended to be flexible, the SRF in East Manchester had to be adaptable to changing market conditions, with the pace of change speeding up, or slowing down, depending on flow of finance. And, it was experimental with a long-term remit: 10 years worth of planning and development funding were secured in each phase to allow sufficient time for new initiatives to be tried and tested.

Tom Russell's commitment to, and emphasis on, trying to find ways of working in partnership with local residents in East Manchester was a reflection of the revised urban priorities of a late 1990s newly elected Labour government. The express intention was to move beyond the urban policies of the preceding Conservative era, because whilst the Urban Development Corporations (UDCs) of the 1980s had certainly been successful, to some extent, in making urban brownfield (derelict) post-industrial sites available for regeneration on terms that were extremely lucrative for property developers and financial corporations, specific examples, such as the London Docklands development, proved that urban regeneration limited to dramatic physical transformation and extreme prioritisation of business interests completely failed to yield benefit to local working-class neighbourhoods whose residents were still reeling from the catastrophic effects on their lives of industrial and manufacturing collapse.

In the Docklands, for example, people living difficult lives on nearby housing estates had to cope with rising levels of unemployment at the same time as they bore witness to the birth of a thriving new financial quarter for the benefit of white-collar workers. The problem was that the Docklands generated billions of pounds of wealth from skyscrapers that turned their backs on the realities of impoverishment in the east of London. Unquestionably, the Docklands project exposed the inadequacies of the 'trickle down' model of urban development, and, without falling out of love with the idea of entrepreneurial public–private business partnerships, New Labour endeavoured to find a different way to do things in Britain's post-industrial cities. The problem of inner city, urban poverty remained hard to solve and high on the political agenda.

All Aboard

Tom Russell explained, when we first met, that a key part of his job as Chief Executive of the Urban Regeneration Company (URC), New East Manchester (NEM), had been to maintain political alliances with local, regional, and central governments; he also had to cultivate relationships with property developers and business interests, as well as with landowners and stakeholders—all those various organisations and agencies with a stake in the project whose work or interests were implicated in, and affected by, the broad scope of the regeneration company's ambitions and projects. Tom emphasised that through the attempt to coordinate all these vested interests with the aspirations for change of the local population, he not only had to try to get everyone on board with the regeneration project, but also to keep them on board. The challenge was how to fit and hold together what counted, at the local level, as problems in desperate need of attention, with what mattered, at the level of the city, in terms of important strategic ambitions.

The Regeneration Company was, then, not only the means for crafting a vision and narrative that could inspire and rally a whole range of recruits to the cause, balancing commercial priorities with 'community' interests, but it was also a kind of vehicle—a time machine, if you like—for driving forward this assembled network of interests towards a new future, a collective way ahead forged out of the effort to reshape and redefine the space of the eastern edge-lands of the city.

Tom clarified, at our initial meeting, that the problem for any URC is to acknowledge the challenges of life in the post-industrial places that are to be transformed; to understand the cynicism of people demoralised by decades of disappointment; and, still, to be determined to create a feeling of possibility and optimism. After that, the difficulty is to sustain the sense that something exciting is finally really happening, that meaningful change really can take place, and that the promise is to be trusted, of a different and better way forward. The task, Tom stressed, lies not so much in getting started (although that is hard enough, because the political will and vast sums of public funding have to be put in place, and then sustained), but in keeping on going in such a way that none of the critical mass of vested interests who have been brought on board with the project, to support and lend momentum to the new plans, will ever want to abandon ship, because this is always disastrous: it jeopardises the whole mission by destabilising the balance of interests.

Understood like this, and even with an awareness of all the deficiencies and endless disparagement of grandiose top-down state-led projects, it is important to appreciate that though it may be hubris, there is something heroic about people who dare to try and risk their reputations by trying (however misguided they might be) to create the conditions for change and attempt to bring a new urban reality into being; it requires a Herculean effort—a legendary struggle that risks all the time, being nothing more than a futile, Sisyphean frustration.

The Scale of the Challenge

It is immediately obvious to me on being invited into the Legacy Directorate in London that Tom Russell's track record in Manchester, his way of leading, and community-minded but commercially realistic vision for the legacy are a source of inspiration. This reflects an idealistic sense, in some parts of the directorate, that the promises of Ken Livingstone's Olympic bid are to be taken seriously, and that it is OK to be enthused by the wildly idealistic pledge that 'the most enduring legacy of the Olympics will be the regeneration of an entire community [East London] for the direct benefit of everyone who lives there'.[1]

---

[1] London Olympics Candidature File, Volume 1, p.19.

Just as much as elite athletes preparing for Olympic feats in the sporting venues, there is an atmosphere on the top floors of Canary Wharf, in the tripartite Olympic planning team, of a race against time. There is a busied intensity, with everyone applied in different ways to the superhuman effort, not only to prepare for the Games, but also to make them make a difference to what happens after 2012. The seriousness, excitement, and camaraderie are palpable, of people brought together by what they perceive to be an extraordinary undertaking.

In time, I come to think of this elite group of Olympic change-makers as fellow super-achievers to their sporting colleagues; they work tirelessly and with devotion on the Olympic project, trying to achieve in just a few years what would normally take a decade or two, of dogged urban development to pull off, and, in their spare time, many of them are also doing phenomenal things—climbing the world's mountains, one by one; cycling from London to Amsterdam in a weekend, just for fun; regularly running marathons for charity; and generally, driving themselves to the limit of what is possible. Not all of them, but enough employees for it to be remarkable are energised by an incredible, seemingly indefatigable, slightly intimidating, enthusiasm for life.

Part of what comes to fascinate me in the Legacy Directorate is the difference between those people who seem to operate with an understanding that the point of their privileged position, working on one of London's most prestigious development projects, is to be of service to the public and to deliver on what London has promised in its Olympic bid and those who appear to have an elitist sense of excellence for its own sake, and who, for that reason—of competitive superiority—are determined to be involved with, and make the Olympic project a success. The idea of a high-flying, self-serving elite, which competes against itself for supremacy, goes well with the combination, at Canary Wharf, of Olympic planning and high finance; here is a place where urban regeneration expresses exclusivity in economically lucrative and spatially segregated terms, and it is easy to ignore and to be disdainful of the poverty on the doorstep as if it were a cultural contaminant—something that the elite needs to fortify itself against—rather than address as a shared problem to be creatively and intelligently integrated and resolved, as the city develops and transforms.

Those regeneration specialists, like Tom Russell, who express a contrary perspective of public-minded duty and who worry that the view from the skyscrapers of Canary Wharf is 'somewhat colonial', trouble the metropolitan outlook of a self-satisfied urban elite. Tom was adamant when we first spoke that for the project of urban regeneration to work, the Legacy Directorate and some of its staff would have to be brought down to earth. This would happen quite literally, Tom explained to me, when the offices are relocated, as, he said, they must be from the lofty heights of the Barclays Building to the grounded realities of Stratford, close to the emerging Olympic Park, where the people of East London can more properly start to claim some 'ownership' of the project.

Listening to Tom, I get the impression that he fully expects, as time goes on, for the promise of community benefit to be jeopardised, and, because he feels so strongly that this would lead to the failure of the project overall, he seems to be suggesting that the legacy promises are in need of protection, custodianship even. My sense is that there may be a fight—tooth and nail—to honour the commitments that have been made—and I feel as though Tom has given me the 'heads up' to look out for those people in the Legacy Directorate who are equal to the task, as time goes on, of defending the promise of Olympic legacy.

In the face of public scepticism and media cynicism about the Olympic Games in general, and about London's Olympic legacy in particular, I am rather taken aback by the impression I get, inside the Legacy Directorate, of a significant number of people driven by a sense of public-service duty and the privilege of a once-in-a-lifetime opportunity to take part in the Olympic dream of outstanding human achievement. This is nothing like what I expected and it is not at all straigthforward; it is not like the easy idea on the ground that the government must inevitably be in the service of capitalism, and high finance, with the state heedlessly imposing its grand ideas on the people, grabbing land for nothing other than exploitative, commercially lucrative purposes. Something much more complicated and more interesting is happening here.

Against the background of financial recession and imminent political upheaval, a more-than-usually tense dynamic is unfolding between those whose imperative it is to promote the private interest, as if it were synonymous with their own self-advancement, and those who are determined to harness commercial interests to a broader promise and, thereby, take on a greater challenge, which, for the sake of public good, is to defend and drive forward Tom Russell's version of regeneration-proper.

Forward Moving Momentum

With 'community' carrying a heavy rhetorical load at the heart of Olympic Legacy in London and the commercial imperative high on the agenda, all the signs, at the end of 2007, when Tom Russell was appointed were that he was exactly the right kind of dynamic leader and experienced set of hands to try to put the Manchester model to work. His task was to devise and mobilise a strategic vision—a way of action—a battle plan, if you like—to fight for, and navigate a course towards a business-minded but public-focused Olympic legacy in London. In effect, Tom was brought in, because London needed its own URC, and an SRF, to lend momentum, give direction to, and provide guidance for its post-Games plans.

The SRF would describe and prescribe how physical development of Olympic lands could be integrated with the goals of social and economic change for the local government boroughs of Newham, Hackney, Tower Hamlets, Waltham Forest, and Greenwich, which are host to the Olympics in East London. The URC, solely dedicated to legacy planning and delivery, would be independent of the LDA, and at arm's length, therefore, from central government and the mayor, which ideally would give greater confidence to the public and private sector in the negotiations about the purpose and benefits of their involvement with and investment in the project.

What Tom could not have fully anticipated, when he took up his post at the end of 2007, is that 2008 would bring the election of a charismatic Conservative Mayor of London. This is a mayor who has no time for his left-wing predecessor's, Ken Livingstone's, pet project—the LDA—and this creates a problem for Tom, because the shadow of doubt which Boris Johnson has cast over the LDA as a whole raises the more specific question of what the role of the agency and its dedicated staff will be, down the line, in the planning and delivery of London's Olympic legacy. The success of Boris Johnson also puts on the table the possibility of a change of government at the next General Election, with a potential shift of sympathies becoming evident in the nation, from Labour to Conservative. And, as if this was not a difficult enough set of political problems to negotiate, there is also the matter of a global financial crisis, which will have serious economic and political consequences, not least of which, in terms of urban transformation, will be a withdrawal, across the board of financial credit and an increased reticence in investors and developers to commit funds to new projects. There will also be uncertainty about how to deliver 'community' benefit when even commercial returns will now be in jeopardy.

In the face of these immediate pressures, Tom Russell's quiet and composed demeanour is nothing short of extraordinary; there is no sense that he is fazed by the demands of his high-profile post, or that he is particularly nervous about recent political and economic disturbances. The secret, he explained at our first meeting, is to 'hold your nerve', to remain focused on long-term outcomes, whilst also being prepared to adapt, in the short-term, to constantly changing circumstances. One way or another, Tom emphasised, the project must keep moving forward. Knowing what he does about how urban regeneration works and what a painstaking, precarious endeavour it is, I understand that it would be ridiculous for Tom to lose his cool and risk being thrown off course by every immediate danger. Precisely because Tom expects the way ahead to be treacherous, he maintains a sense of calm, because panic is counterproductive to the stability that the progression and forward-moving momentum of the project requires.

The London Plan

Just like in Manchester, one of the main difficulties facing Tom Russell in London is to try to articulate strategic ambitions at the level of the city, with what counts as a problem at the local level in the East End. The Legacy Directorate must ensure that the locally specific regeneration arising out of the Games contributes towards the London Plan. This is the policy document that sets out the mayor's strategic priorities for London's spatial development over the next 20–30 years.

One of the main issues, in London, is how to plan for the growth in its population. The city is already a vast global metropolis, with a population, in 2007, of 7.56 million, which is expected to grow year-on-year, until, by 2030, the number of people in London will be around 10 million. This suggests a need for at least an additional 32,600 homes annually, but because the spatial development of the city has to happen within the confines of Abercrombie's green belt, which encircles the city, there is a pressing problem of where and how to locate additional housing for a growing population. Part of the solution is to increase housing densities in new developments, but this is never a popular solution, since people like and need space; another answer is to redevelop the land that was formerly dedicated to industrial use, and that has fallen into post-industrial decline. Most of this land in London is in the east of the city, and it makes sense, therefore, for East London to be the new centre of London's growth.

There is also an additional strategic imperative given by the fact of East London being the place where most of the disadvantages are concentrated to do with long-term pre- and post-industrial poverty. This means that a person living in the East End of London is more likely, than anywhere else in England, to have to learn how to be resilient in the face of challenges relating to their health, housing, living environment, employment, and education. Tom Russell cannot afford to ignore these realities of life in the areas surrounding the Olympic Park, because part of the original promise of the bid was to make the Games make a difference to the stark reality of entrenched poverty in East London.

Whilst the new housing in the future Olympic Park will necessarily provide a percentage of units for social rent, and part-buy/part-rent, this will only go a tiny fraction of the way towards addressing local need for more affordable housing of all kinds. This creates conflict, because what people would like the Olympic legacy to deliver to London and what it can realistically achieve locally are ambitions that exist in tension, and this tension has to be continuously managed.

Even though the development of new neighbourhoods in the Olympic Park might go some way towards addressing the need, in East London, for more 'aspirational housing', so that those young people and families that do well for themselves do not immediately feel compelled to leave the area once they are better off, there is no denying that there is a chronic shortage of social housing for low-income tenants. There is a constant danger, therefore, about which Tom Russell is keenly aware, of losing the goodwill and support of the people and community organisations living and operating local to the site of the Olympic project, and of this mistrust developing into a popular resistance movement that could, ultimately, jeopardise the whole legacy project.

Part of the reason that the development of the SRF is so important, then, is that it provides the opportunity for the articulation of mayoral plans for localised urban development, in this case in the post-Games Olympic Park, with policy aspirations for improvement in health, environment, education, housing, and employment in the local government boroughs that are host to The Games in East London. This matters because a strong statement of intent about the desire to make the development of the post-Games park make a difference to the areas that surround it, mitigates the risk of a negative legacy building up. Negative legacy slows progress by creating friction and the potential for conflict over divergent interests. Because it matters to him that ownership of the project is claimed by East London, Tom has given the job of designing the SRF to the Olympic Host Boroughs Unit, which makes sense, because it is highly unusual, but imperative for the different boroughs of local government, in East London, to work and collaborate together, overcoming their differences for the sake of the shared endeavour of harnessing positive benefits from Olympic-related growth and development.

Post-Industrial Economic Policy

A further risk to the legacy project, which is rarely ever discussed, is the taken for granted economic policy of post-industrial Britain. The assumption, following on from the decline of industry and manufacture in the UK, is that the Thatcherite investment in the service economy, and in particular, in letting financial capitalism do as it pleases, will continue to pay off (even allowing for periodic and increasingly serious recessions) and yield a future for the nation that no longer relies on Britain being a country that 'makes things'. In this interpretation of urban economics, there is no problem at all in using regeneration initiatives to reclaim and clean up formerly industrial land, changing its use to solve cities' housing needs, and providing space for what the service economy requires, which is new office space, retail locations, creative 'hubs' for the knowledge economy, and homes for new kinds of workers. In the UK, this housing and service sector-led model of regeneration is pursued as if there were no other options for adapting to the transformations of post-industrial society, but other countries, like Germany, have shown that it is possible to take a different approach; there, investment and government subsidy support a mixed economy with new sources of wealth, and growth, existing alongside more traditional forms of banking, industry, and manufacturing production.

In the East End of London, which was at one time London's industrial and manufacturing powerhouse, the gamble might not pay off, in bringing about urban change through a mainly housing and service sector-led regeneration strategy. The same is true, of course, in East Manchester. These are areas characterised by high unemployment where, more than anything, people need jobs and plenty of them. To see posh housing, for new kinds of residents, constructed in the Olympic Park, when, all around, people are in dire need of affordable housing, and an abundant supply of work, could be like adding salt to the wound, creating another potential source of conflict and tension.

Despite successes in some respects, Tom Russell is cautious, for example, about describing his work in East Manchester as a success, because an atmosphere still prevails there of a profound rupture caused by the loss of industry and manufacture. There is always a risk that the disruption of long-standing, predominantly working-class neighbourhoods, alongside a short-sighted failure to preserve or to properly commemorate industrial heritage, will be perceived as a general lack of respect for, and misunderstanding about, the cultural histories of local livelihood that preceded the long-awaited but less-than ideal dawning of a service sector city. In East London, a place that once stood for the spirit of inventiveness and working-class industriousness, there is a risk that bad feeling locally towards a project imposed from above, which is perceived not to meet or to be oblivious to local needs, will foster resentments that could eventually undermine the value of new housing developments planned for the post-Games Olympic Park.

Olympic Debts

Another serious constraint in the planning of Olympic legacy that Tom must come to terms with relates to the obligation to return to London, central government, and The National Lottery, the additional public funds allocated in 2007 to Games expenditure when a review of Olympic finances led to the controversial announcement of a tripling of costs from the estimated £2.375 billion stated in the original bid to £9.25 billion. Important about this arrangement for the repayment, from Olympic legacy, of monies redirected to the Games in 2007 is the assumption, which can in no way be guaranteed, that the legacy, at some point in the future, will be financially lucrative enough to pay for the unexpected extra costs of preparing the land for the Games, and their aftermath. This financial pledge was never an original legacy promise, but it is an obligation in the background of everything the Legacy Directorate does. The demand from government that a commercial return is created for the repayment of debt owed to the public purse means that the legacy has to make good economic sense. The business plan must account for debts that are to be repaid, and this means that the commercial imperative, at the heart of the Legacy Directorate, is not at all about simply privileging business interests just for the sake of it, or, because, as cynics would have it, this is what governments inevitably do to secure their own interests but, rather, because the books have to be seen to balance. In particular, the problem hangs in the air of how to repay to the National Lottery the extra £675 million that was diverted from other good causes to pay for the Olympics.

The Olympic Stadium

Just like in Manchester, one of Tom's top priorities in London is to quickly deal with and resolve the issue of the legacy use of the main sporting stadium. Most important is that London is not left, like other Olympic cities, with an embarrassing white elephant that has no use, is costly to maintain, and impossible to dispose of. Tom is staking his reputation on finding a tenant for the nearly half a billion pounds worth of stadium long before the Games take place in 2012, with the idea that it will be occupied and made use of as soon as humanly possible after the Games are over. This is the Manchester model, which if realisable in London would be a real coup not just for Tom, but for London too; it would signify that Tom is, indeed, the man for the legacy job, and because the stadium is symbolic of Olympic legacy overall, a stadium tenant secured early would immediately boost confidence and send out a strong signal to the nation, and the world, about London's capacity to deliver on the Games and its legacy promises. This matters because the reputation of London, and especially of New Labour, when it comes to the planning—and delivery of other relatively recent mega-projects, like Wembley Stadium and the Millennium Dome—is of humiliation over fumbled ventures plagued either by missed deadlines, cancelled events, and extortionate overspends or the shame of wondering what to do about redundant venues languishing at tax payers' expense.

The stadium also poses a political problem to Tom, because the history of the Olympic bid is inseparable from the promise to deliver, as a main legacy of the Games, a national athletics stadium with local community benefit. This is an issue with a fraught political history. In 2001, Tessa Jowell, the Olympics Minister, when she was Secretary of State at the DCMS, withdrew funding of a national athletics stadium in preparation for hosting the 2005 World Athletics Championship because of fears over escalating costs for the building at Picketts Lock in the Upper Lea Valley, in Northeast London. This was a cause of terrible international embarrassment to Britain, and to UK Athletics, because it meant that the championship had to be hosted at the last minute by Helsinki in Finland. This humiliating debacle also led to the resignation of Chris Smith, Tessa's predecessor at the DCMS, because he had signed off on Picketts Lock after his already-existing humiliation over the too costly, over-budget, way-past-the-deadline redevelopment of Wembley, which was originally supposed to host football, rugby, and athletics, but which arrived in the end as a football-only stadium, leaving the problem unaddressed of where to situate a new home for athletics in London. With the famous British athlete, Sebastian Coe, at the helm of LOCOG, the political pressure is increased to use the Olympic Games to deliver what the bid promised—a stadium that will become a prestigious national centre for UK Athletics.

Tom's experience in Manchester suggests, in contrast, that the most economically viable use of the stadium, in legacy, would be for it to be occupied by a Premier League football club. Very early on, in 2001, when the idea of bidding for an Olympic Games in London was first mooted, bid organisers had approached West Ham United, in East London, and were given a positive response to the suggestion of their occupation of the stadium after the Games. This positive expression of interest from West Ham was reiterated in 2004 (as well as interest from Tottenham Hotspur), when the actual bid team had been determined to prove to the International Olympic Committee (IOC) that there would be 'no white elephants in London'. West Ham is the most obvious choice of legacy tenant because it is a celebrated local Premier League football club and securing its involvement would send all the right messages about delivering a local legacy from the Games. However, by the time the final bid was actually submitted, in November 2004, the specifics were changed to include a new plan for a stadium that could be significantly reduced in size in legacy mode, with athletics use, and not football, at the heart of the design. This dashed any hopes at Spurs, or West Ham, about use of the stadium for football, and pinned London's hopes of winning its bid on a gamble that London would have to prove that it was serious about making up to athletics for its very recent, and spectacular, failure to be prepared to host the 2005 World Championship.

More than a year before Tom's arrival in London, as early as March 2006, Ken Livingstone had again publicly reinforced the legally binding commitment of London's bid to provide an athletics-focused legacy stadium, which was to be reduced in legacy from a Games-time capacity of 80,000 to 25,000 seats. Only a month later, however, Sebastian Coe created confusion by announcing that the use of the stadium by a Premier League football club would not be ruled out on condition that the athletics track remained as a permanent fixture. This finally put Spurs off due to the common perception that stadiums with athletics tracks, in which fans cannot get close enough to the action, ruin the atmosphere and lead to a decline in attendance.

By October 2006, Sports Minister Richard Caborn was happy to be able to suggest to the media that with Tottenham ruled out, West Ham were now in serious talks about moving into the stadium after the Games on the basis of dual use: football and athletics. Just one month later, however, controversy erupted over stadium plans when Tessa Jowell contradicted the sports minister and emphasised that both the government and Ken Livingstone, the Mayor of London, as well as Lord Moynihan of the British Olympic Association (BOA) were committed to the promise to honour provision of an athletics legacy, and to reduce the stadium capacity after the Games. This was because, Tessa Jowell suggested, the combined costs of leasing the stadium, converting it to Premier League use, and retaining the track were off-putting to all football clubs she had spoken to, including West Ham. Tessa's announcement made it clear that there was no shared agreement behind-the-scenes about plans for the stadium, and Richard Caborn had obviously been swiftly brought 'back on message' to give an appearance among the politicians of strategic coherence.

As a result of this political to and fro, in February 2007, much to the dismay of the Sports Minister, the plans were finalised for the Olympic stadium designs without a major football tenant on board. This meant that the opportunity was lost to ensure that combined Premier League football and athletics use was planned into the designs from the beginning. With a fixed athletics track, without retractable seats, and expensive post-Games conversion costs, the attractiveness of the stadium, even to smaller football clubs, diminished, and Leyton Orient, another local East End lower league football club, which had been enthusiastically involved in early negotiations around occupation of the scaled-down stadium, became frustrated and also withdrew its expression of interest.

So, when Tom Russell took up his post, at the end of 2007, he inherited a nightmare scenario; the reduced-size stadium would not be viable for athletics-only use, because there just is not the same demand for athletics events as there is for football, and only football could deliver both weekly use and commercially sustainable occupation, but the designs for the stadium, as submitted, made it unfeasible and unaffordable for both Premier League and smaller team football tenancy. As a result, it was beginning to look increasingly unlikely that a legacy tenant could be found for the stadium according to current plans. Already, then, there are signs, despite best intentions, that just like in every other Olympic city, the Olympic stadium in London will become the lightning rod of the legacy project. It is likely to attract fierce criticism on all sides for the foreseeable future, and become the talking point when anything else to do with post-Games planning comes under question.

Only the change of mayor, in June 2008, allowed Tom to get beyond this impasse. Boris Johnson immediately started pushing for a more ambitious legacy use for the stadium and endorsed the idea of a Premier League football tenant, but the problem is that Boris also used the 'lack of progress' in LDA negotiations about the stadium, as a stick with which to beat the agency, and, by definition, to undermine Tom Russell's leadership on legacy issues. Losing no time in stealing a march on the Olympic legacy, Boris quickly launched his own 'Legacy Board of Advisors' and suggested that before it was too late, more commercially viable uses had to be found for the Olympic venues. Boris also announced that a consultation was to be launched by government to see if the Olympic legacy was better off in the hands of a dedicated, sole purpose URC. Of course, this made sense to Tom Russell, since this was always his preferred Manchester model for the planning and delivery of urban regeneration, but for Boris to own the idea was a political coup.

Poor Tom, he is less than a year in post, but I fear his days might be numbered. His fate is likely to be sealed in the new politics of a mayoralty that will, I suspect, be determined to put an end, not just to the LDA but also everything visibly associated with the ideas and previous way of doing things of Ken Livingstone, the former mayor. Like a conquering king, and all new rulers before him, Boris Johnson is likely to claim the spoils, and then put to the sword—laying to waste—the standard bearers, institutional structures, and landscapes that stand for the old world—the way things were before the new reign begins to make its own mark.

No wonder Tom says that 'regeneration is like trying to push a boulder up a mountain'; it seems like an impossible and thankless task. Just as you think you are beginning to make progress, something happens to destabilise the balance of interests, and precious time is then lost in desperately trying to regain equilibrium so that the balancing act can be resumed. With a change of leadership, things are even more precarious; the massive load has to be transferred—mid-mountain—onto a new and inexperienced set of shoulders and all of this has to happen without sending the boulder crashing back down the mountain. I fear this is the circus act my research will bear witness to: mid-mountain, on treacherous terrain, the transfer of the load.

Meanwhile, I notice that as political intrigue intensifies at the top of the organisational and political hierarchy, the everyday staff members of the Legacy Directorate teams are keeping their heads down and making busy as usual. There is no time to get distracted, because there are deadlines to meet and battles to be fought on the ground about the kinds of decisions that will actually make a difference to what will come to pass after the Games are over. When everything might change because of a new political cycle, there is a narrowing window of opportunity in which to get things done, and the pressure is on to deliver projects/work streams that might later be axed if they have not already been brought to fruition.

Land Assembly

Famous for meeting seemingly impossible deadlines is Gareth Blacker, the dreaded Director of the Land Team at the Legacy Directorate. Dreaded, I say, because his job at the LDA has partly been, in double quick time, to assemble in the Lower Lea Valley, the 500 hectares of land for the creation of the Olympic Park. For a public body, like the LDA, to 'assemble land' is for it to produce a larger land holding that can be pieced together through the purchase of individual plots from private or public sector owners. This happens either through negotiation or, failing that, by force of law.

To assemble the lands for the Olympic Park required negotiation with 2200 different business, residential, and community interests. It was the largest and most complex land assembly process ever undertaken in Britain. For it to happen so speedily was, therefore, a remarkable and unprecedented feat of urban redevelopment. It took only 2 years from the time the Olympic bid was won in July 2005, until July 2007, for the land to be acquired and handed over to the ODA for work to begin on the construction of the park, sporting venues, and associated infrastructure.

Normally, land acquisition processes are extremely time-consuming and costly, because of the likelihood of appeals, public inquiries, disputes about compensation, and, therefore, uncertainty about eventual overall costs of acquisition. The gamble is that the amount paid out to land owners might be more than the value of the land at the point of redevelopment so that a loss is made rather than a gain, and this is never more risky than during a financial crisis when the development value plummets, of land set aside for regeneration. Not surprisingly, the breakneck speed at which Gareth Blacker moved the land acquisition process forward, and his almost immediate use of the power granted to him by government to issue Compulsory Purchase Orders (CPO) for the assembly of Olympic lands did not win him any friends in the East End of London.

A CPO can only be issued if the development of the land to be acquired is said to be in the public interest. This immediately weighs the greater interests of a broader and unspecified public, who might gain from the regeneration of the Lower Lea Valley, against the particular welfare or benefits of certain individuals, community groups, or businesses who are displaced from highly specific locations and activities. This justification for displacement 'in the public interest' places an even greater onus on the delivery of an Olympic legacy that is perceived from a public perspective to be positive, because otherwise it will be impossible, in retrospect, to find any ground from which to defend or excuse the disruption to a few for the good of the many. Similarly, the enforcement of the sale of the land is, ideally, not supposed to lead, for affected parties, to a material decline or loss of any kind; land is supposed to be purchased at market value and compensation is supposed to be offered for the full costs of relocation and associated loss of business. For community groups and groups of residents, the same applies; an equal or superior offer has to be made of accommodation/new location and, even though it was not compulsory for the LDA to do so, it endeavoured to follow 'best practice' by ensuring that it supported affected parties in their transition to new environments and/or provided land, for example, in newly formed industrial parks for relocation of affected businesses.

At a time when public and media scepticism about the Olympic project remains high and the legacy boss, Tom Russell, is desperately trying to win allies to the cause and sustain momentum for the forward moving motion of the project, Gareth Blacker has faced an almost impossible task: his challenge has been to hastily assemble the land without creating so much alienation, and resistance among those people being displaced (and fuelling a greater sense of injustice among their growing numbers of supporters) that the reputation and momentum of the overall project would be jeopardised. By the skin of his teeth, and with a budget of £995 million for land acquisitions, Gareth Blacker seems to have achieved his objective even though, as in all Olympic projects, to greater or lesser degrees, displacements in the Lower Lea Valley have caused considerable controversy. For many, Gareth Blacker has come to symbolise the tough treatment of the LDA, as it sacrificed the usual way of doing things to the by-any-means-necessary attempt to harness the Olympic dream to ambitions for urban change in London. This is especially true among those in the Lower Lea Valley who feel that their interests have been ridden over—roughshod—as the Olympic juggernaut has come powering through their part of town.

The Lower Lea Valley

After the River Thames, which flows eastwards through London out to the Thames Estuary, and the North Sea, the River Lea is London's second river. It runs north to south from rural Bedfordshire and Hertfordshire, meeting marshy ground, and then, industrialised riverbanks and associated canal systems, before it flows into the Thames, in East London, at Leamouth. In the nineteenth and early twentieth centuries, the lower valley of the Lea was the perfect location for industry and manufacture in London; water and electricity were in plentiful supply, and it was far enough away from the city centre for dirty and smelly industries, like chemical manufacture, to develop and prosper, away from residential areas. It is not difficult to imagine an atmosphere of intense activity and industriousness applied to all manner of experimental endeavour. Not far from the thriving dockyards of the Thames, which were the bustling centres of international shipping employing thousands of workers, the River Lea and its associated canals were busy transport corridors too, with water traffic constantly moving up and down the valley. At the mouth of the river, where it meets the Thames, there were bustling shipbuilding yards, and the Thames Ironworks, where the iron was produced for Brunel's revolutionary iron bridges and Britain's first warships, made of iron.

The river also yielded sand and gravel, and the ready supply of water led to an abundance of mills whose energy was applied to various kinds of production from electricity, to flour, to gunpowder. In contrast to the Upper Lea Valley, where the rich soils of the valley led to the development of market gardening and the world's largest concentration of greenhouses, the Lower Lea was characterised by factories for the manufacture of porcelain, matches, paints, and other noxious products whose emissions were masked now and again by the sweet smell of confectionery being made at Clarke, Nickolls & Coombs, Britain's largest producer of sugary treats. Trains were manufactured at the Stratford Works for the Great Eastern Railway, which connected the industrial powerhouse of London's East End to East Anglia, and a dense network of rail lines intersected and divided the area. An abundance of entrepreneurial spirit led to many important technological breakthroughs, such as the invention of petrol and plastic, and as a result of Michael Faraday's experimental workshop in the lighthouse at Leamouth and the development of businesses dedicated to the manufacture of electrical goods, the area became associated with innovation in electronics.

A spirit of resistance arose here too, in 1888, when the women and girls at the Bryant and May match factory went on strike to protest against conditions of employment that meant unbearably long hours of work with little protection from the ill effects to health of handling phosphorous for the production of matches. In the later twentieth century, the decline of industry and manufacture, and the rise in residential population in the surrounding areas of the river, led to the development in the Lower Lea Valley of a hotchpotch of smaller, light industrial businesses, scrap yards, textile production, food processing concerns, and so on.

By the beginning of the twenty-first century, in 2005, when the success was announced of London's bid for the Olympic Games, the area had become a strange combination of both post-industrial dereliction, largely out of sight and out of mind, on the margins of London's eastern periphery and a diversity of ongoing productive activities, with 300 businesses (employing 2500 people) keeping alive the last remnants of a 200-year-old industrial culture. Alongside the possibilities for legitimate undertakings, with cheap rent and affordable land classified for industrial and light-industrial use, there was a sense, too, of space for illicit activity and the possibility for crime to flourish, because the eyes of the city had always been turned in the other direction, to the West, leaving the East of London overlooked and long neglected.

Despite heavily polluted waters and industrial contamination of the land, the unique geography of river valley, associated waterways, expanses of marshlands, pockets of green space, and nature reserves, as well as a long period of post-industrial decline in the Lower Lea Valley, led to the emergence of a relatively undisturbed series of habitats where wildlife of various kinds was able to flourish. Part of the controversy of the land acquisition process, and the earlier planning permissions, was that plans for the development of the Olympic Park would mean disruption to and/ or destruction of many of the habitats of the Lower Lea Valley, which, in a densely populated urban environment, are appreciated locally for the proximity to nature that they bring. The river system itself and some of the rare wildlife to be found there are protected by national conservation laws, and, at the phenomenal cost of £450 per newt, both smooth newts inside the planned area of Olympic Park and great crested newts at Hog Hill, in Redbridge, where the Eastway Cycle Circuit is to be relocated, had to be carefully rehomed before construction projects could continue. Also listed in the inventory of species to be affected by the construction of the Olympic Park were bats, lizards, many rare and less common vertebrates, 204 species of invertebrate, kingfishers, black redstarts, coots, moorhens, mallards, mute swans, green woodpeckers, grey wagtails, great crested grebes, grebes, dunnocks, sand martins, kestrels, thrushes, fieldfares, gulls, herons, and cormorants.

Equally controversial as the disruption to wildlife was the fact that the plans implied permanent, and temporary, changes to particular areas of Metropolitan Open Land (MOL). These are lands designated, like London's Green Belt, as open spaces for public enjoyment, which are protected from development and cannot be built on other than for exceptional reasons that have to be agreed not just by the local borough but also by the mayor and central government. Hackney Marshes, in the Northwest of the Lower Lea Valley, in the host Olympic borough of Hackney, comprise London's largest area—136 hectares—of protected commons; 16–18 hectares of this land are to be temporarily used for the Olympics as car parking space. This means not only disruption to the existing leisure use of the land, mainly for amateur football, but also the loss of 350 mature trees, including pear, cherry, ash, mulberry, southern beech, weeping poplars, and 110-year-old native black poplars.

Another area of officially designated common land in Hackney to be affected by Olympic development is Arena Fields, on the west side of the planned park. Arena Fields was given to the people of London by an act of parliament in 1894 to be retained as MOL in perpetuity. The loss of these lands to public use is scandalous, arousing deep suspicions, not just because all Olympic Games (since Sydney 2000) are supposed to be 'Green Olympics' demonstrating a cutting-edge environmentalism, commitment to the emerging values and practices of 'sustainability', but because of the history, in England, of the acts of enclosure. Between 1604 and 1914, these acts led to the privatisation of over 6 million acres of common lands whose original purpose was to facilitate self-sufficiency in a peasantry benefiting from access to land—in an open field system—for common grazing and crop rotation. The historical precedent of an association between forced enclosure and the creation of a market for land, whose monetary value can then be extracted, means that those who see the Olympic Games as nothing more than an elaborate 'land grab' for the benefit of commercial interests are, as they should be, on red alert. Organisations, like Games Monitor, have been hawkish in their attention to what the promised Olympic legacy will mean for a public, which has not only funded the Games, through its taxes, but is paying a high price locally for its disruptions in terms of losses that cannot be calculated. The existence of Games Monitor, and other resistance movements like it, are an important part of the Olympic legacy that should not be underestimated.

Although Arena Fields is to be lost forever, the promise is for the area to be replaced by parklands of a similar size nearby, in Hackney, after the Games are over, but again the loss of easy access to green space and destruction of mature and diverse species of trees is irreplaceable. Accessed by a footbridge across the other side of the Lea Navigation Canal, the fields were directly opposite Gainsborough Primary School and a public housing estate called Lea Bank Square. Only time will tell whether the loss to that school and those residents of their open fields, and the disruption they are experiencing as a result of having to live cheek by jowl with the Olympic construction site will be outweighed by what the Olympic legacy promises to deliver, in the long-term, as a greater public good.

The problem is that no cost–benefit analysis can account for the destruction of common lands, or the disruption of wildlife habitat, and these incalculable losses help to make a broader point—whilst land values can more easily be calculated in terms of market value when the negotiation involves the acquisition of land via commodity transactions, the same does not apply when the displacement involves environmental disturbance and alienation of people from what they understand to be deeply personal and collectively shared bonds to the land. Such things cannot be compensated for in monetary terms. The most extreme example of what this means, in terms of the Olympic land assembly process, is the displacement from their plots of the tenants of the Manor Garden Allotment Society.

The Allotments

Given as a gift to the allotment holders, and therefore understood by them to be inalienable, that is, not to be taken away—theirs to use forever by right—was 4.5 acres of land between the River Lea and Channelsea River in the Lower Lea Valley. The gardens were established in 1900, by Major Arthur Villiers, an old Etonian, son of the seventh Earl of Jersey, a descendant of the Duke of Buckingham and director of Barings Bank, the oldest merchant bank in London. The gift of land was a philanthropic act, and part of a broader sporting and educational mission in this area, by Eton College, to provide small parcels of land for working-class people living local to that area to improve their livelihoods, and well-being, and in this case, to grow vegetables, which, in the face of real deprivation, meant people could obtain a degree of food self-sufficiency and improved quality of life.

As a result of this gift, 80 individual plots have been consistently cultivated for over a century, many by three generations of family, which has led to the formation of a stable, self-organising collective called the Manor Gardens Society. Group members include long-standing white working-class East End families, as well as a diversity of working-class people from different racial and ethnic backgrounds and, in more recent times, a few middle-class people attracted to the allotments by the publicity surrounding the fight by the allotment holders against their Olympic eviction.

Trying to explain the degree of connection to place forged through three generations of devoted cultivation, and participation in the social life of the gardens, the current secretary of the society—Mark Harton—explains to me, with great sorrow, that deceased allotment holders' ashes are scattered on the land. His point is to emphasise that the substance of 'the diggers'—as particular kinds of persons, who are fellow gardeners of the Manor Garden Society—has become inseparable from the soil. The loss to the gardeners of their plots is, therefore, a highly emotive issue concerning the displacement not just of land, but also of a way of life, and sense of community, and personhood forged through a long history of working the land.

In 2007, the gardens were demolished to make way for the landscaping of the Olympic Park of the 2012 summer Games. The land of the Manor Garden allotments was inside the designated boundary of the park-to-be and destined to become, of all things, a concrete concourse. Plot holders were told that they could not stay, and when they protested it was impressed upon them that their displacement was inevitable; they could not stay within the perimeter of the 11-mile security fence that was to be erected around the construction site. Sparking a fierce resistance in the gardeners, the imperative for them to move was fought. A support group called Life Island, backed by Friends of the Earth, was created to struggle for the right to remain on the land, and finally, after a protracted legal battle against eviction, it was agreed that the allotments would be destroyed, but only on condition that they had to be temporarily relocated outside the park and then reinstated somewhere in the Olympic Park after the Games are over. The victory means that the allotment holders are to be the only group affected by the land assembly process to have won the right, post-2012, to return, in some shape or form, to the land that is to become the Olympic Park.

On the fateful day of their eviction, the allotment gardeners joined groups of protestors outside Hackney Town Hall to register their discontent and to loudly proclaim their mistrust of the political promises made by the government, and local borough councils, that the Olympic

Games would deliver a positive legacy and transform the heart of East London for the benefit of everyone who lives there. No wonder, given this deep sense of attachment to the land, that the gardeners were the last to leave the Olympic Park site; no surprise that they wept as the bulldozers moved in and levelled their plots, and no wonder that solidarity with the gardeners has become the reason for, and symbol of, a more general anti-Olympic sentiment in East London.

The eventual fate of the Manor Garden Society will become one of the most important litmus tests of what the Olympics can deliver in terms of promised legacy to people living locally to the park. Overall, what matters here is that the attempt to create a new future for a post-industrial urban area—and the laudable endeavour to bring to it, though innovative development—new life, purpose, activity, and opportunity must properly account for and incorporate the past of what a sense of place entails. What has happened in the Lea Valley, its unique history and character, and what it has meant to the people who have inhabited it must be part of the story of Olympic legacy, and even a very brief exploration of the life-world of this place before the Olympic Games reveals that the Lower Lea Valley was most definitely not a 'wasteland', as it was frequently described by the LDA and the ODA, in order to justify its development. Part of the measure of post-industrial developments must be the extent to which the rich and locally meaningful history of industrial life and labour, in a particular kind of environment, is incorporated and put at the centre of how urban transformation is designed. A lack of respect for the depth, and significance of working-class histories, and places of habitation is not an acceptable outcome for projects of change led and conceptualised by a mainly white middle-class elite of public sector urban regeneration specialists who mostly live elsewhere and have nothing to lose.

Olympic Opportunities

Designed to reflect the pan-London priorities of the LDA, as the agency tasked with maintaining the economic growth, and 'global success' of the city, whilst also reducing urban inequalities of all kinds, the project, known inside the Legacy Directorate as Oly. Opps. is a pre-2012—build-up to the Games—multimillion pound programme of opportunities and engagement, around the themes of employment, business and skills, as well as sport and sustainability.

Director of Olympic Opportunity at the Legacy Directorate is Geoff Newton. His remit across London and, more specifically, in the Olympic host boroughs is to create 'Legacy Now'. Geoff's ambitious, Olympic-inspired agenda for social and economic change both in East London and across the capital includes a diverse and complex range of projects with a focus on reducing high levels of 'worklessness'; promoting public and private sector partnerships to provide local and pan-London job brokerage as well as more relevant training opportunities linked to available employment; improved business engagement to develop the long-term capacity of small and 'ethnicity-minority' businesses; facilitation of the access of businesses of all sizes to Olympic contract opportunities through an e-portal called CompeteFor; improvements in access to quality, affordable childcare; encouragement of greater job readiness through skills development projects in media, construction, retail, and hospitality; investment in training centres for construction, hospitality, and transport; higher levels of capital investment in sport, sport-related training/employment, and sporting participation; an increase in cultural activities through project funding; provision of training opportunities for employment in the arts and cultural sector; support for the Cultural Olympiad; promotion of a cultural and arts-focused approach to regeneration; touring a series of promotional events to raise awareness among Londoners about the Games (and the opportunities they make possible); and the development of a pre-volunteering programme called Personal Best, the model which has been imported to London as a result of its unprecedented success in the Manchester Commonwealth Games.

The vast array of projects and initiatives, as well as the focus on employment and skills, and sporting and cultural engagement is a reflection not just of excitement at the LDA about the transformational potential for London of hosting the Games, but also of the left-leaning orientation of the LDA as the agency responsible for delivering Ken Livingstone's vision of London as a city characterised by greater equality of opportunity. However, the focus on socio-economics also conceals something important. Firstly, the social and economic organisation of the legacy project itself, and of the ODA and LOCOG, could have been put much more directly centre stage as examples of how the overall ambition to address problems of unemployment in London could be delivered in practice. For example, by the time of the Games in 2012, and long afterwards, hundreds, if not thousands, of individual contracts with private companies will have been awarded as a result of London winning the Olympic bid. Imagine if each of those contracts came with a legal requirement that a certain number of paid internships/apprenticeships/jobs were created for young people of the Olympic Host Boroughs for the duration of the contract and beyond. This would have led to the development of thousands of opportunities for young people not just within the various work streams of LOCOG, the ODA, and the Legacy Directorate itself, but also in the huge variety of companies lending their expertise to the Olympic project. These include specialised legal and accountancy firms, engineering and architectural practices, urban planners and designers, construction companies, energy providers, transport specialists, project management companies, sports and leisure consultancies, property developers, environmental agencies, sustainability consultancies, and so on. The expansion of the career horizons that this could have led to would have been an invaluable gift to the young people of East London.

Secondly, another unintended consequence of the narrow framing of the socio-economics of the Olympic planning operation, a socio-economics which places the social and the economic outside of the corporations and organisational structures involved in the Olympic Planning operation, is that the opportunity is lost to analyse that operation as a social and economic endeavour in itself. What is needed is a reframing and broadening out of the notion of 'socio-economics' in urban regeneration so that it also includes attention to the sociality, and financial implications, of being involved on the inside of the business and bureaucracy, entailed by state-led urban change. For example, the steady increase in the staging around the world of mega-event urban transformation projects has produced an elite international cadre of planning, design, and many other kinds of specialists who travel the world, circulating from one event to the other, lending their expertise in the build-up to bids and the preparations for events. The proliferation of urban mega-events, like FIFA's World Cups and the IOC's Olympic Games, to name just two examples, ensures that a middle-class wealthy elite sustains itself regardless of whether or not the events it plans are successful, and irrespective of whether the hosting of the event promises anything to the more general public, which has usually funded the event through its taxes. Greater attention is required to the political economy, and the socio-economics, of what is going on behind-the-scenes in the planning of mega-events, rather than continuously perpetuating the idea that the social and economic aspirations of these projects relate solely to the lives of the urban poor who are to be affected by them.

Thirdly, another critique of the Oly. Opps. programme is that it cast its net too widely; in trying to make sure that London, in general, was not neglected by an exclusive focus on East London, initiatives were dissipated that could arguably have been more productive with clearer, more meaningful outcomes at an intensely local level in the Olympic Host Boroughs of East London. My earlier research, in the post-industrial docklands of Bermondsey, to the south of the River Thames, taught me that life in predominantly working-class neighbourhoods is experienced socially at the level of place, which means that often, where a young person lives, and is growing up matters a great deal. In Bermondsey, for example, people would make careful distinctions about who was 'born and bred' in Bermondsey, and who really knew, as a result of this closely defined sense of belonging, what it meant to be of this place, and to be a person in a certain kind of way, with specific values and a particular orientation to life. This means that young people in Bermondsey, and in predominantly working-class urban neighbourhoods in London, tend to categorise each other on the basis of which social housing estate they hail from, and/or which postcode they belong to. This makes it no surprise that young people living in predominantly working-class neighbourhoods can easily get into trouble for being in the wrong place at the wrong time in an area where masculine reputations are forged on unforgiving streets. This is as true in the East End of London as it is in Bermondsey, in the Southeast.

In places like this, family, kinship, and networks of friendship have historically been critical to how place is experienced and, in some cases, dense networks of family and familiarity have developed over time, and these were traditionally an essential resource in the face of life's hardships. This makes me want to suggest that the place where change has to happen, in any attempt to bring meaningful transformation to the predominantly working-class neighbourhoods of East London, is at the level of the housing estate. This is especially the case when change is deemed, from on high, to be desirable in terms of the conventional socio-economics to do with overcoming the limitations of opportunity associated with poverty.

Rather than operating solely through agencies of government and the employment and training organisations of the local boroughs, it might have proved productive to specifically locate the Oly. Opps. programmes, (in association with the voluntary sector organisations in the host boroughs that are already reaching out to these more narrowly focused geographical areas), in those 11 politics wards and their housing estates, surrounding the emerging Olympic Park. This would have made it possible for the Legacy Directorate to cultivate the ongoing, sustainable development of personable relations with particular estates, families, and young people, and to make this lead to the development of exciting new opportunities for these young people in terms of employment, training and skills, as well as sporting participation and cultural engagement. Without matching investment in financial terms to investment in terms of social engagement on the estates, the opportunity may have been lost to assess, over a significant period of time, what difference it makes to particular local housing estates and specific families, and individual young men and women when the Olympics comes to town.

I would argue that it is only the building of localised significant relations of person-to-person understanding and, therefore, awareness of how life is actually lived in the East End of London that can lead to the development of meaningful and sustainable transformation, as a result of state-led projects of urban change. Without this, the risk is very real that the Oly. Opp. projects will, from the perspective of young people on the streets of East London (and the community organisations that try to serve them), appear to be nothing more than a drop in the ocean.

It remains to be seen how the ambitious scope of Oly. Opps. projects will feed into The Host Borough Unit's SRF, but the significant investment in and sheer range of 'socio-economic' projects at the LDA make me fear that Geoff Newton too will be a casualty of the new mayoralty. Boris Johnson's Legacy Board of Advisors signifies a wholesale review of the approach to legacy planning, with an urgent focus on the need for greater commercial investment in the project, and a focus on the legacy use of the venues. In difficult financial times and with so much economic uncertainty in the air, I suspect there will be little tolerance in a Conservative leadership for the proliferation of Oly. Opps. or what are often called 'soft' legacy projects in contrast to the 'hard' facts of the need for physical development of land, buildings, and infrastructure. I imagine that there will be a cull of some of the Oly. Opps. programmes, but I can also see how this will create an internal battleground in the Legacy Directorate, as people committed to these projects fight to preserve a broader perspective of what they stand for, which is the commitment of London to deliver on its legacy promises.

Suggested Reading

Blakely, G., & Evans, B. (2013). *The regeneration of East Manchester: A political analysis.* Manchester: Manchester University Press.
Comfort, N. (2013). *The slow death of British industry: A sixty-year suicide, 1952–2012.* London: Biteback Publishing.
Davis, J. (2011). *Urbanising the event: How past processes, present politics, and future plans shape London's Olympic legacy.* Ph.D. Thesis: London School of Economics and Political Science.
Fainstein, S. (1994). *The city builders: Property development in New York, and London, 1980–2000.* Cambridge, MA: Blackwell.
Foster, J. (1998). *Docklands: Cultures in conflict, worlds in collision.* London: UCL Press.
Marshall, P. (2010). *Before the Olympics: The Lea Valley, 1981–2010.* http://www.blurb.co.uk/books/3488533-before-the-olympics
Robertson, A. F. (1984). *People and the state: An anthropology of planned development.* Cambridge: Cambridge University Press.
Sinclair, I. (2011). *Ghost milk: Calling time on the grand project.* London: Hamish Hamilton.
Ward, K., & Peck, J. (Eds.). (2010). *City of revolution: Restructuring Manchester.* Manchester: Manchester University Press.
Williams, K., Erturk, I., Froud, J., Johal, S., Leaver, A., & Moran, M. (2011). City state against national settlement: UK economic policy and politics after the financial crisis. Working Paper 101. *CRESC working paper series.*

3

Future-Scaping

One of Tom Russell's first announcements in January 2008, a month after his appointment as Chief Executive of the Legacy Directorate, was news about which of the six shortlisted master-planning teams had won the LDA contract to come up with an overall vision, detailed landscape design ideas, and, eventually, planning applications for what the Olympic Park could look like in future and be used for, post-2012, in legacy mode. It was no great surprise, bearing in mind the London/Manchester connection, that the winning consortium was led by EDAW, the landscape architects' firm known for having successfully transformed Manchester City Centre after the devastation of the Irish Republican Army (IRA) bomb in 1996, and celebrated for the early master-planning work, commissioned by the LDA in 2003, in preparation for London's Olympic bid.

This early pre-Olympic bid work had been put out to tender before Tony Blair had even decided, in May 2003, to give the full backing of government to the idea to bid for the Games. It signified that whether London was successful or not in its bid to host the Games, the LDA was determined to make early legacy gains from the bidding process itself.

The brief from the LDA for the 2003 work required that the master planners focus on the possibilities for regeneration in the Lower Lea Valley and come up with two plans—one, for what could be possible in this area if London won their bid to host the 2012 Olympic Games, and another showing how transformation and development could unfold without the Games.

The team of master planners had to work at breakneck speed, with only 6 months available—between August 2003 and February 2004—not just to work out what kind of change could be possible and desirable in the Lower Lea Valley, but also to seek collaboration with and consultation on their ideas from the four most affected East London boroughs—Newham, Hackney, Tower Hamlets, and Waltham Forest—whose planning authorities had to come together as a Joint Planning Advisory Team, to review and agree on the Outline Planning Applications. This coming together, of what would later become the Host Boroughs of the Olympic Games, was a considerable feat of collaboration, and an early indication not only that collaboration across all levels of urban governance was essential to the success of the bid and the development of plans for an Olympic legacy, but also that it mattered that the idea to host an Olympic Games in East London was, from the beginning, a grass roots, local-government movement, with support from the East End of the city.

Community-Led Planning

The man responsible for driving forward the idea for an Olympic Games in London is Richard Sumray, a local councillor from north London, in Camden. Richard was inspired by the idea of greater sporting provision for London's youth, and dedicated himself over a period of 20 years to the development of an idea for a London Olympic bid. He did the early groundwork to ensure that by the time he presented, in the year 2000, a serious Olympic bid proposal to London's new mayor, Ken Livingstone, he was already able to demonstrate that he had the backing not just of key players in the East End, but also support across the whole of London.

Two key East End strategists, who supported Richard Sumray wholeheartedly because of their existing commitment to from-the-ground-up locally based community-focused urban planning, were Reverend Lord Andrew Mawson, and Professor Paul Brickell. Lord Mawson is the founding director of the Bromley-by-Bow Centre, in the host borough of Tower Hamlets. The centre, which started life in 1984, arose from Lord Mawson's Christian ministry in the area and was the UK's first Healthy Living Centre. A highly innovative community organisation and health care/well-being centre, the Bromley-by-Bow Centre also provides job brokerage and employment and skills training, as well as opportunities for local people to develop and gain start-up funding for their own businesses, through the not-for-profit model of social entrepreneurship. Lord Mawson, who is also a founder member of Poplar HARCA, a housing association in Tower Hamlets, with community-led regeneration at its core, is vehemently anti-government bureaucracy and a firm believer that to get things done, that is, to effect sustainable changes in urban neighbourhoods in a state of decline, requires that decision making is worked out collaboratively in such a way that those people who are to be affected by processes of transformation have a say in, and are empowered by learning about how their own plans for change can be brought to fruition.

Professor Paul Brickell is a 'born and bred' East Londoner, a professor of molecular biology who once led the cancer department at Great Ormond Street Children's Hospital. He is a local Labour councillor in one of the Olympic host boroughs—Newham—and also Olympic advisor to Newham's ambitious elected Labour mayor, Sir Robin Wales. Paul was inspired by Lord Mawson to join him in lending his energy and intelligence to the cause of community-led regeneration in the East End of London, and Paul became Director of Development and then Chief Executive at Bromley-by-Bow, before then leading a regeneration company, Leaside Regeneration, in Tower Hamlets.

To explain to me the difference between top-down and community-led regeneration initiatives, in which processes of planning are used as problem-solving devices, and to address those issues that local experience reveals are most in need of attention, Paul introduces me to Crissy Townsend on the Teviot Estate in Tower Hamlets. Crissy tells me the story of her journey to community-led regeneration and begins with the account of how she once broke down the door of a derelict shop on the estate. Crissy says she had hit rock bottom; she had just thrown her alcoholic husband out of the home in their flat on the estate; the flat was in a terrible state of disrepair, and was the constant reminder not just of the decline in her own living standards, and life experience, but also of a local council that, from her point of view, could not care less about its tenants. She describes how in winter, wind rattled through the windows of the flat, lifted the threadbare carpets, and no repairs were ever attended to. Crissy admits that she felt defeated and had become depressed. Meanwhile, she was working out how to take care of her children on her own, and lamenting that she had no education or employment-relevant skills. Crissy stresses that she could not read or write, could not find any work, and had become resigned to a life lived on benefits. She describes feelings of hopelessness and helplessness.

Crissy then goes on to explain how, one day, suddenly everything changed: she was walking past the small parade of mostly abandoned shops on the estate and saw two very young children playing near the road outside; their ball went into the road, and Crissy watched, helpless, as one of the children very nearly got knocked down by a passing car. Crissy tells me that something in her just snapped; in desperation, she looked around, saw the derelict, boarded up shops behind her, and angrily began to break down the door of the one that looked the most abandoned. Once inside, she started to furiously empty the contents of the shop onto the pavement outside. Before long, other residents came by and asked what she was doing, wondering if she had gone mad. She told them, 'I am making a play house. I am making a safe place for these children to play, because no one else cares.'

Impressed with her obviously furious determination and surprised that finally someone was taking into their own hands the idea to do something about the dereliction, and neglect on the estate, instead of waiting in vain for the local council to do something, Crissy's fellow residents asked her what she needed. She asked them to bring brooms and buckets, mops and paint left over from DIY jobs at home. Before long, the shop was cleared, cleaned, and repainted, and she then went back every day to keep the shop open with other women who agreed to be there every day to get the message out to the estate that there was now a safe place for young children to play.

Crissy took in donations of toys and games, and over time, step-by-step, she tackled a recalcitrant council, fought for the right to stay in the shop on a very low rent, and slowly, but surely, got herself an education, gaining a university degree in Community Management. On the day I visit Crissy at the transformed shop, it has obviously become much more than a safe place for young children to play; it is a small community centre where residents can pop in to use computing and photocopying facilities, seek advice about training and employment, and generally find what the best kinds of community organisations provide, which is a welcoming place to simply chat and spend time, or seek assistance to actively facilitate life changes of all kinds, either individually or by joining in with various projects.

While I am chatting to Crissy, a young Asian man comes in to use the facilities, and Crissy introduces him to me; he tells me that before Crissy started the community organisation—Teviot Action Group (TAG)—the far-right, racist, BNP were a strong and hateful force on the estate, and life for the Asian residents was becoming increasingly frightening and miserable. The young man explains that once Crissy started to make a difference everything changed, and residents had reason to begin to see what they had in common. Crissy describes how people started coming together across racial and ethnic divides to work together as people who were now more able to recognise their similarly difficult social and economic situation, and to decide for themselves (without waiting anymore for the council to do anything) how to improve their shared conditions of life on the estate.

Being aware that a lack of transport facilities made local residents feel trapped and isolated on the estate, which also prevented them from accessing job and other life opportunities, Crissy worked tirelessly with Paul Brickell at Leaside Regeneration to start the process of developing plans, seeking funding for, and eventually seeing to fruition the construction of a new Docklands Light Railway (DLR) stop near the estate. It is called Langdon Park. The opening of the station, just last year [2007], was a triumph of community planning and a transformational moment not just for Crissy, but also for the whole estate and everyone who lives in the surrounding area.

Important about this case study is that a sense of community has been created through urban regeneration itself, contradicting what most top-down urban regeneration projects assume, which is that in post-industrial, mainly working-class areas there must already be, out there, somewhere, pre-defined, pre-existing communities to be consulted, and impacted upon. Because of a long history of association between urban working-class neighbourhoods in London and the idea of closely knit communities, defined by connections of kinship and long-standing multi-generational residence, there is an idea that relative poverty and 'community' go hand-in-hand, but the reality of life for residents on London's social housing estates is often far from this historical ideal. The problem with the assumption of 'communities' out there, unspecified and undefined, is that the concept of community is used rhetorically by projects of urban regeneration as the counterpoint to commercial interest.

Corporations, collectively defined as investors or developers, have a profit motive, and money to spend and gain; their involvement in the project of urban regeneration is backstage, often international, and commercially confidential. Communities, in contrast, are collectively defined as groups of residents living locally to the development. They have more visibility and an ascribed social motive, which empties money out of their expectation of gain. This clarifies that the category of community does a particular kind of frontstage political work in those regeneration projects that are being imposed as central and local government imperatives. This work makes 'community consultation' stand in for democracy and creates a largely unexamined assumption that commercial interests will be capitalised in monetary terms and 'communities' will become richer only in terms of social wealth, which, in often unspecified ways, is imagined to be the outcome of improvement in the quality of life, for example, in the provision of improved infrastructure, environment, and increased access to new amenities.

Fighting against this more passive view of community benefit are organisations like The East London Communities Organisation (TELCO), which is an alliance of the very many community organisations and faith groups operating in East London, which come together in solidarity around single-issue campaigns, to build leadership skills to fight for social, political, and economic change. Just two examples of such initiatives are, firstly, the campaigns for a Living Wage for Olympic workers, which TELCO persuaded LOCOG to endorse in November 2004, when the Olympic bid was submitted, and, secondly, the promise that 30 % of Olympic employment opportunities in the park construction and actual event stages would go to people living locally to the park. If these promises are fulfilled, London will be the first Living Wage Olympics and proud trailblazer to a broader set of campaigns for a Living Wage in other sectors of the economy.

Crissy's efforts, as much as those of the urban dynamos, inside the Legacy Directorate are heroic. Crissy too has undertaken a super-human journey akin to the sporting triumphs of Olympic heroes, but she undertook this long before it became clear that the Olympic Games were coming to East London. It is this kind of self-directed personal transformation that other local leaders, like Paul Brickell and Lord Mawson, believe in, and are determined so passionately to facilitate through the community provision they offer in the East End of London. In Paul's mind there is no difference between the spirit of determined enterprise that Crissy has shown, and what the industrial East End was once famous for, which is an experimental, entrepreneurial drive to bring about productive change through innovation, and inventiveness. This image, which Paul and others like him are so keen to reinstate, is the very opposite of the rather depressing idea, circulating in top-down regeneration rhetoric (which many people in the East End find highly offensive) that East London is a place entirely defined by a sense of lack, and limitation, related to the realities of material and social 'deprivation'.

It is no surprise, given Crissy's achievements, that she was so excited, in 2005, about London winning the bid for the 2012 Olympics; she tells me that she was full of expectation about what this would mean in terms of new and exciting opportunities for the young people on the estate. And it is little wonder, at the end of 2008, that I find her frustrated and enraged, because, as she perceives it, the chance has so far been squandered by the Olympic planning authorities to build enduring and transformational links with the housing estates that are a stone's throw from the future Olympic park, but whose residents still feel, as she describes them, cut off from the action, as if 'they may as well be in Timbuktu'.

This sense, of a lost opportunity to systematically incorporate residents and, especially, the young people living on social housing estates local to the development of the Olympic Park, in a pre-Games legacy programme of momentum and capacity building, mirrors the frustration I often hear in East London that young people had been placed at the heart of the Olympic bid and felt themselves to be instrumental in its success, but were now sensing that they have been dropped by the wayside, as preparations for the Games motor ahead.

Urban Change-Makers

Rather than waiting for the Games to come to them, urban change-makers like Paul Brickell and Andrew Mawson have, through their own dogged determination, taken up the challenge to proactively seek ways to create opportunities of Olympic legacy for the East End of London. Both of them are adamant that it is not the Olympics that are bringing change to the Lower Lea Valley because they, and others in the Olympic host boroughs, have long been invested in transforming the area and seen steady change as a result of their combined strategic efforts. However, they all agree that because of the catalyst to development, and transformation, they will provide, the Games are extremely welcome. The challenge is how not to allow the Olympic juggernaut to run roughshod over existing East End initiatives and strategies, and to work out how to harness the Games and the flow of public and private investment, they promise, to what locally based planners, motivated community organisers, and locally elected politicians understand to be the kind of change that is most needed in East London.

As the city reorientates itself and starts to look eastwards, the Olympics will undoubtedly contribute to a change of perception about the East End, and what it has to offer to London, but still, the frustration, which Andrew Mawson and Paul Brickell express is that, for the most part, they feel that the politicians and bureaucrats of central and London government, and the planners of the Olympic and Legacy operations tend to have scant regard for, or understanding of, East London and its history, as if nothing important has happened or is happening here, as if no one knows what they are doing in the East End, and as if, without the Games and 'the expertise' that comes with them, nothing would ever get done in the Lower Lea Valley. Determined to fight against this perception,

Andrew Mawson and Paul Brickell are making noise, and in different ways they are becoming the go-to people for politicians and planners to consult for 'the local perspective' on what is happening in East London and how to make things happen there. These men refuse, however, to be the means for an Olympic or Olympic legacy tick-box exercise; they will not allow themselves to stand for local community in a way that makes the powers-that-be feel that all they have to do is prove that they have spoken to 'local people' and those who understand or represent local interests, but without promising genuine change in the interests of those people.

Another strategist and long-term resident of Newham, with an impressive record of public sector service history in East London, is John Lock; he has been a school governor for over 20 years, worked first as a local councillor in Newham, and then became a board member on Newham's Primary Healthcare Trust (PCT). The trust welcomed London's bid for the Olympic Games as a potential opportunity to create the means for greater equality of health and well-being outcomes in East London, which is notorious for being the part of London with the least active lifestyles, and worst outcomes for health, and John is active in the struggle to articulate the ambitions of Olympic legacy to the realities facing East London public sector organisations. John is now Director of Strategic Development at the University of East London (UEL), where he has been instrumental in the development of the iconic Docklands campus and the creation of the Stratford Renaissance Partnership to promote Stratford as one of London's primary destinations for investment. John has also played a leading part in ensuring that the UEL is at the heart of plans for Olympic legacy, and has especially been involved in strategic planning around the legacy use of the Olympic stadium.

Determined to situate the Games in the context of ongoing transformation in East London, John describes to me a continuous trend in the area, from industrial times to the post-industrial present, of innovation and technology, international business and trade, and infrastructural development. He speaks to me about the history of existing regeneration initiatives in the area, and how vital these have been to a gradual story of revitalisation that will culminate in, and not start with, the 2012 Olympics. John mentions (despite all the problems associated with it) the London Docklands development, which was started at the beginning of the 1980s, and is still growing; the City Airport (1987); UEL campus (1999) at the Royal Docks; the Jubilee Line (1999), and its extension to Stratford; the International Rail Line to the Channel Tunnel (2009); road upgrades to the A13; the ExCeL Centre (2000); the Dome (2000), which was transformed into the 0^2 entertainment centre in 2005; and in 2008 the beginning of Crossrail, which is the new East–West rail route across Greater London.

Because of the dedication to East London and hard-won achievements of people like John Lock, Paul Brickell, and Andrew Mawson, it is no surprise that they watch with some trepidation as a legion of Olympic outsiders muscle in, determined to decide what happens next. All eyes are on the LDA, which does not have the best of reputations in East London, because the perception is that before the Olympics came along it, and the London Thames Gateway Development Corporation (LTGDC) (which is the organisation responsible for the regeneration of 40 miles of Thames riverbank from the Docklands to the east, towards the Thames estuary where the river meets the sea) were too bureaucratic, unwieldy, and obstructive to the self-generated local development plans of East End strategists. The Legacy Directorate and URC that is to come out of it are more welcome, because these innovations represent a new and potentially more independent organisational interface than the LDA, and there is a greater chance, therefore, that East End strategists will be able to find a fresh chance to build alliances and advance their own interests. Under the spotlight too is the EDAW consortium, which won the prized contract to design the long-term, 30-year vision, and planning applications for the Olympic Park in legacy mode, and that is about to produce its final ideas about what the future in this part of London could look like. The expertise of EDAW is beyond question, and they have been on board with the Olympic project from the very beginning, so they are a tried and tested entity with strong credentials in terms of a commitment to urban regeneration, but, nevertheless, they are a central London practice whose client is the LDA, and this makes for a healthy degree of scepticism among East End strategists about what this will mean for what they perceive, protectively, to be their patch, their part of London. The question is whether or not the plans will be ambitious enough to satisfy the aspirations of

East London change-makers whose lives have been dedicated to bringing about a significant change in the Lower Lea Valley.

Early Master-Planning Work

The aim in appointing a master-planning team very early on, in 2003, before it had even been agreed or not by government to begin a formal bidding process had been to get the planning applications for proposed development in the Lower Lea Valley, submitted in January 2004, so that London could make a strong statement of intent in its response to the Candidature Questionnaire of the IOC. The outcome of the master-planning process was essentially an approved proposal to release a significant portion of industrial land (173 hectares) to new uses and to create, thereby, a new city housing district—a Water City (inspired by Andrew Mawson's vision for the area)—making the most of the waterways, industrial heritage, and a network of green spaces running the length of the Lower Lea Valley as far as the Thames.

The plan involved removing the electricity pylons, which dominated the landscape, addressing the industrial legacy of dangerously contaminated land and water, and overcoming barriers to movement across the valley created by heavy-duty through-roads and rail routes. Using the newly created place to 'stitch' together the 'urban fabric' separated, on either side of the river valley, by post-industrial isolation and infrastructural obstacles, the idea was to create new neighbourhoods, cultivate connections between the new site and existing/emerging regeneration initiatives, and to further develop existing centres of activity to make the Lower Lea Valley amenable to more intensive habitation, new kinds of employment, and leisure uses.

A vision statement was designed to send a clear signal to potential public and private investors and affected stakeholders (all those with a vested interest in the Lower Lea Valley) about the mayor's intention to support the creation of a future place of exciting new urban possibilities. The statement recognised the need to account for and to articulate what was imagined for the future Olympic Park, with the local plans for development in the affected local Lower Lea Valley boroughs of Newham,

Hackney, Tower Hamlets, and Waltham Forest, and this meant that the logic of the Olympic bid was absolutely clear—success would simply add a catalyst to already existing plans to transform an area of the city earmarked for significant regeneration. London was to grow and develop in an eastwards direction, no matter what the Olympic Committee decided.

The granting of the Olympic Planning Permissions in October 2004, just before the Candidate File was formally submitted to the IOC, in November, meant that if London was successful, work could begin the very next day on its plans to prepare for the Games, and their post-2012 legacy. This made the London bid look credible and deliverable. So serious was London about its Olympic bid, and the part it would play in the strategy for the regeneration of the Lower Lea Valley, that negotiations were begun early with landowners and businesses occupying the relevant land for the construction of the Olympic Park. The overhead electricity pylons, which once dominated the skyline, are now in the process of being dismantled and routed underground.

The land on which the Aquatics Centre is being built, for example, was purchased by the LDA as early as 2003/2004, long before London knew, in July 2005, that its bid for the Games had been successful. In January 2003, the 12-acre site of the Hackney Wick Dog Track, which had closed in 1997, lain derelict, and been brought to life once every month as a giant outdoor car-boot market, was purchased by the LDA and immediately demolished; that space (which some local residents feel represents another significant loss of working-class history in the area) is to become the Olympic Broadcast and Press Centre.

In 2007, the evolution of strategic urban design thinking about the Lower Lea Valley by the LDA culminated, in association with the ODA and the LTGDC in the publication of the Opportunity Area Planning Development Framework (OAPDF) for the Lower Lea Valley as part of the mayor's revised London Plan. The Opportunity Area Framework included the future Olympic Park in an area of 1450 hectares linking the Thames, in the south, to Leyton, in Waltham Forest in the north, to the green spaces of Lea Valley Regional Park that extend into Hertfordshire.[1]

---

[1] Lower Lea Valley Opportunity Area Planning Framework. http://legacy.london.gov.uk/mayor/planning/docs/lowerleavalley-pt1.pdf Accessed 15th May 2015.

To avoid the kind of hotchpotch, piecemeal development that often characterises urban transformation, the OAPDF, like a form of SRF, established a set of seven development principles that landowners, developers, funding and delivery agencies, and local and strategic stakeholders would have to incorporate in their planning and policy documents. These included renovation and activation of waterways; clustering of community infrastructure, and new and existing transport provision to create vibrant 'Places of Exchange'; co-existence of new housing with new social infrastructure such as health, education, retail space, and green spaces; retaining some sense of a Working Valley through the intensification of key employment spaces, including some retained areas of industrial use and development of sites for creative industries; sustainable transport strategies to encourage cycling, walking, and cross valley connections to overcome traditional obstacles to freedom of movement in this area; cleaning up contaminated land, enhancing the unique environmental, and historic legacy of the Lower Lea Valley; and optimising the Olympic investment of parklands, sporting venues, open space, and new employment spaces. The overarching framework, guided by these seven development principles, would integrate, like a patchwork quilt, 15 separate subareas and the Olympic Park with additional infrastructure, facilities, and services, including transport, to facilitate projected levels of growth of households and employment for London.

Accompanied by a whole suite of technical documents (covering topics such as Flood Risk Assessment; Strategic Land Use Assessments; Strategic Environmental Assessments; Socio-Economic Strategies, and Delivery/Investment Strategy), the OPADF demonstrated, in 2007, the scale of ambition and the seriousness and rigour of the approach of the LDA for regeneration in the Lower Lea Valley. The fact that this work, and the earlier master-planning work in preparation for, and post-Olympic bid, was undertaken by master planners, EDAW, meant that the consortium formed in 2007 by EDAW to bid for the master-planning work, focusing specifically on the post-Games legacy use of the Olympic Park, stood the best chance not just of winning the contract, but of quickly advancing the work in relation to an overall appreciation of the place of the Olympic Park in the context of the plans for the regeneration of the Lea Valley.

Asked by the LDA to join forces with rival bidders, the Dutch firm, Kees Christiaanse Architects and Planners (KCAP), EDAW were forced to accommodate to the international reputation of urban design and planning in the Netherlands, which, not surprisingly, is to do with achieving a successful balance between land and waterways. The Dutch are also famous for urban experimentation and for translating this flair into new design standards that lead the way in terms of both the contemporary pre-occupation with minimising the effects on the environment of urban development, and enhancing city living through the creation of sustainable urban neighbourhoods.

As the Director of the Land Team at the Legacy Directorate, Gareth Blacker and his small team of planners, are clients at the LDA, of the EDAW master-planning consortium. Not satisfied with the completion, in 2007, of the rapid assembly of lands for the construction of the Olympic Park, Gareth has another breakneck deadline on his hands, to oversee the master-planning process and to submit the planning applications for the post-Games legacy uses of the Olympic Park by the summer of 2009. At the beginning of my research, in November 2008, the master-planning team has already produced, after a summer of public and stakeholder consultation, the third iteration, Output C, of the scheme for an Olympic Park master plan. The next and final step, in early 2009, is to advance to 'Scheme Fix', which is the finalisation of a set of plans that, subject to a final round of consultation, will lead to the submission of the planning applications. No wonder that there is an air, in the Legacy Directorate, of heightened activity and anticipation, surrounding the master-planning process. With a new mayor hovering over the LDA, and its legacy plans, and with the prospect of the transformation on the cards of the Legacy Directorate into some kind of new URC, there is every likelihood that Gareth Blacker's plans will be compromised in some way, but there is nothing to do, but press on in the hope that the risk to the Olympic legacy will be too great of compromising the momentum generated so far. After all, the whole point of an early submission of planning applications for the park in legacy mode is that it will send a strong and clear signal to private and public investors that the Legacy Directorate is about to be 'open for business'.

The Legacy Master Plan Framework

Fashionably described as 'place-making', the process of producing a master plan framework is very different to the more straightforward procedures involved in urban planning, which, in any local government constituency, is about the management, through a system of state-organised regulatory controls, of individual applications for private development. A master plan is more comprehensive; it is often commissioned by the public sector and involves the imagining of ambitious, large-scale, long-term, and complex schemes for development that may, as in the case of the Olympic Park legacy plans, cut across local government boundaries.

Quite often, however, the commissioning, and envisioning of a master plan, is as far as these grandiose projects for spatial development may get, which means that even as a lucrative industry of master-planning proliferates, it may be the case, for any particular location, that a littered trail of master plans, all lead to the disappointing realisation that, for various reasons, attempts have failed, to make development happen. It is the failure of so many master plans in the UK that makes the successful realisation of any one plan all the more interesting. It begs the question of what conditions needs to be met for new urban futures to come into being.

In the attempt to avoid the hotchpotch, or haphazard kind of urban development that can arise from the accumulation of individual, small-scale planning applications, each of which serves only its own needs, the master plan sets out broad aspirations and a clear vision for the wider area under consideration. The aim is to imagine in a more integrated, cohesive way of thinking and strategising what kind of place could be brought into being in the future. The focus on 'place' is about synthesising existing understanding in urban design about what makes places work, that is, what makes them live-able, enjoyable places to inhabit, to work in, or to visit. For example, the south bank of the Thames is celebrated as a constantly vibrant visitor destination, and a highly desirable place to live and work, because it has evolved, over a long period of time, in such a way that it now combines just the right balance of attractive riverside location with a mix of building developments whose uses bring waterway, housing, offices, restaurants, cultural institutions, and entertainment into close, but varied kinds of proximity. It is often said of Canary Wharf, in contrast, that it does not work 'as a place', because the way it was designed—as a citadel containing the skyscrapers of high finance, with shopping outlets hidden away, underground—means that during the day it might be a good place to work (from a certain perspective), but in the evenings and at weekends, it is not a good place to live. This is because it is cut off by infrastructural obstacles from surrounding areas, and, internally, it is 'dead', because it was designed with a sole purpose—to facilitate the business of the finance sector—so that once the tens of thousands of workers empty out of it at the end of the day and at the end of the working week, it risks becoming a soulless place, which is not helped by the fact that it is also heavily policed by a private security force.

Accounting for the highly specific geographic features of the location, which, in the case of the Olympic Park in the Lower Lea Valley, is to do with the engineering challenges posed by a river valley, with varied waterways, steep river banks, marshes, flood plains, and heavily polluted land and water, the master plan combines physical—land and infrastructure (transport, waste, bridges, utilities, etc.) plans—with proposals for what else needs to be considered to make the location work as a viable place. The master plan works to a red line boundary, in terms of what can be imagined for the actual land that has been assembled for consideration, but it also situates the questions about what kind of place could be brought into being on this land, in the broader context of its surrounding location. It asks how the new place will work in terms of immediately neighbouring areas, and in the best-case scenario, it asks how the development scheme for the new place can derive worth from and add value to the already existing spatial context. For example, in the case of the Legacy Master Plan Framework (LMF), the spatial master plan (in keeping with the early master-planning work that preceded the Legacy plans) is accompanied by a whole suite of strategy documents, including socio-economic calculations about the levels of necessary additional social infrastructure, such as schools, health, and community facilities, that will be necessary to the successful evolution not just of the new place, but also its existing environs.

The LMF maps out the key spatial elements of the Olympic Park site such as the possible relationship between the waterways, and the land that can be used for the development of new housing, and employment spaces. It also shows how the land could be divided up into 'development platforms', which is the next stage in the materialisation of the intention to transform industrial land to new uses.

The plans for the use of development platforms are designed to be indicative and flexible—they might change in time, but they show, spatially, what could be done where, when, and how—and they signify to the market that investment opportunities are going to be made available in this place. The plans work like a kind of persuasion device, and are central, therefore, to the Legacy Directorate's, and Tom Russell's main mission, which is to recruit allies to the cause, to get people on board, and keep them on board to build momentum, and encourage both investors and people who live locally to the development to imagine, in positive terms, the future post-Games possibilities of particular places currently under construction.

The plans also indicate to the Legacy Directorate, how it is that the scheme could lead, through the gradual materialisation of plans, to the generation of the kind of property development that might yield the financial return needed for the repayment of Olympic debts. The challenge for master planners is to provide a degree of certainty, to encourage local residents and investors, and to placate government, whilst also promising a degree of adaptability over the long period of time—more than 30 years—that it is imagined it will take to bring development plans to fruition.

The current iteration of the Master Plan, which is called Output C, envisages the possibility of 76 individual development platforms, 65 % of which will be dedicated to residential use, with a potential for 10,000–12,000 new homes, over 40 % of which will be family housing, with at least 35 % of the homes designated as 'affordable'. The affordable homes will be split 50:50 between those dedicated to social rent (borough council or Registered Social Landlord [RSL] allocated homes) and those to intermediate tenure—part buy/part rent housing—which allows those people who are doing well economically to get on the housing ladder even though they cannot yet afford an ordinary mortgage, to buy a home on the open market.

Based on a rigorous analysis of London housing policy, the various needs and aspirations for housing of the Lower Lea Valley Olympic host boroughs, and the plans of the Lower Lea Valley Opportunity Area Planning Development Framework (LLV OAPDF), the Legacy Master Plan presents, in its socio-economic strategy, a proposal for a priority, in the future Olympic Park, on family housing. This is to locally address the problem of there being insufficient aspirational housing for those who are doing well for themselves to stay, and grow their families in the area, rather than moving out to Essex. The aim, by encouraging people to stay in East London, is to develop sustainable, stable neighbourhoods and communities that will start to turn around the problem in the area of a high level of population turnover, or 'churn'. The same rationale is given for the commitment to the provision of Lifetime Homes, which means that housing should be designed to be adaptable, over time, to the changing needs of families and individuals, as life circumstances transform. In this way, people do not have to leave their homes as they go through different phases of their lives, and the hope is, therefore, that neighbourhoods will remain the focus of a long-term commitment to urban living. Similarly, the idea is to provide a whole range of housing types, from one bedroom apartments to four bedroom family housing of various kinds, so that as any person's needs change, there will be the possibility for moving, within the Olympic Park, from one kind of housing to another without having to leave the area all together.

Urban Stitches

The focus on family housing is also designed to address the problems locally, in the Lower Lea Valley host Olympic boroughs, of serious overcrowding and overprovision, privately, of smaller apartments in new housing developments. Recognising, too, the need for appropriate density and space standards, with more space per housing unit in social rented family accommodation, as well as provision close to family housing, of open space, play space, social infrastructure, schools, and transport, the Legacy Master Plan reaches towards the latest and highest standards in housing policy. It also breaks new ground, in the sense that rather than planning in the building structures first and then implying a forced fit of people to place, it has begun, instead, and is trying to work innovatively, with the idea that a better approach is to work out what kind of people are going to be living, working, and travelling through the Olympic Park and its immediate surroundings, and then, designing the place and the housing to reflect that. Ideally the mix of housing types and tenures, with integration of surrounding areas, as well as a commitment to mixed development, with, in some areas, employment spaces provided alongside housing, will lead to a residential combination of people from different social and ethnic backgrounds reflecting the wider area, which is a part of London characterised by a young and ethnically diverse population.

Similarly, the in-depth analysis of the need for social infrastructure relative to planned housing demonstrates the seriousness with which the master-planning consortium is treating the regeneration brief from the Legacy Directorate. The projection of an additional 10,000–12,000 homes as a result of the long-term development of the Olympic Park will lead to an additional population of approximately 19,100 people, and this is on top of the rise in population of 51,800 people, in the areas immediately surrounding the park over a 20-year period to 2028. Inside the park itself, the additional population will lead to a need for three more primary schools, a secondary school, up to ten more nurseries, eleven general practitioners (GPs), ten more dentists, additional emergency health and social care, community space, outdoor play space, library space, multi-faith facilities, and safer neighbourhood teams.

The planned location of the LMF social infrastructure within the park takes into account both the different 'character' of the new neighbourhoods that are being imagined, as well as the most pressing needs for additional services and facilities in the immediately surrounding areas. In this way, the provision of infrastructure to combined populations, in and outside the park, becomes another means for the integration of the park with existing neighbourhoods. This is to avoid the Canary Wharf effect, where a prospering, well-to-do, well-cared-for population can easily ignore a wider population nearby, whose needs are sorely neglected.

The idea, to make possible the integration of the park into its surrounding context, is to 'stitch' the park into the urban fabric, by embedding the LMF in the broader context of the SRF, and by also planning for social infrastructure, transport links, and bridges, to increase possibilities for 'connectivity', so that the red line boundary marking out the land on a map is not perceived as an impenetrable border in real life, but rather is the means for the forging of new relationships between new and existing neighbourhoods.

In addition, a whole set of Fringe Master Plans are in the making, which will ensure that the areas closest to the edge of the Olympic Park will have also been thought through, and their development strategically planned in conversation with the LMF and the SRF. Five Fringe Master Plans have been commissioned, including Hackney Wick and Fish Island to the northwest of the park: Bromley-by-Bow; Sugarhouse Lane and Three Mills to the southwest; Stratford High Street; Stratford Town Centre to the southeast; and the Northern Olympic Fringe to the northwest.

Character Areas

Output C describes a plan for the development platforms to be divided into six new neighbourhoods inside the park. These are 'character areas'—Hackney Wick East, Stratford Village, Stratford Waterfront, Old Ford, Pudding Mill, and Olympic Quarter—designed in such a way that each has its own distinctive sense of place and character based on a combination of the location's history, its Olympic inheritance, and relevant geographical features. In each neighbourhood area, depending on its location and surrounding context, a different balance is envisaged for the use of development platforms for residential and employment use, with space for education, social infrastructure, employment, retail, leisure, cultural activities, and car parking. The ambition is for 9000–10,000 new jobs in the creative and media industries, the service sector, financial and professional services, and tourism and leisure, but because the whole development is going to take 30 years, or more, the plans for the evolution of these ambitions and each character area are phased with investment opportunities staggered over time.

Because of the long time period for development, when some development plots will be idle for much longer than others, it is imagined that a 'festival landscape' will provide for an ongoing series of events to animate the park and to contribute to the growth of a visitor economy.

The plans make clear that this is not a quick fix; the regeneration of the Olympic Park involves a long-term scheme of transformation, which will take decades to come to complete fruition, and this will lead to the necessity for the careful management of public expectations about Olympic legacy after the Games.

The Park and Sporting Venues

Other key spatial elements[2] in the scheme include the waterways, the 102 hectares of MOL that must be set aside for open space and parklands, and the 'Olympic Inheritance', which makes this place a future park like no other. This is to be a park, which, after the Games, will contain not just housing and spaces for employment and infrastructure, but also the set of sporting venues that are to be left at the site—the Olympic stadium, the Aquatics Centre, the multi-use sports venue, the Velodrome, the BMX track, the road cycle circuit, the hockey centre, the tennis centre, and five-a-side football pitches.

The master planners have also shown a careful attentiveness to the sightlines in the park so that the height of any planned building does not obscure the view of what is considered to be the right kind of architectural form for housing and employment space in any other character area. Thus, each new neighbourhood must stand alone in its distinctiveness and work as a place overall, but it must also relate to the whole park in the way that the geographical features and built form, complement and speak to each other in a mutually enhancing way. The focus on the views from the different locations of the park has led the master planners to propose a special focus on the highest point in the west of the park, which they have named, rather pompously, The Belvedere, and suggested that this becomes a point for the development of ideas for an important cultural focus for the park.

---

[2] For a visual sense of the evolution of the Illustrative Masterplan, Output C, see pages 164, 165, 174 & 179 of the PhD thesis of Juliet Davis http://etheses.lse.ac.uk/382/1/JulietDavisPhD.pdf. It is no longer possible to access these maps online, and the analysis given in this PhD, of the evolution of the spatial development of park plans, is invaluable.

In relation to the site's key elements, it becomes clear in the masterplanners' outputs, not only what is going to be distinctive about this new place, but also that a particular kind of rationale underpins the strategic thinking that goes into the task of future-scaping this location. Holding to the original development principles of the earlier master-planning work for the Lower Lea Valley, and within the limits of what the site makes possible, (without compromising the waterways, open space, and parklands), a certain number of post-industrial development platforms are to be created, to contribute to the generation of sufficient new housing for London, and from which sufficient value must be created to repay Olympic debts. And, all this must be done without undermining both the overarching ambition of the project, which is to make this scheme make a difference to the overall physical, social, and economic regeneration of the Lower Lea Valley, and the desire in the Olympic Host Boroughs in the Lower Lea Valley for a set of plans that will transform the perception of East London in the minds of its inhabitants, making the east of the city a new destination of choice, rather than a place that no one wants to visit unless absolutely necessary, and that current residents want to escape as soon as possible.

This is no mean feat, and it is no wonder, bearing in mind just how much careful work has gone into the plans, that the Legacy Directorate's Land Team is feeling nervous about the new mayor, who is throwing his weight around and implying that the LDA has made a mess of legacy planning so far. I cannot help but feel, just as I do about Tom Russell and Geoff Newton, that Gareth Blacker's days are also numbered; Gareth is the driving force behind the LMF, as client at the Legacy Directorate, and his reputation depends on the super fast and efficient progression of the plans towards next summer's submission of the planning application for the scheme.

It is hard to have to say this, and perhaps cynical of me, but it only seems logical on the basis of what I am learning about the political landscape of legacy that regardless of the dedication of the EDAW master-planning consortium, and all that time and money spent on the process so far, that a politician who wants to lay claim to the future of the Olympic Park and its legacy is going to bring the momentum of the master-planning process and future-scaping work to a stop, so that it can be appropriated and restarted in a new and more politically palatable form.

Suggested Reading

Abram, S. (2011) *Culture and planning*. Surrey: Ashgate.
Abram, S., & Weszkalnys, G. (Eds.). (2013). *Elusive promises: Planning in the contemporary world*. New York: Berghahn Books.
Bernstock, P. (2014). *Olympic housing: A critical review of London 2012's legacy*. Surrey: Ashgate.
Bullivant, L. (2012). *Masterplanning futures*. New York: Routledge.
Imrie, R., & Raco, M. (Eds.). (2003). *Urban Renaissance?: New Labour, community and urban policy*. Bristol: The Policy Press.
Imrie, R, Lees, L., & Raco, M. (2008). *Regenerating London: Governance, sustainability, and community in a global city*. New York: Routledge.
Minton, A. (2012). *Ground control: Fear and happiness in the 21st century city*. London: Penguin.
Raco, M. (2015). Sustainable city building and the new politics of the possible: Reflections on the governance of the London Olympics 2012. *Area, 47*(2), 124–131.
Raco, M. (2013). *State led privatisation and the demise of the democratic state: welfare reform and localism in an era of regulatory capitalism*. Surrey: Ashgate.
Rutheiser, C. (1996). *Imagineering Atlanta: The politics of place in the city of dreams*. New York: Verso.

4

Fighting to Be Heard

Tom Russell puts me in the capable hands of Emma Wheelhouse, Senior Consultation and Engagement Manager of the Legacy Directorate. I know of Emma already, because she led the autumn of 2008 consultation events for Output C of the LMF. To try to find a way into the mysteries of the Olympic legacy, I had attended community consultation and technical stakeholder events in the host Olympic boroughs, and observed and participated in workshops, which sought feedback about the master planners' detailed design briefs for each of the six 'character areas' for the Olympic Park in legacy mode.

Emma is one of the indefatigable champions of the Legacy Directorate. She has boundless energy, motivates everyone, and is an inspiration to her small three-woman team of dedicated Consultation and Community Engagement staff. Passionate about East London, Emma has worked in the area for years, and explains the project of regeneration, to me, in terms of a public service commitment to facilitating the changes people want to make in their own lives:

> I did always want to be involved in regeneration, I wanted to do stuff with communities, with real people, around helping them in a practical way

that probably wasn't medicine or counselling, but was about trying to help people transform their own lives, and regen. [regeneration] is an extremely good way to do that. And, the East End represents the very best place to be doing that. Way before the Olympics, it was the East End where, if you look at all of the different urban regeneration projects, and problems, and challenges, and opportunities, this is where it's at. So I was drawn to the East End, because I knew I wanted to work in that field, and it's such an exciting place to start to do some of that. And, so I've been here for quite a few years even before the Games was bid for, really, really enjoyed it as soon as I arrived. It's just such a warm, and welcoming part of London. It's about all the composite different parts, and it is the diversity that makes it, and the energy that makes it so fun, and so exciting to be here, and to work here. I know it better than anywhere else in London, even where I live in South London [because my fiancé works there]. It's easier to connect to, in some weird way. Not everywhere, but I don't know central London that way, I certainly don't know West London at all, all of the tourist patches I get lost in. But in the East End I feel at home. I know the streets, I know the networks, I know how to get to places—I know the people.

Flying the flag for Tom Russell's regeneration agenda, Emma takes seriously her work on the consultation process for the LMF. She is committed to the vision of regeneration that was promised in the Olympic bid, and she too, like Tom, believes that the whole project of the Olympic legacy will be compromised if those stakeholders, local residents, and community organisations living, and working locally to the emerging park, are not brought on board with the plans, and kept on board as the plans transform over time:

> I think regeneration is about using this particular area, and I'm not going to say park site, because I think it shouldn't be a site with a red line boundary, but it's to use this particular part of East London on the back of the investment from The Games to really start a process of genuine regeneration across social, economic, cultural, and environmental, physical levers, and actions, if you like, that start to improve the life chances, and the opportunities of this area. It is about really investing in this part of East London at the grassroots community level, as well as the economic level, investing in skills, and training, and social development, as well as raising the profile, the perception of East London, by creating an iconic visitor

destination, and investment-type focus. So, it's about taking a real long-term regeneration approach to how you can create uplift in this area, and also bring the communities, and the businesses with you as part of that uplift. So it's not replacing what's here, it's supporting, and developing, and improving what's here, and it's doing that in a way that's respectful, and genuine, which mainly takes a long time, but that has the end ambition of creating a much better place.

Emma has overseen the 18-month programme of consultation for the LMF. Like other aspects of the legacy project, the intention for the consultation programme has always been to set new standards in 'best practice', which means that the LDA has, via the Legacy Directorate, dedicated significant time and resource to going far beyond what is required for a statutory period of consultation. This involves creating a long-term relationship built out of ongoing conversations, which means not just seeking comments and queries about the evolution of the master plan, in a way that opinions can potentially affect the planners' decision-making process, but also designing a programme of outreach work to make sure that the process of providing information about the planning of Olympic legacy leads to a growing sense among people living in East London, in the host boroughs, that the Olympic Park is theirs, that it is for them, that they feel a sense of 'ownership' of it, and that the changes taking place there can be transformative of their lives in various ways. Speaking proudly about her work, Emma describes the challenge of trying to get people interested in the post-Games Olympic Park, curious about plans for legacy, and engaged with the future of the place:

> ... a big part of the [legacy] has to do with the planning, and design work for how this space [The Olympic Park] is going to function, and a key part of how we connect people into that is making sure that it serves their [local residents'] needs, and interests. So, formal consultation, done in lots of different ways, but also really properly engaging, and consulting on ideas, and developing them with people's buy in, and involvement, is one of the best ways that we can hopefully achieve the right end result. We have to respect the fact that [at the moment] the park is a massive building site, and will be for a while, even after the Games, and there are people that live right around it. So, how do we mitigate, and reduce those impacts? How do we

give people access to the park? How do we get more people into the park, school groups into the park, tours, all of that sort of stuff, to really try, and open it up as much as is possible? Sometimes that's physically with things like park tours, sometimes it's with things like outreach projects, trying to find ways that people can understand a little bit more about what's going on behind the blue barriers, you know, the security fences.

I ask Emma to explain the particular challenges of the work that she and her team are involved in, and she elaborates:

I think what makes it really challenging is the fact that it is all done under a media spotlight, and that means expectations are set, but sometimes not by us. So, how do you manage those expectations? And that's very, very important when you're working with the communities, because a lot of what they learn first hand is through what they read in the media, or what they see in the media. And a lot of those opinions are formed, and ingrained by what they pick up, which isn't necessarily where you want to start your dialogue. So, it takes a lot of time to build the respect, and the trust, and the understanding of these communities. We've had that advantage of being around for a lot longer than any other host city in terms of the legacy project, which is brilliant, really, really good, and it's been essential to work alongside the ODA [Olympic Delivery Authority] and LOCOG [London Organizing Committee of the Olympic Games] right from the start, but it doesn't necessarily mean it's still an easy ride, because those expectations are so ingrained, and so challenging in terms of what's been said, and it's also really quite hard to explain why things [the planning and realization of legacy] take so long. So I think managing expectations is a number one challenge, and that's made so much harder, because we are under this media, and political spotlight, and we always will be, and that's only going to increase after the Games. And I'm particularly worried about that period, because I feel like the media is hungry for a failure. They're just waiting for it, because that's what makes a good headline. So it doesn't matter all the fabulous work that we have already done, you know, and all the good progress that we've got in train, it's like they don't want to give us the time to prove that we can do it.

Emma describes how difficult it is for herself, and her team, to be the forward/public facing front of the legacy operation, responsible for forging a relationship with the communities and organisations living locally to the park, getting to know about what life is like in East London from residents' perspective, learning about what changes they would like to see happen, and then, also fighting the cause of a community-led regeneration inside the Legacy Directorate. All this whilst also having to be realistic about what the legacy project can and cannot achieve. Emma explains that maintaining this two-way dialogue, communicating about what regeneration means inside and outside the directorate, is a difficult balance to strike:

> It hasn't been an easy ride, because it's been constantly positioning the importance of regeneration in terms of community benefit, fighting for that, proving that internally. You know, that's what's really hard about my role, it's a lot of what feels like fighting, and the day-to-day reminders, and rationalisation of why we should be doing this, and why does business benefit. It's always positioning, and campaigning on an internal level to say this is the right thing to do, and this is why. I would say perhaps what [the process of consultation] did highlight, which is interesting, and which we need to do more on, is going back to that point about trying to understand what hasn't really stuck with people, what doesn't really resonate. So it might have been key messages that we had, or key points we were trying to get across that still people are saying, "I don't get it'", or, "I want more on this", or, "I don't understand that", or, "can you explain it?" And that makes me think, "oh okay, we're obviously not clear about this, or people just aren't relating to that". So, where I think we need to be a little bit smarter is adjusting our message, or our work to respond to some of those blanks if you like. And I think that's an on-going process, and I think that's part of informing the communications strategy. I think it's how we tell the story, and trying to make sure that we pitch that story correctly for the different stakeholder groups. And it's always important to be able to kind of listen, and learn, and adapt. I think we're now in the adapting stage. You know, we have listened, we'll continue to listen, we're always learning, but we have to be able to adapt the way that we kind of translate that intelligence and then play it back again.

The point that Emma makes, about 'the story', is important. It is a reminder that the Community Consultation and Engagement initiative is part of the Communications, or Comms. Team of the Legacy Directorate.

Part of Emma's job, alongside those in the directorate who are working on marketing, press and media, as well as public affairs (which is about speaking to, liaising with, and cultivating political support in central and London government), is to get 'the message' out about the emerging plans for an Olympic legacy and to communicate how the process of designing and envisaging that legacy is taking shape. As Emma says, it is about crafting a 'story', and the whole point of this is to be persuasive, because it is confidence that drives the project forward. The making of these messages, which constitute the ongoing production of a story—a coherent narrative—about Olympic legacy is part of what Tom Russell is talking about; it is about the necessity to recruit allies to the cause, to get people on board with the plans for Olympic legacy, and then, to keep those people on board. And, it is about trying to keep a positive spin on things, even in the face of a political and media machine, as well as a general and East London public that are unsurprisingly highly sceptical both about the Games and their legacy.

Rather than dismissing this narrative as nothing more than a rhetorical device, I would argue that the 'lines' and 'messages' that are the creative output of the Comms. Team about the current state of legacy affairs, as well as the documents and visuals which embody and represent the story, are to be understood as the materials that allow for the construction of a network—a set of supportive, if critical, relationships—that gets people on board and lends momentum to the project, partly by preventing it from being slowed down by the friction of furious resistance from people and organisations, who might otherwise feel run over, roughshod, by the Olympic machinery.

Emma is not naïve about the difficulties involved in the legacy project; she has a clear sense that the Legacy Directorate cannot do everything by itself, and that as just one part of the organisational landscape in East London, it can only ever be part of the picture. She is also aware that the challenge of regeneration in East London is about sustaining political interest and public sector funding for the project in the long-term, so that public money and political influence can be used to entice private investment to play a part:

> I think the challenges are about being quite clear about what we can and can't take responsibility for, being clear internally, and action-ing work

accordingly, being clear externally, and developing partnerships accordingly, so that whatever needs to be done can still be done, but we might not be the lead organisation on some things, we might just facilitate some things, or we might just need to be aware of other things happening. So, being really clear about what our strategy is, and why it is, and then what we are investing to support the delivery of that, and where there are gaps, trying to work with others to fill them. I think there are some very practical challenges about sustaining political buy-in over such a long period, sustaining financial commitments from the public sector to mean that you can actually lever in the private sector investments that we know we can do, but you've got to seed fund that, you've got to enable that, you've got to work at that. It's kind of like you have to put in, to get out, which everybody understands, but it's keeping that going, which is really hard, because [after The Games are over] what we'll lose is the reason, the 2012 umbrella that's allowed all this investment, and all this focus. When that goes it could almost be counterproductive, because it could be seen as well, "you've had it, you know, there was your £9.3 billion". So, I think it's about being clear about exactly what we need to do, and how we're going to do it, and what we're responsible for, trying to fill in those gaps through partnership working, and really effective relationships with other delivery partners, and bodies. I think that's really important. So, being humble enough to recognise we have a key role to play, but we are not going to be, you know, the single entity that dictates success, or not in this area. And it is vital that we bring people along with us, because it's going to be a long journey.

The Consultation Process

Professor Paul Brickell, one of the East London change-makers, is—through his involvement in the regeneration company, Leaside Regeneration, part of the master-planning consortium with responsibility, alongside the consultancy Beyond Green—for the design and delivery of the LMF consultation process. He has been working closely with Emma, who learned the ropes of community engagement with Paul, when she worked at Leaside Regeneration. Paul's approach to consultation is that it should not be a tick-box exercise; people's opinions should be sought, but rather than just facilitating the voicing of thoughts, feelings, and ideas, the process of consultation ought to, and can, in the best-case scenario, lead not just to a more collaborative approach to urban planning, but also to a life-changing process of learning about planning as a problem-solving device for effecting urban and social change.

For example, Emma has just launched the Legacy Youth Panel, in association with Fundamental, the independent East London-based architecture centre, which provides training, skills development, and confidence building to people whose lives are to be affected by processes of urban change. The aim is to create better places in cities, by enhancing the capacity for people to actively engage with planners and developers. From a position of in-depth knowledge, and greater understanding, people are taught how to engage in the process of consultation, so that it is more likely to lead to a genuinely negotiated series of changes in the urban environment.

Fundamental leads Architecture Crew, the UK's first architectural youth forum, which aims to educate young people about the process of urban planning and development so that they can develop the skills to participate effectively in the changes that are going to affect the places where they live, and are growing up. The idea is to also educate planners and developers about how engaging with young people might lead to the design and creation of places that work better for everyone. Drawing on the model of the Architecture Crew, and working with Nick Edwards, the Chief Executive of Fundamental, Emma and her team have collaborated in the creation of a Legacy Youth Panel, and also a schools' programme, reaching out to inform and get local school children engaged with, and thinking about the Olympic legacy. The Legacy Youth Panel is a forum of young people, 14–19 years old from the host Olympic boroughs who are being trained to participate in the consultation process for the LMF and, through this process of participation, develop life-changing skills. Each year, twenty-five young people are to be recruited to the programme to undertake training in order to develop their expertise, learn about the specific planning and development process relating to the emerging Olympic Park in legacy mode, and also to find out more about the evolution of the urban environment both in East London, and in London more generally.

Twelve to fifteen of these young people will take part in the consultation process itself, which will involve dedicated meetings with the LMF master-planning team, and lead to the production of an official response to the most recent iteration of the legacy plans in Output C. The young people are expected to communicate their aspirations for the future of East London, to explain what they want for the Olympic Park in legacy mode, and to contribute their perceptions of what it is like to live and grow up in East London. Some young people have already expressed, for example, how important a sense of place, and especially postcodes, are to youth identity. Some of the young people who are participating in the project have never left East London, or even their own local area, and this begins to explain what kinds of problems are posed to young people by the activities of territorial street gangs, and how important it is to them to address this problem, and to change perceptions of young people in East London.

What matters about the project, from Emma's point of view, is that the views of young people are to be taken seriously, and they are going to have the opportunity to develop their CVs in significant ways as a result of making a long-term commitment to the project. The members of the Youth Panel are to design their own logo, organise events to raise awareness among other young people in the East End of London about the legacy planning process, and, as the project progresses, to use Fundamental's mixed media approach to produce music and visuals to demonstrate their process of learning and development.

The View Tube

Apart from the insistence on consultation as a potential for life-changing opportunity, Paul Brickell is also adamant that the process of community engagement must contain possibilities for lending support to entrepreneurial social enterprise in the host boroughs of East London. He explains to me that he has tried numerous times, in numerous ways, to explain what he means by this to senior people both in the ODA, and in the Legacy Directorate, but they just 'don't get it'. So, he is determined to show them what he means, and to show them at the same time that it is vital, early on, to create a meaningful relationship between people and the park so that they begin to get a sense of 'ownership' and accessibility, even during the pre-Games construction phase. Paul describes this as the need to make 'dents in the fence'—spaces where people can see in, and are welcomed to come forward to overcome the sense of exclusion created by the securitised boundary of the park. He explains to me that unless the consultation and engagement programme can create 'a thousand golden threads', linking people to the park, he is sure that the legacy project will fail.

One of the social enterprise initiatives Paul is developing with the team at Leaside Regeneration is the View Tube project. This is going to be a place where people can go to get right up close to the Olympic Park construction site, and, from the southern end of the park, close to the Pudding Mill DLR station, from the heights of The Greenway (the cycle way and footpath that runs from Tower Hamlets to Newham, on top of the length of the London's Victorian Outfall Sewer) get a look at the Olympic stadium coming into existence, and feel a sense of excitement about all the activity that is happening on site.

The way the enterprise works is by developing an idea that makes good business sense, but for all profits to be ploughed back into a social endeavour, whose objective is to inspire community engagement with the park. The View Tube plan is genius, because it makes use of recycled shipping containers to house a café, a classroom, cycle hire, and exhibition space, all without being heavy enough to be impermissible as a construction. Paul has fought hard to obtain funding for the project from the ODA, Thames Water, and the LTGDC, and it should be up and running by the end of next summer.

The Strategic Regeneration Framework

Compared to the frustration of losing battles over what would have been big wins for local legacy initiatives, like West Ham football club in the Olympic stadium and a leisure pool in the post-Games Aquatics Centre, the View Tube is a small, but not insignificant victory. It signifies the determination of East London strategists, like Paul Brickell, to keep fighting for the cause of an Olympic legacy that supports and adapts to what is already understood about community-inspired regeneration. From this perspective, it is perhaps no surprise that Paul was once a Professor of Haematology and head of a successful cancer research laboratory; he continues to engage in experiments about revitalisation, only now his laboratory is in the urban environment.

Paul reiterates that the struggle, in the host boroughs, is to fight against the imposition of a top-down vision of Olympic legacy, and he explains that this is what has led, this year, to the formation of the Olympic Park Regeneration Steering Group (OPRSG), which brings together, for quarterly meetings about prioritising regeneration in East London, the chief executives and mayors of the host Olympic boroughs, with Tom Russell from the Legacy Directorate; the Mayor of London; Tessa Jowell, Minister for the Olympics; and Hazel Blears, Secretary of State for Communities and Local Government. This is in addition to the creation, last year, of the Host Boroughs' Unit, which is leading on the design of the SRF. The unit is led by Roger Taylor, who is another Manchester import, with a wealth of experience in the public sector from his recent experience as Chief Executive of Waltham Forest Council and, before that, Manchester City Council.

Part of the Olympic Opportunities team at the Legacy Directorate, working in partnership with the host Olympic boroughs and leading on the development of socio-economic legacy, is a small three-person team, which is seconded from the Legacy Directorate to the Host Boroughs Unit, to inform the work on the SRF. Michelle May leads this work. She is another irrepressible legacy champion, an inspiration to her team, and defender of Tom Russell's version of regeneration proper. Michelle was also 'born and bred' in East London; her father is an ex-docker, who now runs a pub in the area, all of her family still live in Newham, and Michelle knows more or less everyone in East London who is working in the field of urban regeneration and economic transformation. She explains to me that part of what motivates her is the fact that coming from the local area herself, and getting paid such a lot of money to do what she does for a living—working in regeneration—she wants to be able to 'look people in the eye', and feel that her work is really making a difference; she needs to believe that there is a reason for these large pay packets, and that this project is not about exploitation. Michelle says that it is important to her that this project does better than anything she has worked on in the past, and she is ready to fight for this outcome, because she cannot bear the frustration of feeling that it might all come to nothing. This would be unacceptable, she says, for families, like her own in Canning Town, where young boys, like her nephews, are going to leave school and, most likely, face limited opportunities and disillusionment about the promise of urban regeneration:

> I do get disillusioned, because I've worked in regeneration now for 20 years, and really I've done some good projects, but actually has any of it, apart from for a few beneficiaries of projects, has it really made a difference? Realistically, we have to make, create a development, which makes sense to the area that it fits into. It can't be seen as a development that has no relationship with anything that sits outside of it. And that is about whether existing residents in the future live on the site, go to school on the site, have jobs on the site. So, the task is to make it a part of the existing place so that you almost wouldn't know that you've stepped over a boundary. So, to develop without a visible red line, and just to be really bold, and brave about what is a once in a lifetime opportunity. We have to set the bar. But to do all of that, and make it a viable scheme, and pay back [the government], that's a huge challenge.

I ask Michelle to explain what kind of work her team is involved in, and she elaborates:

> The work is about [supporting the host boroughs], [job brokerage projects, and the initiatives of employment and skills agencies], getting local people into jobs, increasing qualifications, skill levels, or trying to increase the number of local businesses involved in Olympic, and legacy supply chains. So, for example, we are responsible for delivering the local employment training framework (LETF), which is a £9 million employment [constructions and other] skills programme for the five host boroughs. We were always meant to be the glue between the Olympic Land Team who were doing the physical stuff, and then Geoff [Newton's] pan London [Oly. Opps.] team. We were the team that tried to do a very localised socio-economic programme linked

to the emerging [LMF] master plan. And you can't ever under estimate how much good relationships, you know, managing to keep them, [the host boroughs] trusting us, and wanting to work with us, you can't underestimate that as a sort of success really. I think partners [host boroughs] do trust us, and that we're here to do a good job, and that we share their ambitions around local regeneration, and I'm proud of that.

In the same way that Emma's Consultation and Community Engagement Team are creating and cultivating the relationships necessary to keeping local residents and community organisations informed about, contributing to, and challenging plans for the post-Games legacy, Michelle's Socio-economic Team is also building relationships with a key set of organisational bodies in the host Olympic boroughs and, in doing so, is building momentum for the legacy project by supporting East London in its aspirations for social and economic change. The contribution of Michelle's team to the work of the Host Boroughs Unit in developing the SRF is, in the Tom Russell version of things, about putting in place the policy context in relation to which all efforts and work streams of the Legacy Directorate, and other relevant agencies and organisations become geared towards a shared aspiration of improving opportunities and living standards for residents of the Lower Lea Valley.

What worries me is that if the change in political climate leads to the axing of Geoff Newton's Olympic Opportunities, as I predict it will, the work of Michelle's team, and the priority given to the SRF, may go with it. This would potentially jeopardise the opportunity to articulate the LMF with an overarching set of regeneration priorities determined by the host boroughs. Meanwhile, it is clear from the latest round of consultation activities for Output C that East London strategists are not waiting around to find out what the future will bring; on the contrary, they are making the most of the consultation process as the chance to find out about current plans and to enter into supportive and critical dialogue with planners. The opportunity is not lost on them to persuade and to harass the Legacy Directorate about what support they need to realise their plans about what they already have in mind for the places they are trying to transform.

Technical Workshops

Because the participants in the Output C technical consultation workshops tend to be involved, like Paul Brickell, in leading the combined effort to address the particular challenges of East London living, they are more likely to have an understanding of the strategic landscape, in terms of already existing, often pre-Olympic plans for transformation, as well as an awareness of the organisational frameworks, and social networks through which public service and private enterprises are currently being delivered. They are in a good position, therefore, to pose questions not just about the details of the plans for the legacy park and its particular 'character areas', but also, more generally, about how the LMF, the Legacy Directorate, and the SRF can support and add value to a local scene of proliferating home-grown initiatives.

Local leaders and strategists, from over fifty-two different organisations, have been regularly attending a series of Legacy Master Plan technical workshops on a variety of themes (housing, transport, social infrastructure, environment, sports, arts and cultural infrastructure, employment and economic renewal). These provide the opportunity for challenges to be made to the most current ideas. For example, John Lock of the UEL, one of the key East London strategists, in one technical workshop, responds to the idea of attracting a world-class higher education institution, like Loughborough (a university famous for its sporting excellence), to develop a campus and research institute in the legacy park. John says to the planners and Legacy Directorate consultation team:

> Talk to us! If there is something we can't do, talk to us! Don't import Loughborough. We have had ten, or more years of experience working together to bring creative, and media education institutes to the East of London—Ravensbourne College, Goldsmiths Fine Art, UEL Institute of Performing Arts, and LABAN. There is no need to import 'world class'— we are already creating that momentum for ourselves. UEL can come together in a community of educational organisations in the Olympic Stadium, with a research institute located at the Media Centre (in Hackney Wick). We can add partners, but don't parachute 'world-class' institutions in. Think about working together with us.

After the workshop, John explains to me the importance of UEL in the context of East London. It gives a second chance for people to get qualified after what he describes as 'a crap education at school', and he describes to me the determination at UEL to generate legacy from the Olympics. They have been involved, early on, as soon as the success of the bid was announced, in developing, at UEL, a sporting infrastructure and academic programme, and creating new partnerships with sporting bodies in the UK, and around the world, so that UEL will be in a position, by 2012, to play host to foreign athletes, and their teams, training for the Games, as well as officials, and Olympic-related visitors.

John's relentless determination has meant that UEL is centrally involved in the plans for legacy, including the proposal, which is currently included in the Legacy Master Plan, for a sports specialist secondary school to be located at the Olympic stadium. Rather than waiting for the Olympic legacy to come to UEL, it is clear that UEL has been instrumental in creating legacy from the Games for itself, and is actively lending its initiative to the Legacy Directorate. This means that John, and others like him in the host boroughs, are in a good position to make the most of the technical workshops, and to use them as an opportunity not just to challenge the planners about their ideas and make suggestions about what the Legacy Master Plan needs to offer, but also to pester the Legacy Directorate, in an effort to persuade the powers that be, and to promote their own causes.

Sharing with me his sense of the strategic context—the organisational and institutional background against which legacy plans are developing—John emphasises that the public sector alone cannot solve the problems that need to be addressed in East London. He explains to me how important the right balance is, in urban change, between public and private collaboration. Public service provision in East London must, John says, be better integrated, and the opportunity to develop a SRF, and a Multi-Area Agreement (MAA), across the host Olympic boroughs, provides the opportunity for this articulation of interests across health, housing, education, environment, and employment. John acknowledges that work on the development of the SRF, which is being undertaken by the Host Boroughs Unit, is running seriously behind the LMF, which means that planners cannot yet say anything about how it is envisaged that plans for the legacy park will contribute to, and be articulated with, the broader aspirations for change of the host boroughs more generally, but expectations remain high about the potential for integration of policy and planning across the various issues most affecting the population of East London.

John emphasises the importance of the private sector. This is why, he says, the evolution of the Legacy Directorate is so important. It must move away from the public sector way of working of the LDA into an URC (which is currently described, by those in government who are designing and bringing it into being, as a Special Purpose Vehicle [SPV]), with a private sector chair and an appropriate public/private split on the board. This is not only because guarantees need to be given, John explains, about the long-term management of the future Olympic Park, but also so that ambitions remain high, even in hard times, about the scale of transformation needed to effect sustainable change in the area. John has no doubt that given the right leadership, the direction of travel of Olympic legacy can be steered carefully between the need to inspire confidence in investors, to attract private finance to the project, and the necessity to keep public sector and local community organisations' interests at heart.

Continuing in an entrepreneurial vein, John describes how important it is to support and develop the active, commercial aspirations of the diverse working-class communities of the East London, and he contrasts this business-minded grass roots energy to the loss of hope in many of the long-standing white working-class families in East London, such as in Canning Town, who have lost everything with the loss of industry, docks, and manufacture, and also feel abandoned by a new kind of Labour politics, which no longer represents their interests. The grievances of these people need to be heard and acted upon, John suggests, especially because regeneration initiatives in Canning Town have been less than welcome by local people, and far from successful by any measure. Part of the problem, John suggests, is that housing-led schemes without associated economic revival strategies are always going to be doomed to fail. These kinds of schemes come about, he says, because all too often well-meaning policy-makers do not live in, or properly understand the places they plan to change. People like himself and Paul Brickell, who live and work in the areas they are dedicated to serving and transforming, are, John says, all too rare.

The public/private collaboration is also important, John explains, because it overcomes the idea that only politicians know what is best for the areas they govern, and that they should retain control over decision-making processes. That model of local governance in which decisions were made by committees of risk-averse politicians behind closed doors, John stresses, is the past, and a more entrepreneurial, but arguably less democratic model of urban decision-making is now the norm. This helps me to understand that the political atmosphere, at the level of strategic thinking in East London, is very much New Labour. Following in the footsteps of the Conservative transformation of urban governance, New Labour has continued courting the commercial advantage, and the aspirations of local change-makers, in East London, like John Lock and Paul Brickell, are pragmatic, and far away from the socialist vision of a politics of the people with no need to get into bed with big business. On the contrary, the trick is to harness private finance to the vehicle of public sector aspiration and to inspire the people who are to be served by these changes to join in with the momentum for urban change. This is the very opposite of what John describes as 'local whingeing', which, he says, he is tired of, because it is a repeating and unhelpful refrain that makes endless claims on government for more welfare benefits for the poor, but never makes anything better. The aim, rather, is to overcome entrenched poverty in East London through the transformation of opportunity, and to address the constant 'churn' of people moving through the area by creating mixed-class communities, mixed-class schools, and the kind of new neighbourhoods that anchor people in places, because they want to stay.

From this perspective, I begin to sense that the change of mayor, from the left-wing independent socialist, Ken Livingstone, to Conservative Boris Johnson may well be more welcome than could, at first, be anticipated in the Labour-led host Olympic boroughs in East London. This does not bode well for Tom Russell, or the LDA, and neither does it inspire confidence in me that the integrative idealism at the heart of EDAW's LMF will necessarily be welcome in East London. Despite the depth and rigour of its analytical work, if the LMF sacrifices a big ambition to use the Olympic Park as the springboard to create a new, 'aspirational', 're-branded' identity of place for East London, to a pragmatic design for returning value to the treasury and creating neighbourhoods that are well connected to, and supportive of, surrounding locations, plans for the legacy will be met with circumspection and critique.

Multiple Voices

Echoing John's insistence to planners that they learn better how to work with the existing initiatives for change in East London (but contradicting John's thoughts about a higher education institute in the Media Centre building that will remain after the Games, on the Hackney side of the park), a local councillor, Chris Kennedy, from Hackney uses the technical workshops as a place to fight to be heard:

> Start with the positives of what is already growing here organically, start from what we've got already. What we've got already is creative industries. We are worried about what kind of higher educational institute will be attracted to the Media Centre location, we want it to compliment what we are already planning, which is creative industries. This is where we are coming from, where we have been coming from for a while, long before The Olympics, so why aren't we talking about that today?

Chris is referring to the Wick Master Plan, which, pre-Olympic Games bid, was Hackney Council's vision, using funds from the Single Regeneration Budget (SRB), in the 1990s, to develop, for themselves, the area of post-industrial land that is now inside the boundary of the Olympic Park, and which is now to become the place of the Press and Broadcast Centres. Their aim was to work with an anchor tenant private sector partner, to create an iconic employment space, a headquarters, ideally, around which a cluster of employment-focused initiatives could be grown, centring specifically on media or cultural industries. This was to complement what was already happening in Hackney, which was the proliferation and eastwards expansion of artistic and creative innovation, and transformation of formerly derelict post-industrial buildings for new and vibrant purposes. This artistic renaissance of Hackney Wick, for example, where there are now 600 artists' studios, inhabiting old warehouse spaces, on the periphery of the Olympic Park (amongst housing estates inhabited by long-standing, mostly white working-class residents, who would have been involved in the old industrial and manufacturing economy), was to be the inspiration for the cultivation of an already existing movement for change, into a master plan strategy for creating new kinds of employment for at least 3500 people.

The problem, and the reason for Chris Kennedy's indignation in the technical stakeholders' consultation meeting, is that whilst the idea of a higher education use for the Media Centre is now being bandied about, no one seems to be talking about the plans that Hackney already had for the area, and which Hackney were persuaded to put on hold when the Olympic bid process was begun. The political promise was that the catalyst of the Games would lead to the expansion of Hackney's own ideas, improving on the aim to provide employment, and improved infrastructure, whilst honouring the desire for a creative industries hub of some kind. The recession has, however, put paid to the certainty of that promise, and what might become of the Media Centre remains to be seen because the private investment behind it has pulled out, and as a result, it has now been 'value-designed' in such a way that the government can afford to build it without private sector money, and most major broadcasting and media tenants will no longer find it an attractive proposition after the Games. There is even talk that instead of trying to find legacy tenants, it might be a better idea to pull the buildings down after 2012.

Not to be thwarted, however, Hackney are completely determined, with the support of the East London Business Alliance (ELBA), to lobby for and to realise the legacy they originally envisioned for this area. At every opportunity Hackney mayor, Jules Pipe, is fighting, with local councillors, like Chris Kennedy, to remind legacy planners and central government of the promise that was made to grow a cultural quarter in this part of the park. What most annoys Chris, he says, is that so many people in Hackney are sceptical about the Olympics and the promise of legacy, and he hates to have to imagine that they might be right; he really believed that the Olympics could deliver a more expansive, better supported version of what they had in mind to bring about, and it is a soul-destroying prospect for him to think that after having persuaded people to get on board with the plans, that things might not come to fruition as planned. This is especially difficult for a local councillor in

Hackney when the residents of Lea Bank Square, right on the perimeter of the Olympic Park development, are having to suffer, day and night, the noise, dust, and disruption of the construction project.

The issue with the Media Centre, just like with the Olympic stadium, is that all this headache could have been avoided if, like in Manchester with Manchester City and the football stadium, the anchor tenant had been identified in advance, and then (within the confines of what Games-time use also requires) the building designed to suit that tenant's purposes so that the building could very quickly be used again after 2012. Without this, it feels a bit like locking the stable after the horse has bolted. The desperate attempt to find legacy uses for buildings that have only been designed for the sole purpose of hosting an Olympic Games, and the fact that the remit of the ODA is to build venues, on time and on budget, without concern for legacy use means that pretty quickly, if the window of opportunity is lost for the design-review that builds legacy use in from the beginning, things start to look hopeless.

Echoing Chris Kennedy's concerns at the technical stakeholder workshop, Richard Dikstra, an independent digital media consultant, asserts that 'Hackney doesn't want undergraduates; it wants employment. There is already a plan for this.' I speak to Richard after the workshop, and he explains why and how he got on board with the Media Centre project:

> I got introduced to it through some other people who had gone along to a presentation that ELBA people had been doing, which is the East London Business Alliance, and a couple of media people went along to this presentation without any great expectations of what it was about, and then suddenly thought—there's something there, this is interesting, and then it was a bit serendipitous, that the right people got talking to the right people. And then, with all these things it needs somebody who actually is willing to run with it really, because I mean one of the things that we're actually quite good at in the UK is actually thinking of some ideas, and then thinking, oh no, that's a wee bit too difficult isn't it, and everybody backing off, but a couple of people actually just got really enthused with it, and moved forward, and now we've got talking to them, and I said, "right, okay, I can see how that might work".
>
> I think in this situation it's actually saying, right, there is a building being built, and a site, which actually hasn't had a lot of advantages for

years, and years, and actually couldn't something be done there? There are certain things, which suggest that people in media are looking to actually change what they're doing with looking for new premises, and maybe to look to cheaper areas, just as a confluence of different kinds of vague ideas floating around, and people saying, well hang on a minute we could do something. But the point was passion really, that actually, this idea, you can see that it can do good, but equally it's got a commercial position to it. Some people are actually fired up with the fact that here is this once in a lifetime opportunity, it's crying out for something to happen, and actually if people get talking about it, something might come of it all. But it takes a couple of people who have got a bit of vision really to actually drive it forward.

And the folk at ELBA I think have got a nucleus of that position together, but I think what they've found is that there's an awful lot of vested interests around the place, I mean it's perhaps too strong a word to say this, but it's an awful lot of people who, say, "no, no, just build this", and you know, as long as it's built, and it's built on the day, and it's more or less built to budget we'll be okay, you know, and then someone else can have a look at the legacy stuff.

I think there are people who are turning around, and actually saying, commercially if we could get that space for the sort of price that we would like to pay, which is presumably below the West London market rent, what you might regard as the market rent of a new development on it, then actually it would be good for our business, and we would move out there, so there's a commercial underpinning of it. But it's based on the fact that there's been some pump priming by other people, because the facility really is built for another reason.

Richard suggests that post-production facilities have reached their capacity in their traditional home of Soho, and the BBC is going to be moving out of White City. This as well as the political move to take the BBC to the regions, to Manchester, to placate its critics, [might mean] it could be persuaded to also take up space in the Media Centre. Richard suggests that what really needs to happen is some proper thinking around the business case that would make all of this happen:

> What do we believe the industry will pay to move there? Bearing in mind the fact that what we're actually asking them to do is to effectively relocate

some of their business, and no one wants to be the first, and only tenant there, because never mind anything else, we are in the fringes of Soho at the moment, so it's quite pleasant, so to get people to move, it has to be somewhere which is attractive. So, as I say, I think if they actually turned around, and said, "It's going to cost ten pounds, 15 pounds per square foot, is this something that the industry would sign up to?" I think they could actually find out quite quickly if they were going to be sensible in terms of their negotiations. And then they could turn around and say, "okay, so that's what we have here, what we need is X number of tenants, we need to get Y amount of café space, or restaurant space, and a few other bits, and pieces around it to make it attractive, what does that require us to do versus the other use that we have?" If someone was given that as a project, which is actually to turn around and say, "Right, you have to make it viable for the tenants that we want to attract there, because we think they're a growth industry, something that we actually want to do, something there seems to be an interest in, plus we've got to make it attractive for them anyway, plus we've then got to accommodate the needs of this four week [Olympics] broadcast event, what do we come up with? And how much is that going to cost us?"

Obviously passionate about the legacy potential of the Media Centre project in Hackney, Richard explains that he thinks the problem with not having designed the legacy use, in advance, around the plans that Hackney already has and, with an anchor tenant in place, is that it will be left to 'the market' to find the solution. The problem with this, he says, is that the financial crisis has already shown us what happens when everything is left to the market. It does not take care of itself and it does not take care of anything else, it just makes a lot of money for a while, but for what purpose? Richard suggests that if the government is serious about legacy employment uses, it needs to put its money where its mouth is, not just propping up the banking sector, but supporting industry and the growth of creative industries at the Media Centre would be a perfect example of, and experiment in what pump-priming can achieve. As an example, Richard reminds me of the totally different approach in Germany:

> We've allowed ourselves to have most of our industries collapse over the last few years in the view that, well the market was right, and everything should

be outsourced to China, or whatever, but I think one of the interesting things is that until very recently the biggest exporting economy in the world was still actually Germany. And in fairness, because manufacturing in Germany is very high end, you know, precision pieces, and actually putting lots of investment into developing that high end base, in the long term, you can't judge these things on short term decisions. And I think that that's part of the problem—the political cycle—works against longer term planning cycles.

Richard puts his passion for this project in personal context, explaining something about his personal background in Scotland, and what motivates him to be involved in trying to get Hackney's initiative off the ground, even whilst he is sceptical about whether the politicians will ever grasp what is required:

> Originally, I'm from Glasgow, and I suppose I think that a lot of factories have closed down, and the people have ended up not knowing, or able to move out first of all, and then secondly, I know that obviously as an area where lots of immigrants come into, and actually don't have any skills which fit together, you get into this cycle, and then you go, and see some run down factories, and closed up, and boarded up places, and you know that's the place that a business doesn't want to go to.
>
> Well, the people who are trying to do the Media Centre, they want to work with local schools and bring in people, and have training programmes, and actually try to anchor it into the community. It's actually a coming together for the whole industry there. But as I say, the opportunity has to be grasped at a political level with somebody actually turning around, and saying, "God, we would be stupid not to give this a go."
> Richard Dikstra, Director, Belle Media

Community Workshops

Also frustrated about consultation workshops that focus on the legacy park and its imagined new 'character areas', but fail to put to rest the anxieties of people who are deeply worried about the issues they most urgently want to see addressed, are local residents who attend the Output

C community consultation meetings, and take the opportunity they find there, to vent their fears and frustrations. For example, at a workshop I attended in Newham, there was a strong sense of frustration about the experience of regeneration so far, in East London, as a series of projects, which disappoint hopes for genuine change in the best interests of everyday residents, and confirm deeply held suspicions that despite all the talk, any transformation that does occur, even if successful, will be for the benefit of everyone else—'yuppies'—'rich people'—and not 'ordinary people' like them.

The main topic of concern of people attending the workshop was the chronic housing problem in East London described in terms of high levels of homelessness; a lack of adequate family housing; the termination, by Margaret Thatcher of a government commitment to social housing; the introduction by the same Conservative government of the right to buy social housing; and the negative effect on neighbourhood cohesion of increasing buy-to-let apartments whose owners have no investment in the local area. These kinds of concerns created resistance, and hostility to what the planners, and Emma's community engagement team, were there to try to seek comment about—the details of the LMF's 'character area briefs' for the new neighbourhoods of the Olympic Park.

One Newham resident, who had very little to say in the workshop itself, was extremely vocal when I visited her at home to talk things through. She felt that the consultation workshop was a sales pitch, about a place that she could not imagine working well, because that is her experience of other regeneration projects, a place not for people like herself, and unlikely to persuade East London people to venture out of their parochial pre-occupation with their own 'manors', where each is to their own. I asked her what she thought was for sale, and she explained:

> Well, this big idea, and everything was going to be fine, and dandy afterwards, and we were going to have all this beautiful green space, and, you know, all this posh housing. But is it going to be another place that operates only Monday to Friday? You can go over to Docklands on a Sunday. You can walk all around it. Or you can go up into the city. You've got no life on a Saturday or a Sunday, you know, they are both business communities. You do not walk along the road, even amongst the houses, you never

see washing hanging out on the line, or anybody walking around shopping or anything like that. Oh, by all means, you'll see them all at the big shopping centre, all in their cars. There's no community. When I first came here, [to East London] there was an awful lot more community. And I personally have seen the community spirit already go, you know. You see, you've got the original East Ender. They would be out there. They would scrub their steps. They would wash their paths. You've got some little terraced houses just along. Most of them, they're split into flats, two apartments, downstairs, and upstairs, it's housing associations there. They're quick turnaround. There's no pride of place, and people are just too busy now, it's how things are. The children, they're all backwards, and forwards in cars, because they're being shipped further on, or the parents haven't got the time to walk them there, because they're going to have to get on, and get to their own job. So they've got to get cracking.

You know, I like architecture. I am interested in buildings. I think Richard Rogers, he wrote a book, The Ideal City, where you've got all these spaces all together. And if you're going to have a site like that [the Olympic Park], why on earth—you know, they've got to do these things, but I do think there's going to be so much of a 'them and us', because of the posh housing. It all depends on who is in charge.

Suggested Readings

Carmon, M., & Fainstein, S. (Eds.). (2013). *Policy, planning, and people: Promoting justice in urban development*. Philadelphia: University of Pennsylvania Press.
Cohen, P. (2013). *On the wrong side of the track? East London and the post-Olympics*. London: Lawrence and Wishart Ltd.
Evans, G. (2001). *Cultural planning: An urban renaissance?* New York: Routledge.
Florida, R. (2004). *Cities and the creative class*. New York: Routledge.
Florida, R. (2014). *The rise of the creative class revisited*. New York: Basic Books.
Jacobs, J. (1993). *The death and life of great American cities*. New York: Random House.
Rogers, R. (1997). *Cities for a small planet: Reith lectures*. London: Faber & Faber.

Sinclair, I. (2010). *Hackney, that Rose Red Empire: A confidential report.* London: Penguin.

Wagg, S. (2015). *The London Olympics of 2012: Politics, promises and legacy.* New York: Palgrave Macmillan.

Wates, N. (2014). *The community planning handbook: How people can shape their cities, towns, and villages in any part of the world.* New York: Routledge.

Part II

The New World

5

Odyssey Becalmed

June 2009

Everything has come to a standstill. The Comms. Team is in disarray. The master planners are dismayed. Gareth Blacker has been suspended. Tom Russell has gone.

In a team meeting at Canary Wharf, with Emma and the rest of the Consultation and Engagement team, Adam Williams, the usually suave, impossibly cool Associate Director of Planning at EDAW and lead planner on the LMF, makes no attempt to hide his shock and disappointment. A sense of disorientation and hopelessness prevails over the meeting, and even Emma, who usually could not have a sunnier, more optimistic outlook, is overcome and dispirited. It is difficult to sit in on this meeting and witness the inspiration and energy gone from the team. As they flounder, trying to work out what is going on and what it means for the work they have dedicated themselves to over the last half decade or more, I take notes. I listen and wonder what the current state of play means, both for the momentum that has so carefully been built up and also for the regeneration principles Emma and Adam's teams abide by. I have the sensation that I have had as an anthropologist, so many times before, of being invited to bear witness to a process of impossibly difficult change.

The new entity, the URC—the SPV—has finally been established as the Olympic Park Legacy Company (OPLC), and whilst recruitment is taking place for new senior appointments and members of the Board, the company has a skeletal structure under the leadership of Baroness Margaret Ford, who is the new Chair and figurehead of a more commercially driven legacy agenda. It is too soon to say what the formation of the company means for the Comms. Team of the Legacy Directorate, but things are not looking good, and uncertainty hangs in the air.

A new interim Director of Comms. has been given the task of containing the situation, which, at the moment, means freezing the Comms. budget and silencing the team until the new company has come up with a narrative, for itself, about what kind of change it stands for. Quite quickly, it becomes clear that the future is to be made out of a repression of the past, which the new interim Director of Comms. describes in terms of the difference between 'the old world' and 'the new'. Everything to do with the LDA, and their way of doing legacy, is classified as belonging to 'the old world' and treated as a threat to the creation of what the new world might be. This threat must be contained, and the process of containment is taking its toll in the Legacy Directorate, because people have no idea what the formation of the new Legacy Company will mean for them.

Rebecca Haves, Emma's constant support and more outspoken member of the Consultation and Engagement team, jumps straight in, starting a team meeting by explaining that none of them are allowed to speak to the new interim Director of Comms., unless she decides there is a need for her to speak to them. For people who have spent the last 6 years developing the kind of project knowledge that precisely allows them to know just what to say, and when, this is frustrating to say the least, especially because they know that the woman they are now answerable to, and silenced by, has absolutely zero knowledge about either the Olympic Games, their legacy, or regeneration in East London. The fact that she is a physically imposing woman, who strides through the open plan space of the office like the captain of a rugby team, only adds to the intimidating impression of a hostile takeover, enforced by an imposing henchwoman whose job is to inspire fear in her subjects.

5 Odyssey Becalmed   105

Emma, in frustration, explains to the team that her hands are tied; they are not allowed to continue as normal. The new interim director is to oversee all lines and messages going through the press and PR team, and is to be informed of everything that has been done by the Comms. Team to date so that she can decide what needs to be done for the future:

Rebecca: Meanwhile, the consultees are getting nothing.

Emma: And, there are still no lines on the LMF [Legacy Master Plan Framework] timeline programme.

Adam Williams: Since the company [OPLC] was incorporated on the 1st May, all the HR [Human Resources] stuff is starting again, from scratch. And, Andrew Altman, the new Chief Executive is to start on the 1st August.

Rebecca: Meanwhile, Margaret Ford is meeting people randomly, with no oversight from us, as the Comms. Team, about what message she is giving out, and with no briefing about who she is seeing.

Emma: This is all about putting distance between the Olympic Legacy Directorate, and the Olympic Park Legacy Company, and where it wants to go—the direction of travel. There is going to be a hiatus, waiting for things to fall into place, and a battle about the remit of the company.

Adam: Who is that battle between? The LDA, the GLA [Greater London Assembly]—who?

Emma: Everyone. Everyone is pitching in. One issue is whether or not the socio-economic visions should be integrated, as Tom imagined they should be. The current direction is that the LDA and host boroughs will take charge of the SRF [Strategic Regeneration Framework], which will be separate from OPLC [Olympic Park Legacy Company] but with very close working, and no funding or responsibility in the OPLC.

Adam: What is the remit of OPLC? There is talk that it will now include the Fringe Master Plan areas, but who is bouncing these ideas around? Is it Neale Coleman? Richard Brown [Director of Corporate Strategy]? Boris?

Emma: Neale drives them.

Adam: I suppose this hiatus is not surprising.

Emma: Yes, they have to double-check everything before they put their name to anything.

Adam: But Margaret Ford doesn't understand that the LMF is designed to be flexible. Imagine if they do start the process of Master planning again, [as rumoured], they will still have the same constraints, and politics; they would still end up where we are now, and all that would be different is the number of housing units. There is no need to start again, but only to discuss possibilities, and limitations in relation to what people have in mind.

Emma: The problem is that people are hungry for real detail.

Adam: (exasperated) It is not our job to fix the details, this has to be a flexible framework! We can't model any detailed options until the Scheme Fix is agreed.

Emma: Even Neale, and the mayor, as well as Margaret Ford want detail.

Adam: We don't have a lot of clarity [from OPLC] going forward.

Emma: We know as much as you, and we're Comms. A letter is going out this week to all stakeholders explaining that we are waiting for the new people [new executive appointments] to be in.

Adam: What are you going to say to them about the scale of the delay?

Emma: It will be an open-ended comment, because we are waiting for lines.

Adam: Well, we submitted the Scheme Fix on Friday, so we are keeping to our end of the bargain ha! We have kept to our contract. Meanwhile, Bill [Bill Hanway—EDAW Director, and project lead with Jason Prior] has been told that everything is on ice—everything is frozen—that we need to reduce our involvement, and continue only with process around the stadium until the new Scheme Fix is agreed, with the planning application to be submitted now in late spring/summer 2010—autumn even—but for the EDAW consultancy, this is not good news. What is the programme of work? Do we need to reduce to a skeleton crew? Our contract runs out in a couple of weeks, remember.

Emma: All I can say is that I have been told the same—that EDAW work will be scaled back greatly, with just behind the scenes work.

Adam: Yes, just stadium, and sporadic pieces, nothing compared to what we were preparing for, which is to submit planning applications. The point is that this is about the assessment of the Master Plan Framework, but what about all the rigour that sits behind that? What about the stakeholders? The

LDA are taking a big step back after having shared so much, and to then submit a limited document?

Emma: Will you follow this up with Irene [Irene Man, Gareth Blacker's second in command], and let us know?

Adam: (look of absolute amazement because the flow of information should be going the other way—the Comms. Team are supposed to be informed, internally about what is going on, and, then, as legacy clients, inform Adam about what is happening. It is not his job to tell the Comms. Team what is happening inside their own organisation).

Emma: (silent, a moment of quiet despair).

Adam: What about the feedback on the draft consultation report?

Emma: I have been told that I can't come straight back to you on it—they don't want to be held to anything that has already happened.

Adam: (look of disbelief—shakes head).

Adam: Our people won't work at risk of not being paid. If the consultation report is not going out, what about the individual letters to stakeholders [those who have made formal written responses to Output C]?

Emma: No letters have gone out, and this is seriously bad.

Adam: The process has to be managed properly.

Laura Eyres (Public Affairs): It is confusing for stakeholders. With Tom gone, momentum is lost. We need to get the stakeholder list to Margaret Ford, so that she knows who to be speaking to. And we need more of a steer at the moment.

Emma: Who is going to take people through their fears? What about timelines? What are the lines?

Rebecca: Could we release the LMF consultation report, what we did, what we heard, how it changed the plans?

Emma: No, there is too much fear of having to retract what we say later down the line.

Samantha Sifah (Community Outreach Manager): We have to put something out.

Rebecca: Everything is on hold—even the external agents who are taking the Media Centre to market.

Emma: All we can do is try to continue with our outreach, and engagement work. The problem is that if we delay the work on the LMF until early 2010, which is a General Election year, there will be six weeks of pre-election purdah, [when central and local government cannot make any announcements about projects to the press] and then everything will be delayed again.

Adam: What about the SRF [Strategic Regeneration Framework]?

Emma: That is delayed too. There is a risk of who we are speaking to— Roger Taylor is talking to the borough mayors, the leads [Chief Executives of Host Boroughs], and the heads of regen. [each borough has its own Head of Regeneration and Planning], but not the 2012 heads [each host borough also has its own person leading, and advising borough leaders on Olympic issues]. They [the 2012 leads] feel dislodged, and they are venting their frustration on us.

Adam: The SRF was Tom's baby. If it hasn't died a death already, there is a risk it won't have any teeth. (Sarcastically) How many work streams are there now—9?

Emma: The host boroughs are leading on it now, aiming for a launch-able vision statement, which we've already heard (over and over again), in October.

Emma: This is all making me feel really low—(tears in eyes)—there's only a tiny budget that's the problem.

Adam: Well, at least we are all in the same boat.

Rebecca: It's really depressing.

Emma: (ends the meeting, really low, dispirited).

This record of the Consultation and Engagement team meeting captures a moment of profound uncertainty following recent scandals, in which Tom Russell 'resigned' (or, more truthfully, was pushed out) last month, because he has not been appointed as the new Chief Executive of the Legacy Company. And, to make matters worse, Gareth Blacker has just been suspended. Ironically, this is in the same month that planning applications were due to be submitted for the LMF, so no wonder the master planners are dismayed. There is now a power vacuum in the place where a strong and forceful director once stood. This comes after having been told that the formation of the new company, and the appointment of a new Chair, and Chief Executive, means a freeze on master-planning work, while the whole legacy scheme is reviewed.

The suspension of Gareth Blacker relates to an overspend of £159 million on the payments to the last few landowners who were still negotiating about payments for their land, which was acquired by Gareth Blacker's Land Team at the LDA, for the land assembly process. The £159 million is in excess of the budgeted, £995 million, and the overspend has come to light, because an audit of the Legacy Directorate's work has been undertaken in preparation for the transfer of legacy assets to the OPLC. Even though the overspend is controversial, especially in the light of Boris Johnson's forensic investigation of the LDA, which has made everyone paranoid about financial process, it is not exactly surprising. The largest land assembly process ever undertaken in Britain was never going to come in on budget, and it was a miracle that it came in on time. That is the whole problem with complex land assembly processes, it is an inexact science; the likelihood of appeals, public inquiries, disputes about compensation, and changes in market conditions over time make it impossible to be certain about eventual, overall costs of acquisition. It is a pity that the overspend should have come to light through an external audit, but the LDA were less perturbed about the problem than those who were baying for the agency's blood. Efforts have been made to provide reassurance to both the mayor and the media that the overspend could be soaked up through cuts to other projects, but to no avail, the damage is done, and Gareth Blacker has now been dealt with.

The timing of the finance question is not great for other reasons too, mainly because it follows on from the announcement, in February, about the effects of the recession on falling land values, and, later in the year, in May, the announcement of the withdrawal of private funding from the Olympic Village. The plummeting land values do not inspire confidence about the £650 million loan that was taken out by the LDA for the land assembly process. And, Grant Thornton, who have done a lot of financial modelling and business consulting for the legacy project, have suggested that Olympic Park legacy developments will not be in a position to start yielding surplus revenue until at least 2025. This is not great news for those, like The National Lottery, who are waiting for debt repayments from an uncertain legacy future. The LDA has been in dialogue with The Treasury about refinancing the land assembly debt, but now, it looks as though negotiations are underway for the land to be transferred to the OPLC, which leaves open the contentious issue of whether or not the debt will go with it. If the debt goes with the land, the company will not only be bogged down before it even gets started, but it will start to look as if the special purpose of the vehicle was to transfer the risk of debt-laden assets.

With Gareth goes the LMF, which seems like madness, because the value of the land would have gone up as soon as planning permission was granted. Like others in the Legacy Company, I cannot help, but have the feeling that 'the big men' of the old world are being carefully moved out of the way. Even though Gareth Blacker managed to drive the work on the LMF through, to February of this year, when the Preferred Option was launched to a media fanfare, and rolled out to the public and to stakeholders, for a final 6-week consultation period (prior to submission of planning applications), the parallel announcement, at that time, of advertisements in the *Sunday Times* for the recruitment of a Chair and Chief Executive of the OPLC cast a shadow of doubt over proceedings. Up front, press releases, taken up enthusiastically by the media, were full of the newly launched 'vision for a vibrant new look East London', but behind the scenes, the question on everyone's lips was about what the formation of the OPLC would mean for the Legacy Directorate of the LDA, and the future vision of the Olympic Park of the legacy master planners.

Exactly what the significance is of the final arrival on the scene of what everyone has been waiting for, which is a new organisational entity—the SPV/OPLC—still remains to be seen 4 months after the adverts were placed for the chair and chief executive, but the expectation has always been that no matter what reassurances are given about continuity, a new broom is going to sweep clean. At that time, in February, I was trying to make sense of the story behind the scenes, about the SPV, the SRF, and OPLC, and conducted a number of interviews. An interview with an academic specialising in cities and urban development was portentous.

5 Odyssey Becalmed   111

He suggested that I was putting too much emphasis on the LMF, that I should think of it as little more than a political statement, and a way of testing responses to ideas about housing densities. I asked what the point was, then, of a sustained process of consultation, and he explained his perspective on the situation:

> Gentrification is the only way to bring change in cities, but we live in a democracy. We have to be seen to be letting people know what we are doing, and planning. With the arrival of the SPV, the LMF will be ripped up, and started again. Next month a new Chief Executive will be appointed, and next month the company will own all this [the land of the Olympic Park].

The interview worries me, because I feel that it tells me too much about what is about to unfold—the appointment of a new chief executive, the commercialisation of legacy that this appointment is likely to signify; the sidelining of Tom Russell; the sidelining of the LMF, in its current form, and with it, the commitment to socio-economic transformation, rather than gentrification, as the driver of change in East London. This is the opposite of what I have understood East London change-makers to be fighting for, and it is contrary to what I have come to appreciate about those members of staff in the Legacy Directorate, and at EDAW, who are dedicated to the public service vision of regeneration that Tom Russell stood for. I fear that the strong desire in East London for the SPV and, with it, an increased commercial focus and grander ambition for the Olympic Park's future, and East London in general, may come at the expense of the careful work necessary to the task—already long in the tooth—of trying to work out how to harness incoming investment, and big ideas, to the promise of the Olympic bid to transform the heart of East London for the benefit of everyone who lives there. I have a stronger-than-ever sense that those in the Legacy Directorate, for whom the promise of regeneration proper stills matters, are going to have a fight on their hands to stay on board this new vehicle, as it mobilises and works out what direction to take. As the SPV picks up speed, I can see that certain people are going to have to hang on, for dear life. Meanwhile, I begin to wonder what a 'gentrified' version of the LMF would look like.

A Big Idea

By March, among many other formal responses from stakeholders, the Host Boroughs Unit had submitted their formal response to LMF Output C. Partly because the housing densities appeared to be driven by a business plan in which debt repayment, rather than place making, was the absolute priority, and partly because, as predicted, they were less than satisfied with the overall ambition of the scheme, the Host Boroughs Unit expressed its dissatisfaction:

> We welcome some of the central elements of the Output C plans, particularly the maintenance of the Olympic parklands at the heart of the proposals, the attempt to form stronger links with the fringe areas, and the idea of creating a variety of neighbourhoods with differing characters.
>
> But we feel the plans lack a 'big idea' with the potential to transform perceptions of the wider Lea Valley. The emphasis on neighbourhoods and centres, focusing on existing communities, and their integration with new developments, is welcomed, but this should not be at the expense of a strong identity, defining character, and sense of place for the Olympic Park, and wider Lower Lea Valley as a whole.
>
> [Our suggestion is for] early establishment of an iconic visitor attraction within the Park (e.g. at the Belvedere) to stamp a unique "personality" on the park, provide a lasting reminder for future generations of the staging of the Olympics, and reflect the rich heritage of the Lea Valley. One possibility could be an Olympic variant on the Eiffel Tower, incorporating restaurant/legacy gallery. Whilst not disrupting the "flow" of the open spaces of the valley, nor East-West connections, it would mark this pivotal point in the Park. A permanent London exhibition space for a major museum/gallery such as the Hermitage, or the Guggenheim, could also be a possibility if a suitable sponsor could be found.
>
> We recognise that meeting all these objectives will require careful balancing of competing pressures, and can only be done as we place the LMF in the wider context of the strategic plan for the boroughs as a whole, initially through the SRF. It will also be necessary to consider some innovative approaches to designing the Belvedere area in particular.

Frustrating, as I know this response must be to the master planners, it speaks volumes. More than the socio-economic and physical integration of the park with its surroundings, the desire of the host boroughs is for a 'big idea', something to attract the attention of London, something to bring tourists to the park, something to catch the eye, and make a statement about the new image of East London as a place to visit. The demand will be challenging, because it asks too much of the master planners; the decision is not theirs to decide on what proposals should be made about what the cultural offer, or visitor attraction could be at The Belvedere. Rather, it is their job to suggest where in the park such an attraction might best be placed. After that, it is the job of The Legacy Company, in partnership with the Host Boroughs, and, ideally, stakeholders and members of the public, to contribute to plans for what they want to happen, in terms of 'an iconic visitor attraction', in relation to what the site makes possible.

The request for an 'Olympic variant of the Eiffel Tower' also makes sense of plans, hatched late last year, by Tessa Jowell and Boris Johnson, for something extra in the Olympic Park during the Games in 2012—something like a sixth venue. The idea is for an iconic piece of art in the park. This project was described to me, with raised eyebrows, as 'Boris Johnson's Helter Skelter'—a pie in the sky idea—as the economic recession deepens—for Britain's biggest piece of public art. A design competition has been launched, but the mayor is said to favour an iconic tower, with a slide around it—an amusement ride—to symbolise the fun of the Games. I could just imagine the press opportunity, of Boris taking the first ride, and arriving dishevelled, but happily triumphant at the bottom of the slide where a critical media waits, to capture the mayor clowning around.

No wonder the Host Boroughs Unit is on board with Boris. Whilst the Legacy Directorate is in transition, and the Legacy Company is in its infancy, Boris is waiting for no one. He continues to steal a march on the legacy, taking advantage of the opportunity to make his presence felt with bold ideas that might be spoken of behind the scenes as being 'completely bonkers', but that attract attention and grab headlines. No doubt this reassures the Host Boroughs Unit that Boris is working in sympathy with their vision for an attention-grabbing transformation of East London.

The Doldrums

In the moment where Boris seems unstoppable, and even as Tessa Jowell's star is rising, with a place at the table in Whitehall again, as Minister for the Cabinet Office, she increasingly has her work cut out to keep hold of the legacy headlines. It feels like the Conservative/Labour battle for London, and the nation is ramping up. It does not help Labour's case that they recently haemorrhaged support in the European elections, allowing the far right BNP to gain its first seat in the European Parliament, and coming third, overall, after the anti-immigrant, anti-European, United Kingdom Independence Party (UKIP) also managed to make significant gains.

Meanwhile, the SPV appears to have brought the momentum of the LDA's legacy project to a standstill. Or, rather, what is happening is the horizontal move, which I was dreading, because it means having to watch, as the responsibility for the burden of legacy is being shifted onto a new, and inexperienced, set of shoulders. And, meanwhile, those for whom carrying the load has been a life's journey and special vocation for the last 5 years, or more, are now bewildered and feeling undermined.

At this moment, when I am also wondering how to secure my own place, as a researcher in the OPLC, David Ryner gets back in touch. Yet again, this is not a moment too soon. The new interim Director of Comms. is on my case. She recently confronted me abruptly, demanding to know who I am and what my role is. I do my best to explain, but her only response to a description of my research project is to say, in an irritated tone, 'That sounds like the old world to me.' And insists, before she storms off, 'We are trying to bring a new world into being here.'

David puts my name forward to attend Tessa Jowell's Legacy Dinner, at which she introduces the new Chair of OPLC, Margaret Ford, to a select group of legacy stakeholders. Margaret, who is a Labour peer, has an impressive track record in public and private sectors. She was Managing Director of the Royal Bank of Canada's Global Infrastructure Group, has held a number of private sector directorships, and was Chair, twice, of English Partnerships (EP), the national regeneration agency for England, until it became the Homes and Communities Agency (HCA) at the end of last year. Margaret is new to the East London context, new to sport, and just beginning to find out who is who in a complex field of play.

The dinner takes place in a small private room, upstairs, at Elena L'Etoile, in Soho. As I arrive, I wonder if there are no posh restaurants to meet at in East London, but am pleased to see a few familiar faces—Paul Brickell, Andrew Mawson, Richard Sumray—and to get a sense from this, about the purpose of the dinner, which, in part, is clearly about setting the scene for Margaret in terms of key community stakeholders. Present too are Roger Taylor from the Host Boroughs Unit; Geraldine Blake, Chief Executive of Community Links, a long-established community organisation based in Newham, which runs a wide range of projects, meeting the needs of thousands of residents living in difficult circumstances; Graham Fisher, Chief Executive of Toynbee Hall, another long-standing community organisation, working on the front line against the problems associated with poverty in Tower Hamlets; and Christopher Coombe, standing in for Neil Jameson of London Citizens, the East London community organising network, which brings together a host of East London faith groups, and other organisations, to campaign directly for social, economic, and political change.

Other guests include Alan Leibowitz, Chair of the Board of Trustees of Space, which is a social enterprise providing affordable studio space and support for visual artists across London; Charles Allen, media mogul and Chair of the Nations and Regions for LOCOG; and Peter Welton, Executive Director of the ELBA, which is the organisation comprising 100+ big businesses that are committed to fostering relationships with community organisations in East London, to provide employment opportunities for young people. And last but not least, Chris Stendall, Head of Physical Legacy and Security in the Government Olympic Executive (GOE).

Tessa introduces Margaret to the assembled group and explains that the purpose of the meeting is to discuss the legacy (in the same way that the previous legacy dinners have done), thinking about what is 'a once in a lifetime opportunity', and having the chance to talk about what obstacles might be standing in the way of planning and realising legacy. Tessa then asks each person to introduce themselves, the work that they do, and their interest in legacy. As people go around the table, I see that people are on their best behaviour. I know, from post-consultation interviews that third-sector organisations are feeling deeply disappointed that so far, all Olympic legacy planning means for them is being included in what they think of as 'talking shops', like this one, when what they desperately need the legacy to deliver is an increase in funding, so that they can increase their capacities to do what they already do best, which is to contribute to the socio-economic uplift of the area through their own outreach and engagement projects for people living in conditions of often extreme poverty.

However, it is obvious that they are keen, at a pivotal moment, not to antagonise the new Chair of the OPLC when she is all ears, and looking for allies. People take the chance to set out their stalls, and to give Margaret something to think about. And, as people go around the table, I realise that neutral observation is not an option, so I must take a position. I am happy to be able to wait, to hear what others have got to say, before I commit myself.

When it is Margaret's turn, she tells the story of her mother who was a head teacher at a failing school, and how, through changing the physical environment with the help of parents, she was able to turn the fortunes of the school around. Margaret emphasises that she is new to the East End, and that she is looking for mentors. At this point, she winks at Paul Brickell, and this confirms what I already know, which is that Paul Brickell will not have missed a trick, and would have been well ahead of the game, having met Margaret, introduced her to the Lower Lea Valley, and begun to form a helpful alliance long before this dinner was ever planned.

Margaret explains that her current preoccupation, as Chair of the OPLC, is with the visitor experience to the park. She asks us to imagine Phil and Jean, from Buckinghamshire who come to London for the weekend. They go to the museums in Kensington on the Saturday, and on the Sunday, they visit the Olympic Park. What will they do? Margaret suggests that 'Mum might go to Westfield, with the daughter, to do some shopping, and then meet dad, and son later, in the park. What will their experience be like? How will they be drawn from the stadium to the Velodrome for example?' Margaret stresses that she does not like 'red line boundaries', at which point she winks at Paul again, and I suspect that this 'message' is directly out of his mouth. Margaret says she is also 80 % behind the LMF, but stresses that it needs a '20 % change before a new December iteration'. 'At the moment', she says, 'the LMF is too neutral.'

When it is David Ryner's turn to speak, he says only that he is an assistant to one of Tessa's SPADs, and 'a fan of Output C', to which Paul Brickell quickly retorts, 'I suppose someone has got to be!' This confirms for me the massing of the ranks in the host boroughs, where Newham tends to dominate, in opposition to the LMF. This does not bode well for EDAW, but, on the other hand, for Margaret to say she is 80 % behind the LMF is reassuring news. Everyone knows already that Margaret is committed to revisiting the stadium issue, and work is already underway to review the stadium options with a possibility that the upper level will be retained and tenants sought again on that basis.

Finally, when I have the chance to enter into the dinner discussion, I say that at the moment, whatever people think about it, the LMF, Output C is the only material proposition on the table, and the amount of work that has gone into it deserves proper consideration. I then agree that it is important to think about Phil and Jean from Buckinghamshire, and what their visitor experience might be, so that the Olympic Park stands a chance of becoming a regional and national attraction, but what about Patrick, who lives in Canning Town and is unemployed? His dad was a docker, his grandfather was a docker, and he feels a tremendous sense of nostalgia for the industrial history of the Lower Lea Valley; he laments the loss of the industrial and manufacturing economy, and it makes me wonder—what will his visitor experience be like?

I then explain that my experience of interviewing members of the public who live in East London, and who have attended consultation meetings for the LMF, is that they are worried that the Olympic Park is not going to be for people like them. My concern, I say, is that the future vision of the Olympic Park is too ahistorical, by which I mean that I felt that an opportunity was going to be lost to embody the history of East London in the park in some shape or form, so that everyone who visits, whether from Buckinghamshire, Boston, or Beijing, has the chance to engage with, and to learn about, the proud history of the place and its people.

Margaret and Tessa respond positively to my suggestion, and Andrew Mawson backs me up, emphasising that the identity of the industrial history of East London is about the spirit of innovation and entrepreneurialism. Geraldine Blake, from Community Links, says that she is glad that

I have taken the chance to give voice to real people, because that is what is so often missing from this kind of meeting, and Christopher Coombe, from London Citizens, says that he recognises Patrick's story in the history of the Irish Catholics among London Citizens' membership.

Just before the dinner could end on an unnaturally positive note, Charles Allen quickly took the opportunity, while Tessa was listening, to put a difficult question on the table. This was to raise the query that was on everyone's minds about why it was that government was just about to go into summer recess, and there was still no agreement about how the Legacy Company would be funded. Without this, the company would be unable to organise itself, and progress would continue to stall. Charles' point is noted, but the meeting ends with his question unanswered.

After the dinner, David and I go for a quick drink. I ask him why the funding deal is delayed, and he rolls his eyes and tells me that initial set-up costs are being funded by the LDA, but the company is now looking for £4 million in grant funding from government for its first year of operations. David explains that the delay is to do with bickering behind the scenes between DCMS and Department of Communities and Local Government (DCLG). I ask about Tom Russell, and David says he had to go, because he was too public sector, too Manchester, too softly spoken, not strong enough for the current London challenge, and then stresses that everything to do with Tom Russell is now in jeopardy, so I am going to have my work cut out to hold my own in the new Legacy Company.

In the Dark

When I next see Adam Williams, he explains that EDAW have been given an extension to their contract of a couple of weeks, and a restart date of October, by which time the company's board will have been appointed, and the new American Chief Executive, Andrew Altman, will have taken charge of planning and design issues. Adam says he is learning more about what Margaret Ford wants from the trade press than from OPLC, so instead of waiting for direction from OPLC, he is simply doing what he feels needs to be done. He wonders if anyone at a senior level in OPLC actually knows what is in the Master Plan Framework, and the associated strategy documents, or if anyone at that level really appreciates how much work has gone into it.

Adam also speaks about feeling pulled in different directions, because he is, in addition to LMF work, also doing a scoping project for Boris Johnson on the possibilities for a higher education offer in the park. Adam says the legacy is still 'an open book', and 'no one really seems to know what is wanted.' There is a risk, he says, that because of political tussling behind the scenes, and a lack of clear direction, it will end up as 'a pastiche of a place with no coherence—trying too hard to meet what everyone asks of it'. In frustration, Adam exclaims, 'We are trying to create a framework for development—not a spectacle.' He reiterates that their job is 'not to come up with big ideas, but to create a framework of possibilities.'

Meanwhile, I notice, in the offices of EDAW that desks are beginning to be cleared, as staff are laid off, or redirected to other projects in Europe, or elsewhere, to wait out the LMF hiatus. The danger, Adam explains, is that rather than waiting through an uncertain period with the expectation of returning in October, many of those highly qualified and experienced people, with an invaluable depth of 'project knowledge' gained from years working on the LMF and Lower Lea Valley, will move on, apply for jobs elsewhere, and that knowledge will be lost.

Adam explains that what Margaret said at the legacy dinner, which I explained to him, about her 20 % reservation about the LMF is to do with the need for greater clarity about 'transitional uses'. This makes sense, he says, because the majority of the development platforms are going to take years, if not decades, to be developed into business and residential neighbourhoods, and in the meantime, the park has to work as a visitor destination. He explains that Margaret's other concern is with the sporting legacy, making sure that the options for the stadium are revisited (hence no John Lock at the legacy dinner, because his proposals for UEL's involvement in the sporting education offer at the stadium are now up in the air), and that the sporting offer in the legacy park is pitched as part of the new focus on visitor attractions. Adam says there is no problem with any of this, and there is no reason why this direction cannot be thought through within the parameters of the current LMF scheme of ideas.

Adam also tells me that he has heard that Margaret is concerned that there have been so many relatively young people working in the Legacy Directorate, and that she favours 'more experienced shoulders'. Adam says he is worried that this does not bode well for the Comms. Team. I reiterate what I feel, which is that more value ought to be placed on the depth of project knowledge, and dense network of relationships, not to mention a sense of trust and goodwill that have been built up by the Comms. Team with stakeholders and consultees in East London. I emphasise that all this is surely priceless, and Adam agrees.

I ask Adam what he knows about Andrew Altman, who is to be the new Chief Executive of OPLC. I suggest that it was the same with the Olympic bid—bringing in an American to lead the show and make a statement about commercial credibility. We speak about Andrew Altman's experience in the USA, where he was Director of Planning in Washington, DC, and Chief Executive of the corporation set-up to oversee the $10 billion transformation of the formerly industrial Anacostia Waterfront into a mixed development with a baseball stadium at the heart. Adam says that the problem with bringing in an American, at this stage, is that the political, and planning, context in London is very different, and it is going to take a while for an outsider to have the lie of the land. This will make it hard for Andrew Altman to lead effectively. I cannot help, but also express my amazement about the salary his job commands—£195,000 per annum—and realise that this too, is about the increasing commercialisation of the project, which, in part, means competing in the labour market for the people with the very best credentials.

Hanging in There

The aftermath of the change of London mayor, last year, taught me to look out, in the Legacy Directorate, for those work streams where a change of organisational leadership means, more than ever, so far as is humanly possible, having to keep heads down, and press on. At the moment, all the action is with the Venues Team. For example, Karen West has been working on legacy planning for the Aquatics Centre since 2007, when the decision was made that it had to be value engineered and redesigned from its first proposal to get it within budget. This was a disappointment to stakeholders and local residents, because value engineering meant losing the leisure use, which was a huge blow. The legacy that East London clearly wanted from the Aquatics Centre was a pool with leisure use, and not just pools for elite swimming.

Karen's background is in leisure management, sports facilities management, and development; she has worked for Sport England, a number of local authorities, and was the Director of Swimming for London. Because she has sat, as she describes it, 'at all sides of the table'; she felt she could be objective about what was really required for the legacy building. Karen explains to me what happened:

> We basically went right back to the beginning with the building, and it was effectively a stage C design that was then changed, and changed again for stage D, and then it became a very different building. There were some massive challenges with the building, not least of all the fact that value engineered out was an enormous health, and fitness facility, which in financial terms would have driven the business case, and a wet and dry [e.g. with gym facilities too] facility is much more useful for the drive, and participation number one, for cost recovery number two, and for being attractive for users.
> So, linked to this whole re-evaluation of the building and redesign of the building was the fact that Sport England had a 40 million pound Lottery funding arrangement on the table for this building, but they weren't happy with the design [because Sport England wanted the health, and fitness use back in somehow—even though there was nowhere to put it]. So I was kind of, brokering the design, and the redesign between Sport England, the LDA, and the ODA [Olympic Delivery Authority]. So I was trying to get everybody on the same page, so that we could apply for the Lottery funding for the building.
> In conjunction with British Swimming, we have redesigned the dry dive area within the Aquatics Centre, so that it can accommodate more health, and fitness. It's strength, and conditioning for athletes, but it's still there, and it's still a greater provision than we had. I mean, I feel as though, and I think Newham trusts the fact that I've personally never actually given up on trying to get something out of that. And I think we will get something.
> One of the compromises that we agreed with Sport England was that we would actually make the swimming pools much more flexible. And so we

agreed at a huge cost out of the contingency budget, to put a business case together, and we achieved something, which no other pool will have, and that is the diving pool will have a fully movable floor, so it can go from five metres depth to deck level, and that's not happened before. So, that pool is not just a dedicated diving pool, it can do all sorts of other things. The other thing we will do is to put booms in, so we can subdivide the pools, and additional movable floors. So, even though they look like they're very large 50 metre pools, we can subdivide them into smaller pools, and therefore, they're not so intimidating for the community, but you can get a whole mix of different things going on at any one time. So, we can create a leisure environment by putting in a temporary overlay, be it slides, it doesn't matter, it can be whatever we want it to be, and we are going to build that into the management contract. So, there is a bit of a misconception that leisure water has to be a great big flume slide.

Karen explains to me that even though she was brought in as a consultant, by the time she had dedicated herself to the resolution of the design, and legacy problems with the Aquatics Centre, and found a way forward, she was hooked. She explains that it matters to her personally, because her personal reputation and ethical principles are at stake:

> I mean my work with the boroughs, and the sporting governing bodies, I'm really proud of that. And it's also really, really important to me, because they're my peer group. I've worked in leisure for too many years now, I can't get that wrong. So that has to be right. It's a personal reputational risk to me if this company [OPLC] doesn't take the [regeneration] agenda seriously. Because actually, I have goodwill with these people, they trust that I will, even when a project's dead, they trust that I will still be trying to find a way to deliver some part of it. And that's important. So, I almost have to be creatively tenacious. And, I get support in doing that I'm not saying I don't. But I think that's right, because I don't think the company should ignore what its customers are asking for. And that's where I get worried about the outputs of the design because the extent to which we are synthesising the work, the information that we've taken from all of the stakeholder engagement, will be measured only when the doors open.

Karen explains how important the struggle of the last few years has been, because the battle about legacy has to take place at the level of design specification, when decisions are still being made about the design of venues. This means having to work with, and fight against the ODA, whose remit is to deliver the Olympic Park and venues, on time and on budget. Legacy is not their problem, so, as Karen explains, you have to fight to make it their problem, and this means hanging in there for the long haul and battling it out, and making sure that once battles are won, the outcomes are embedded at a contractual level. This is the problem that has not been overcome at the Media Centre, and Karen's experience with the Aquatics Centre shows just how important it is that each legacy project has a champion, someone who is prepared to fight to the bitter end, battling for the legacy cause against the powers that be.

Karen also has plans in mind for sports participation strategies, for each Olympic venue, in partnership with the host boroughs, each sport's governing body, (from elite to everyday engagement), and a vision for community-focused test events in Aquatics Centre in the year before the Games. Her dedication helps me to understand why it is so important that right from the moment the Olympic bid is won, a separate body, like the Legacy Directorate, and now the OPLC, exists to champion the cause of Olympic legacy. There are seven years between the announcement of the successful host city bid and the Games taking place, and it is clear that every single one of those years are vital, in the fight to plan and to realise an Olympic legacy, and, more accurately, to have time to experiment, whilst fighting, with what it means to deliver an Olympic legacy in a locally meaningful way:

> We have protected the interests of all the people that need to have access, and that's really important. Because there is no way that we won't deliver a measurable legacy, because it's in there. That's important. I mean if we hadn't of been so prescriptive, and that was quite a battle 'cause people were saying, "Oh, we mustn't be too prescriptive," and I was insistent, "No, you have to be prescriptive to a point, you can't stifle innovation, and you can't stifle development, but you have to have, if you like, something that you can measure against." So, I think that—the design specification—[for the Aquatic Centre] is probably from a business point of view, and from a legacy point of view the most important document for me.

I ask Karen to explain what she understands the purpose of the Legacy Company to be, and she clarifies her perception of what is, or should be going on:

> When I bring people in I say, "Oh we've got design, build, fund, operate." They are the four cornerstones. And, then, what runs through that are the socio-economic and strategic policies. But for me, it is about building, and operating, to build, and to operate is to regenerate. That's what we're here to do.
> I also think it's incumbent upon us to protect the interests of local people, and it's absolutely critical. And that's not just about whether they come for a swim, but that's about making sure that their lives are not disrupted too much, that we provide a fully developed, and accessible service for them [local people], as well as for new people that come in. And that's a real challenge, that's a real balance, that's a major, major balancing act.'

I ask Karen how far she feels that she has had to fight for that agenda—protecting the interests of local people—and her response confirms what I already know, which is that there is a division in the company between those who 'get' the regeneration agenda proper, and those who do not:

> Okay, if I'm really honest with you, when I first came here I think there were some people that got that, there were others that didn't. If you want my honest opinion, it is because they don't actually feel, live, breathe and, they're not passionate about it, it's just a job and that's—, I've been a consultant, and that's what you do. You do the job, you go, you don't really live, and breathe it. And, I mean on a personal level, I fought really hard … And that didn't win me many friends. Equally when I would bang on, as I've been told I do, from time to time, about the boroughs, and the socio-economic this, and whatever, again, it didn't win me friends because people wanted to talk about performance sport, and medals, and stuff. Maybe some other people would've given up, but I think there's always been enough people in here [in the company], I've always found enough people that believe that I will deliver what I said I was going to deliver. But there are lots of people in here who get it. And, I have to say there was a time where I was like, "oh my God", you know. "Do you actually get what we're here for?"

It was even as fundamental as that, "Do you really get it?" But of course when you've got a project to deliver, it is a really project specific struggle.

Karen then tells me about her relationship to East London, and how this informs her work:

> I was born on Commercial Road, and then I went to school in Wapping until I was eight. Both my parents are from Hackney, and Stepney, so I have a massive extended family, and friendship base here. And then I went to live in Essex, and then the Midlands, I went to university in the Midlands, and I came back to my first proper job in Hackney. I lived in the Isle of Dogs, and I've lived here ever since. Well I've lived in Hackney, Leyton, Tower Hamlets ever since, so since 1985. That's why I am so passionate about it [the legacy project], because I want there to be things for my kids, my friends' kids to do, and for there to be employment, and for people to be proud of where they live. At the end of the day, I can lay my head on a pillow at night, and know that there will be community benefit.

Obviously taking a great deal of pride in their work, those people who are fighting for accessible sporting venues, with legacy uses planned in, are inspiring to talk to. For Karen West, her work on the Aquatics Centre has clearly become a labour of love. No matter how pragmatic the process of project management, the work is suffused with emotion, and that is what makes the fight sustainable over time. People clearly care about what they are doing. Karen is respected by her colleagues for her tenacity, and they tease her, describing the Aquatics Centre as a stick of rock, the sweet kind you get by the seaside, that has writing inside it, all the way through, from one side to the other. They say, about the Aquatics Centre, to Karen, 'It's got your name going right the way through it.'

This sense of camaraderie and solidarity, over a number of years, to the process of experimentation, and negotiation of what legacy can mean in the context of serious budget restraints, had led to a sense of solidarity at the coal face of the legacy planning operation, where the work is being done to forge ahead and sustain the legacy momentum. The work is serious, but the atmosphere is casual, and a mutually supportive environment is sustained in a continuous giving to one's team, or to the whole company, of gifts of food, and especially sweets, brought home from holidays, and trips abroad. Playful notifications are sent by email about new contributions to the cycle of constant giving of edible gifts: 'treats from Iceland, usual place'; 'In what I have come to appreciate as the mark of an "event", I have laid out a load of junk food, in the usual place'; 'Sticky sweet things from the souks of Marakesh, in the usual place'; 'Sweets from New York, usual place'.

It is the usual spirit of camaraderie, playfulness, and solidarity in the face of serious challenges that makes it harder to witness, as the OPLC comes into being, that for some work streams, morale is plummeting. It is in this atmosphere that I struggle myself to stay on board, and to find a way, in the Comms. Team, to move from observation to greater research participation. This means working out, with Emma, how, even when the budget is locked down, and no new lines or messages are coming out, I can contribute to the only remaining task, which is to keep expanding and sustaining the network of relationships, which constitute the activities of the Comms.' Outreach and Engagement Programme.

Suggested Reading

Brenner, N., & Theodore, N. (2003). *Spaces of neoliberalism: Urban restructuring in North America and Western Europe.* New York: Wiley.
Bridge, G., Lees, L., & Butler, T. (2012). *Mixed communities: Gentrification by stealth?* Bristol: Policy Press.
Grix, J. (Ed.). (2014). *Leveraging legacies from sports mega-events: Concepts and cases.* New York: Palgrave Macmillan.
Holt, R., & Ruta, D. (Eds.). (2015). *Routledge handbook of sport and legacy: Meeting the challenge of major sports events.* New York: Routledge.
Lees, L., Slater, T., & Wyly, E. (2007). *Gentrification.* New York: Routledge.
Lees, L., Slater, T., & Wyly, E. (2010). *The Gentrification reader.* New York: Routledge.

Lindsey, I. (2014). *Living with London's Olympics: an ethnography.* New York: Palgrave Macmillan.
Paton, K. (2014). *Gentrification: A working class perspective.* Surrey: Ashgate.
Preuss, H. (Ed.). (2007). *The impact and evaluation of major sporting events.* New York: Routledge.
Tighe, R., & Mueller, E. (2012). *The affordable housing reader.* New York: Routledge.

6

The Doldrums

March 2010

Six months late, agreement has still not been reached between the LDA, the mayor, and central government about the transfer of the land assembled by the LDA for the Olympic Park. Neither has a decision been made about what is going to happen to the debt that accompanies that land. This is adding to the feeling of low morale, and uncertainty in the OPLC, and putting the reputations of Margaret Ford and her new Chief Executive, Andrew Altman, on the line, because they both know that without the land, OPLC will be a toothless tiger, doomed to die an early death.

The fact that the delay is a result of bickering between the owners of OPLC—central government and London's mayor—only contributes to the feeling that the powers that be, have given birth to a creature that they are now starving of life. Not surprisingly, Margaret Ford, whose job it is to manage these relationships, is maintaining an outward air of calm confidence, because forward-moving momentum relies on this, but behind the scenes, a heightened sense of nervous anxiety pervades the day-to-day business of the company.

Margaret Ford is adamant that the land of the Olympic Park should be transferred to OPLC debt-free, so that she can send the necessary message to investors and developers that OPLC is a landowner, free to do business with land that is not saddled with debt. And, a debt-free land transfer would also be good news for Andrew Altman, because the LMF, which he is now responsible for, would then be free of a crippling, debt-repayment business plan that previously tied the LMF vision too tightly to what no one in London wants, which is high density housing. Perhaps more importantly, it may mean that the land of the Olympic Park will not need to be sold to developers freehold, and instead, it can be retained by the company, kept in public ownership, and leased on a long-term basis, so that a coherent estate management-type approach can be taken to the whole park, including its residential areas, with all the benefits that come with that, such as the setting and maintenance of design standards.

Central government has its mind on the General Election, which is to take place in May, and it cannot afford, especially in a deepening recession, the political scandal of an announcement about a possible further increase in the cost of the Olympic project. The LDA, meanwhile, is adamant; it is still paying for the start-up and running costs of OPLC, to the tune of £884,000 this financial year, on top of a grant payment from the Department of Communities and Local Government (DCLG) of £4 million for 2009/2010, but it refuses to pay the price for the land transfer deal, and is resolute that if the land goes to OPLC, the debt should go with it. The mayor, meanwhile, is continuing to distance himself from the LDA, and is determined that the GLA should not be saddled with the LDA's land assembly debts and liabilities. Hence, the stalemate …

The debt in question is almost £600 million that the LDA still owes to central government as a result of the loan it took out from central government (from the Treasury's Public Works Loan Board) to part-fund the £995 million budget for the Olympic Park land assembly process. At that time, the prospective value of the land was estimated in future to be worth £669 million, and the Memorandum of Understanding signed in 2007 between the government and the mayor, who was then Ken Livingstone, was that once the land was sold to developers, the first £650 million was to go to the LDA, and of the second £675 million made, 75 % was to go to repay the Lottery and 25 % to the LDA, with any remaining monies after that being split 75/25 between the LDA and the Lottery, respectively. Since the land was only estimated to have a future value of £669 million, this did not make the prospects look very good of a timely repayment of the debt owed to the Lottery unless land values were to increase significantly in the long-term. And, now that the political landscape is about to change yet again, keeping an eye on these debts, and who is responsible for honouring them, is becoming a bit like watching that street hustlers' cup and ball game in which you think you have your eye on the prize, so you place a bet, in the hope of doubling your money, but suspect, when you lose, time and time again, that it must have been a scam all along. The London Assembly, whose job it is to keep track of these things, has its work cut out to lend an air of accountability to proceedings, and to serve the London public through an ongoing process of mayoral scrutiny.

The Company

Meanwhile, a bit like making cocktails on the Titanic, OPLC carries on, as if it were a self-confident organisation, making high-level executive appointments, testing out the efficacy of its new structure and decision-making process, trying to project a public facing poise, whilst, backstage, it is trying desperately to create a sense of stability and credible corporate identity.

The Legacy Directorate ceased to exist at the end of August, last summer, and with its demise came the office move, from the skyscrapers of Canary Wharf to new premises in Stratford, in the heart of the action. This has not been good news for some, and the dividing line has become a little clearer between those people in the company who were much more comfortable at Canary Wharf, (where they could get good sushi for lunch and did not have to come face to face with what they perceive to be the grim realities of poverty), and those who are happier to be on the ground, in the place that is supposed to benefit from regeneration, and among the people to whom the promises of the Olympic bid were addressed.

Getting to the new offices means a walk from the bus terminal, train, and tube stations at Stratford, and through the old shopping centre, which is soon to be dwarfed by the Westfield mega shopping mall that is to open next year. With the benefit of experience, I can see clearly that the more brassy kind of busyness of the old shopping centre is perfectly suited to its purpose as a retail destination for people on relatively low incomes, who have little disposable income to spare, but can pick up bargains here enough to go home with several bags full of what they want and need. I fully appreciate the true creativity of turning oneself, and one's home out well, when the challenge is how to buy nice things when money and credit are in short supply. I can also be excited by the forthcoming spectacle of consumption at Westfield, but the respect I have for the hustle and bustle of the shops and market stalls of the old shopping centre is beyond compare; this is the place where everything that is gloomy about poverty comes out fighting, refashioned as a brighter day through the fierce fun of cut-price shopping.

Of course, not everyone sees it like this. For some, the shopping centre is a grubby, tacky reflection of what they perceive to be 'urban squalor', an all too obvious reminder of what needs to be 'gentrified', and having to negotiate the journey through it is a source of daily terror, as a new way to get to, and from work, has to be negotiated through the hurly burly of East London living. The expression of this fear of poverty is a stark reminder of just how far the project of Olympic legacy has to go to turn around negative perceptions among Londoners about the East End of the city.

OPLC

Jointly owned by 'founder members'—the London Mayor and central government (the Secretary of State from the Department of Communities and Local Government)—OPLC is a not-for-profit limited liability company. It has a board of executive directors, which was appointed in November, comprising 12 high-profile members, many of whom are from the world of business, and whose main purpose is to prove the company's new commercial credentials and to set and sustain an 'entrepreneurial' direction, (without losing site of regeneration, sporting, and local community interests). The board is then further subdivided into three committees, which meet separately, to oversee particular areas of company priority—the Investment Committee, the Audit Committee, and the Community Committee, which is chaired by Lord Andrew Mawson, the well-known East London strategist. The appointment of two of the Olympic host borough mayors, Jules Pipe, from Hackney, and Sir Robin Wales, from Newham, also ensures that host boroughs' interests are included, and without it having been declared, their appointments also ensure that Labour is well represented on the board.

Reporting to the board is an Executive Management Team (EMT) to which eight highly paid appointments are now being made. The new work streams—Real Estate, Urban Design and Planning, Commercial Marketing, Operations and Venues, Finance and Corporate Services, Governance and Legal services, Strategy and Corporate Planning, and Corporate Communications—and their high-flying new executive leaders are designed to completely supersede the old management structure of the Legacy Directorate. The point is to bring in fresh blood, make a strong statement about the new 'world class' calibre of OPLC, and to leave the LDA, and its public sector way of doing things behind. Last year, in an internal communication to Legacy Directorate staff, Margaret Ford sent out a strong message to LDA staff, many of who have been seconded to OPLC; she describes the intention behind the organisational structure of the new company as follows:

> The OPLC has been created to be a compact company with the capability to mobilise its size, resources, and relationships in a way that can achieve real pace, and purpose. It will be a small family of focused, flexible, and fleet of foot folk whose success will be demonstrated through their adaptable, can do approach, and their ability to work credibly, and creatively, across internal, and external boundaries. In acknowledging the many achievements of the LDA it is important to accept that the OPLC will not be 'son of LDA', it will look, feel, and behave differently … more like a consultancy in style, and less like a hierarchical bureaucracy.

Keeping things on track, a Programme Management Office (PMO) prepares a detailed monthly report on the progress and the associated risks of a lack of progress in each of the company's work streams, relating this always to the broader context in which the company is working. Some of the greatest risks to future progress are, at the moment, perceived to be the potential failure to achieve an effective and clean transfer of land, assets, and liabilities from the LDA; no capital funding (no money for transformation of the venues and parklands, site preparation, and other necessary capital investment projects after the Games, which would result in a compromise to quality of the regeneration scheme, and then, a reduction in the scheme's value); the viability of stadium legacy use; the viability of the Press and Broadcast Centres (which may require OPLC either to demolish the buildings or to invest in post-Games retrofit for which there is no current funding); insufficient operational funding for the venues and parklands (funding must be made available for operating the venues and managing the parklands without which the future visitor experience will be negative, the potential for increased sporting participation reduced, and company and founder members' reputation damaged).

Comms.

Ironically, at a time of such heightened insecurity in the company, part of the brief of the Comms. Team, this last year, has been to provide the appearance of certainty in how the company communicates itself to itself, and to the world. A small, three-person, marketing team has been working on developing 'the OPLC brand' and begun work on 'developing the story' and commercial positioning of the Olympic Park to engage potential investors and partners both nationally and internationally. This has meant creating a new company logo, a new website, internal and external templates for documents, emails, presentations, and so on, and generally, creating and standardising a new 'look and feel' for a corporate company identity, which is to be expressed in the company's first publications that are going to tell the world what OPLC is about, and what it is here to achieve and deliver. This is described, internally, as being to do with creating the right impression for 'the market' (meaning the market for potential investors and property developers), which speaks volumes about the company's new priorities, and Andrew Altman's task, as a salesman, which is to take the park and its opportunities to the market:

the strength of the Company is in its consistent presentation to the market; we are all important players in helping to offer a single face to market. This means making sure that our personal corporate brand representation is in place, such as email signatures, telephone messages, and the way we meet guests.

The paradox is that 'the old world' Legacy Directorate Comms. Team is being asked to design the look and feel of the 'the new world' OPLC. This makes for fraught communication between Nigel Davidson, long-term manager of the marketing team, and the Interim Director of Comms., whose job is, by definition, to devalue the work of the old Comms. Team, and who finds it hard, therefore, to work with Nigel and to sign off on the work that his small marketing team is doing to bring the new world into existence. This is frustrating to say the least. Similarly, it is excruciating for the Comms. Team that all the focus is on the look and feel of communications and the design of the new corporate identity, but without the company actually having anything to say for itself. The head of the small press team expresses this as the feeling of having nothing to report in the last 6 months, other than that the company itself now exists. Other than a top line message, it is still too soon to be able to tell the world what OPLC stands for, and why this is different to what the Legacy Directorate had already been close to bringing to fruition.

Over Christmas, at a particularly low point, the whole Comms. Team escaped the office, and the team meeting took place over lunch in the pub. Nigel, the marketing manager, admitted that he had been looking for other work, and whilst everyone was in sympathy, everyone knew that no one would be leaving, because they all felt the same strong sense of loyalty to a project they have been caretakers of from the beginning. At this time of uncertainty, it felt, more than ever, that the project needed steady hands. Laura Eyres, the Public Affairs manager, tried to be reassuring:

Nigel: (angry and demoralised) Only the venues team has stuff to do.

Laura: Hopefully we will know what is happening in the New Year [not just because of the land deal, but also with the appointment of the Executive Director of Corporate Marketing].

Nigel: I just feel like no one knows what is happening. Who is bringing it all together?

Laura: I am embarrassed about how marginalised I have become. OPLC needs to lobby more, especially the shadow positions (in the Conservative Party).

Gillian: What would a Conservative victory in the general election mean?

Laura: Massive cuts in public spending, elimination of regional government, [the end of the LDA], more power for Boris Johnson.

Emma: What progress on the stadium?

Laura: We are preparing for soft market testing, securing expressions of interest. Lawyers and other advisors [Jones Lang Lasalle, and Eversheds] have been engaged, and the website and press release are being prepared. Pre-procurement legal process means that the press will be sensitive, so information about the opportunity will be posted on the EU [OJEU] website in Luxembourg.

Nigel: Doesn't that create the impression of an open tender? How will people interpret that?

Laura: It is the best way of advertising what we're doing. It covers our backs on all sides, and shows that formal process is being managed and controlled in the right way.

Laura: The Investment Committee has signed off on the Memorandum of Information for the stadium, and a prospectus for interested parties is to be produced, and an ad. placed in The Times [newspaper], for ten days. There will be tours around the stadium, and park for interested parties. And stakeholder letters will go out.

Nigel was right to say that all the action at that moment centred on the legacy planning of the Olympic venues. Whilst this work continues, and continues to attract controversy, the future use of the stadium has, as predicted, become the lightning rod of the legacy project and the centre of a very public legacy drama. The review of the possible design and capacity options for the Olympic stadium, which was commissioned at the request of Margaret Ford, last year, immediately after her appointment as Chair of OPLC, is complete, and the company is now going to market in an 8-week process of enquiry, to seek expressions of interest in these and other potential configurations of the stadium for legacy use. Internally, the detail of this work is sealed off from the rest of the company, because it is vital that conditions of secrecy and confidentiality are preserved to protect the stadium process.

The condition of legacy use of the stadium is that interested parties must take into account the conditions of the Olympic bid, including the desire to retain the athletics track, and the necessity to have to account for the regeneration of East London. The intention is to secure a tenant by 2011. No wonder there is a state of heightened anxiety in the company; this critical stage of evolution around the planning for legacy use of the stadium is happening at the same time that the foundations on which the fate of the company rests are in jeopardy. The stalemate around the land deal begs the question of how Margaret Ford is supposed to proceed with plans, when the founder members of the company are unable to provide her with the reassurance she needs to go confidently to market. This, as well as the General Election, on the immediate horizon, is reason enough to doubt that OPLC is going to be able to create any momentum for its plans, but there is nothing to do, but maintain an outward air of extreme confidence, because no matter what, confidence is what the market requires. Cleverly, Margaret Ford begins to use her appearances before the London Assembly and Government Select Committees, as well as her interviews with the media, to set out her stall and to subtly begin to badger the politicians into compliance.

Socio-economics

Fighting her own corner, meanwhile, Emma Wheelhouse explained to the Comms. Team, at the escape from the office over Christmas, that part of the challenge she has been given, as manager of the Consultation and Engagement Team, is to start working with the Marketing Team to also engage with international business communities, and not just to focus anymore on 'local communities' in the East End. Her small team of dedicated consultation and engagement staff are already demoralised and not impressed by this new development. Emma is trying hard to manage the situation, but her loyalties are obviously with her team and the difficult challenge they are facing:

> Samantha Sifah (Community Outreach Manager): How disappointing. Our work [years of trust built up through consultation, and engaging local communities] is beginning to feel like what I have always dreaded—layers and layers of uselessness.
>
> Emma (trying to be positive): The new idea is to use the excitement from the Games, and the development of each permanent sporting venue left on the park after the Games, as well as an "events' strategy", to "buy people into the Park" and "build [new] community up".

Emma suggests that all they can do, meanwhile, while Andrew Altman works out what his new 'top line' messages about the company are going to be, is to produce a core presentation for him to use in his public engagements. By putting their 'lines' into his mouth, the Comms. Team attempts to exert its influence over the new Chief Executive. Surreptitiously, they attempt to align what he says in the world, while he is still unsure of himself, with their existing understandings of what is considered to be important about the company's aims and objectives, and, especially, the regeneration agenda.

Not surprisingly, the increasingly business-focused legacy agenda has led to the cull of the Olympic Opportunities Programme, and Geoff Newton has become the next high-profile casualty of the commercialisation process. At the point that the Legacy Company was being brought into being, last year, Michelle May's small socio-economics team was split off from the group of staff that was seconded to the new company, and as OPLC moved to Stratford, Michelle's work stream was left behind at the LDA. Keeping a watchful eye on, and fighting against this development, the members of the Economic Development, Culture, Sport and Tourism Committee (EDCST) of the London Assembly have been pestering Margaret Ford about this bifurcation of legacy interests—hard versus soft legacy—commercial versus community interests—at the committee meetings in front of which Margaret must account for OPLC progress.

Margaret Ford could only reply at committee meetings, that whilst a broader regeneration remit was important to the company, the decision to separate a formal focus on socio-economics from the work streams of OPLC was taken before she had been appointed. In practice, this has meant, on the coalface, that Emma Wheelhouse and her small Consultation and Engagement Team have been left alone to fight the regeneration battle inside OPLC. At the other end of the company hierarchy, meanwhile, Andrew Mawson, as Chair of the Communities Committee, is able to exert pressure on the board for an agenda that does not exclude community interests from what counts as 'entrepreneurialism'. He has also started an All Party Parliamentary Group on Urban Regeneration, Sport and Culture to raise awareness at Westminster. And, on the outside of the company, with the highly successful opening, last November, of The View Tube, Paul Brickell is demonstrating what social enterprise means and what difference it makes in practice.

The SRF

Better late than never, one positive outcome of the hiatus in legacy planning and the stalling of the LMF is that it has given the Host Boroughs Unit a chance to catch up and produce the first iteration of the SRF. Its aim is to specify a clear set of ambitions about exactly what the regeneration of the areas surrounding the Olympic Park would mean in practice. The big idea is called 'Convergence', which is the radical aspiration, in the next 20 years, to bring East London up to the same average levels of life experience as the rest of London. Convergence is to be measured across a number of different indicators, including health, housing, education, employment, crime, public realm, and sporting participation.

Just in the nick of time, and at a critical moment in the transition from the Legacy Directorate to the establishment of OPLC, Roger Taylor, head of the Host Boroughs Unit, has delivered an in-depth report, produced by Navigant Consulting, with exact statistics that describe both the scale of deprivation in East London and the ambition for how these statistics need to change for the better in the next 5-year period of joint planning between the government, the mayor, and the host boroughs.[1]

---

[1] Strategic Regeneration Framework: an Olympic Legacy for the Host Boroughs. http://www.gamesmonitor.org.uk/files/strategic-regeneration-framework-report.pdf. Accessed 10 May 2015.

For example, the ambition relating to overcrowded housing is to reduce the current statistic of between 18 % and 30 % overcrowding in the host boroughs to the 7 % London average.

The report is a clear statement of intent about what the host Olympic boroughs have decided amongst themselves needs to happen for the life experience of their residents to be brought in line with the rest of London, and, the SRF, with its buzz word of Convergence, is a campaign calling card, if not a battering ram, for East London to use as the means to knock on the doors of OPLC, the GLA, and central government and insist that all policy ambitions relating to the Lower Lea Valley, and the Olympic Park, take East London Convergence into account.

Remarkably, there appears to have been very little resistance to the report; it was signed off last October by the OPRSG, and has been welcomed, therefore, to a certain extent by the mayor and central government. Its success lies both in the incredibly high aspiration it sets for itself and in its refusal to make a demand on government, or mayor, for additional funding. The report emphasises that what needs to happen first is the more effective co-ordination of partnership working across the boroughs, at a 'sub-regional' level, and across organisations with shared policy areas, such as crime or employment training, whose remits could be better articulated. For example, Jobcentre Plus, the Department for Work and Pensions, and The Learning and Skills Council (LSC) have all collaborated on a host boroughs joint strategy for investment in improving outcomes on 'worklessness' (getting people back to work who have experienced long-term unemployment), employment, and skills.

By describing regeneration in terms of a clear set of well-evidenced ambitions, it is relatively easy to win political support and sign off on the SRF. It ticks a number of rhetorical boxes that allow the powers that be to show that they are supportive of the cause of socio-economic regeneration in the Olympic host boroughs, but without them having to allocate any additional funding to the cause. With socio-economics marginalised from the remit of OPLC, the SRF is just what it needs, just in time, to show that it retains a political commitment to regeneration in the broader sense.

Speaking at the February meeting of the EDCST Committee of the London Assembly, Roger Taylor described the significance of the publication of the SRF as follows:

> Legacy has been a national government responsibility since the day when it published the bid to the International Olympic Committee to say this was going to be the legacy Games.
> Absolutely no efforts were put into thinking about legacy until the boroughs, working with Tom Russell [Former Head of Olympic Legacy Directorate, LDA] when he was still at the LDA, agreed 18 months ago to start working on it because nobody else was doing anything about it. But we are still very, very, very firmly of the view that this is a national responsibility. All we have done is provide a coherent, exciting, and challenging articulation of what needs to be done to breathe some life into those words, which are in the Olympic bid.
> A year and a half ago the host boroughs were charged with the requirement to think about legacy as it was interpreted through the Government's commitment in the Olympic bid to achieve a significant improvement in the overall condition of the communities living round the Games, and we were pretty clear, at the time, that simply thinking about legacy in terms of what would happen on the Olympic Park after the Games was not going to be adequate. That was about bricks, and mortar. It could have a very profound effect, but it was not necessarily, on its own, going to create one more job, get one child out of child poverty, or anything like that.
> So, the origins of the Strategic Regeneration Framework were a very firm conviction that we, the mayor, and the GLA, and the government needed to address the issues around the socio-economic conditions of the people who live in the east, and southeast London boroughs, which made up the host boroughs for the Olympics. When you look at their condition what you see immediately is that you are talking about, statistically, the most deprived community, and the largest most deprived community, in England. It is a harsh paradox that community sits just seven or eight miles from the centre of one of the richest cities in Western Europe.
> So, we were very clear that what we needed to do was, first of all, to think about how we could address directly the problems of disadvantage in the community, and how we could do that across all of the host boroughs. The targets that we have set ourselves, within the Strategic Regeneration

Framework, which are drawn from our assessment of what are the key, and most important drivers of improvement in socio-economic conditions, are ones which, as far as we are concerned, are the absolutely essential group, and those are educational attainment, skills, particularly National Vocational Qualification (NVQ) levels, and worklessness, and its association with child poverty, housing overcrowding, and homelessness, crime, and health.'
Roger Taylor
Item 3, Appendix A, Economic Development, Culture, Sport and Tourism Committee, 12 January 2010[2]

Although there was some scepticism from the committee about the late arrival of the SRF and the lack of an action plan showing how these laudable aims were going to be achieved, committee members were reassured about the positive reception of the document at OPLC. This was because the committee had already expressed concern that without a socio-economic focus, the risk was that the Olympic Park would become just another insular development.

Legacy Lectures

The date of publication of the SRF coincided with the timing of the first Legacy Lecture that I organised last year [2009] for the Comms. Team, as part of their outreach and engagement strategy. Responding to the many requests from students who want to make the Olympic legacy the object of their final year dissertations, Emma decided in 2008 to organise the first of a series of annual lectures hosted by various London universities, with legacy experts as speakers. The turnout and level of engagement from the students had been disappointing, and Emma wanted to take the idea back to the drawing board. At a time when I was trying to secure my position in the newly emerging Legacy Company, Emma asked me to

---

[2] Olympic Strategic Regeneration Framework Item 3, Appendix A, Economic Development, Culture, Sport and Tourism Committee, 12 January 2010 http://legacy.london.gov.uk/assembly/edcst/2010/jan12/minutes/transcript.pdf. Accessed 10 May 2015.

lead on the Legacy Lectures, and left me to get on with it, expecting me to update the team on my progress at the weekly team catch-up meetings.

Glad for small mercies, I relished the task. Finally, like everyone else, I was responsible for something. I had work to do, and could be as similarly preoccupied at my computer as others in the team. Quietly, I began to assemble my own bid for credibility, among the Comms. staff, for communicating well about legacy. My proposal was for a set of three related, but specifically themed public lectures each year, with each event hosted by a different London university and relevant academic specialist. The idea was that panel discussions should generate debate and lead to a meaningful period of audience questions to the panel. The risk I took was to go against the grain; this was not going to be a slick marketing initiative from the OPLC, which would simply deliver the latest 'lines' and 'messages' and tell the audience what they ought to be thinking, without room for critical thinking. The point was to organise a series of events that if repeated at yearly intervals could contribute to the task of gauging academic and public reaction to ongoing legacy developments. With a focus on challenges to the legacy debate, rather than simply information-giving, panels were formed of a combination of relevant urban academics (depending on each lecture's theme), legacy professionals, and appropriate members of the East London set of stakeholders. The events were designed to be high profile, but accessible, taking place in London's foremost inter-disciplinary centres for urban research, and were to be open to members of the public, as well as students and academics.

The first event took place last November [2009] at the London School of Economics, with Professor Ricky Burdett, from the LSE's Cities Programme, as academic host and speaker. The debate explored the relationship between the physical development of the Olympic Park in legacy mode and socio-economic transformation in East London. This theme was timely, with Paul Brickell and Roger Taylor also on the panel, not only because the first iteration of the SRF was about to be published, spelling out the ambitions for long-term socio-economic development in the host Olympic boroughs, but also because Andrew Altman agreed to speak, because of his connection to the LSE and to Professor Ricky Burdett through the Cities Programme. The acceptance of Andrew

Altman raised the stakes for the event, and suddenly, the whole Comms. Team became interested in what I was doing.

The lecture entitled, 'The First Legacy Games: the physical and socio-economic transformation of London'[3] took place in the brand new and slick surroundings of the Sheikh Zayed lecture theatre. During the question-and-answer session, Roger Taylor admitted that if he had to pull a figure out of the air for the realisation of the SRF, it would be something like a few billion over the 20-year period of the strategy. This was an important moment, because up until this point, the official line had been that the SRF was definitively not about going to government with a begging bowl, but rather about getting government, at central and London levels, to get behind local government plans in East London for new and ambitious ways of working towards radical policy outcomes.

Also controversial was the unexpected public announcement by Professor Ricky Burdett, of his appointment as Design Advisor to OPLC. There was nothing that could be done about this in the moment, but the significance of it was not lost on the Interim Director of Comms., who immediately pointed it out to the Comms. Team, who had also been taken by surprise by this announcement, that it was very important that OPLC was wary of using the term 'appointment'. The risk was that if it became clear that Professor Burdett had been 'appointed', it would also become clear that proper procedures had not been followed around advertisement of the role, and the organisation of a fair process of recruitment. It was to be understood that this was about consultancy, and not 'appointment'. Internally, at OPLC and at EDAW, the announcement at the legacy lecture caused a ripple of gossip to circulate, because with Professor Burdett on board as Design Advisor, it was now clear who was to be orchestrating the design-led review and advising Andrew Altman.

Amazed at what I had managed to pull off at the LSE, the Comms. Team were impressed by the event, and incredulous that 400 delegates, including students, academics, central, and London government legacy-focused staff, and Olympic-related personnel, filled a packed out lecture

---

[3] The First Legacy Games: the physical and socioeconomic transformation of East London. http://www.lse.ac.uk/newsAndMedia/videoAndAudio/channels/publicLecturesAndEvents/player.aspx?id=482. Accessed 10 May 2015.

theatre. Radio 4 came to record the event, and it was broadcast on the You and Yours programme, to a national audience of 2 million people. This kept the press team happy, and the Interim Director of Comms. was then officially off my case; begrudgingly, she said to me at the end of the evening, 'you did well tonight', and since then, she has left me alone. The Comms. Events Manager who also kept a close eye on proceedings, said to me, just before she was leaving to go home on the night, 'Gillian, I feel like you are a person now. I can see you. This was a really good event.'

Having proved that I understood what counted as good Comms. work—creating an event to get the legacy message out there; gaining positive publicity for OPLC, and engaging with a large audience—I had secured my position as a person who understands how to participate effectively in the team, and who knows, therefore, how to add value. To do this without jeopardising my academic credibility (by creating the space for critical debate), was no mean feat. I was pleased to have been able to carve out a role for myself and to become recognisable in the Comms. Team as a person with a contribution to make.

'Blue Sky Thinking'

Five months later, and now dismayed by the rhetoric coming out of the design-led review of the LMF, Emma Wheelhouse is incredulous about the talk of a new ambition to make the Olympic Park 'the Notting Hill of East London', where private schools will be needed to attract the middle classes. Excluded from the review process, and waiting for the new Director of Urban Design and Planning to be appointed, the original small team of planners, now led by Gareth Blacker's deputy—Irene Man—are demoralised, and in limbo. Having got just to the point where the scheme was about to be fixed last year and, then, having to let that go, and start again, letting go of any control as the former clients of the process, has been excruciating for Irene and her team, and it is not surprising that morale among the planners is low.

Irene's budget has been slashed, there is no money for consultation, the letters have still not gone out to those stakeholders who made a formal response to Output C, and there will be no more consultation, just a process of statutory engagement (which means information giving, not the kind of opinion giving that could change what has been decided upon), until the autumn. Meanwhile, everyone is speaking in hushed tones about the cost of the LMF review process, which is apparently going to be more than £5 million—five times more than it has been in any previous year—even when the most intensive work was being done by the EDAW Consortium.

Adam Williams, lead of the EDAW master-planning team, tries to explain to me what is going on, but he too is dismayed and incredulous about the ruthless process through which a new regime is laying claim to the spoils. He knew that the creation of OPLC, and the appointment of Margaret Ford and Andrew Altman, was going to imply, quite rightly a review of the LMF, to make sure that they could put their names to, or change the direction of travel, which the flexibility of the scheme properly allows for, but he did not expect this, this throwing of the baby out with the bath water, which essentially means that a sense of ownership can be claimed by the usurpers, for the urban planning and design process already done for the LMF.

Adam explains that what shocks him most is that EDAW is having to absorb all of the risk, being held to ransom, and required to tolerate the impression that is being created that the LMF is failing, and, at the same time, also being asked to make it look as if they have decided to procure the services of a whole new design team. This saves OPLC from having to go through the proper process for the procurement of services, which are being paid for with significant sums of public money, and that allows for a non-competitive allocation of work to a select group of architectural practices, and landscape designers chosen by those in charge of the review process at OPLC.

The point, Adam spells out, is to revisit the whole scheme with fresh eyes, with no limitations, and to apply 'blue sky thinking' to the site, to see what architects rather than planners might come up with. Adam explains that those in charge of the LMF at EDAW, those who got it close to scheme fix last year, are allowed to sit in on the design-review sessions, but they are not allowed to speak. They are literally expected to be silent, and just to observe unless their opinion is sought. This 'don't speak unless you are spoken to' approach is deeply humiliating, and Adam emphasises that the whole situation has brought the most senior members of the team close to withdrawing EDAW from the whole process. I ask Adam why this is not going to happen, since it would seem to be the most obvious way in which to expose what is going on, but he makes clear what it has taken me a while to fully comprehend, which is that just like it was in the Legacy Directorate, so it is in the master-planning team at EDAW; there is a profound commitment to the ideals of the Olympic bid and their promise of regeneration proper. To walk away now would be to jeopardise that legacy just at the moment when it is most in need of protection. Unfortunately, Adam says that there is no one on the OPLC Board who understands the master-planning process, so there is no oversight of what is going on.

Hence, the team at EDAW perseveres in the knowledge that because of the limitations of the site, the likelihood is that the new team of designers, some of whom were unsuccessful in the original competition for the master-planning work (such as Maccreanor Lavington), will come up with a scheme very much like the one that has already been put forward, but now (because of the change in business plan that the possibility of a debt-free land deal makes possible), with a different way of framing and expressing the already existing priority for family housing.

Adam says it is impossibly difficult in the meetings to watch the designers, many of whom are EDAW's rivals, go through the motions of proposing 'blue sky ideas', only to have to realise, in the end, what the master-planning process had already revealed long before, which is that the geographical limitations of the site, the Olympic inheritance of venues and parkland, as well as the political landscape of stakeholder, and host borough demands and expectations, all lead to a series of serious constraints on what it is possible to do with the site.

Worst of all, Adam says, is that it seems that all the work that has gone into the strategic documents that accompany the scheme, like the socio-economic strategy, are to fall by the wayside. This set of documents established the work of the LMF process as 'regeneration best practice' and demonstrated the evidence not only for how decisions had been made, but also how the site was to be integrated spatially, socially, and conceptually with the surrounding areas. It was exactly this kind of dedicated planning and design process that led to the focus on necessary additional social infrastructure, a holistic approach to the socio-economics of the wider area, and the need for a focus in the Olympic Park on family housing. The fact that this was family housing of higher density, because of the need for the repayment of debt, did not in itself, make the scheme unworkable, because there is an argument to be made that a larger number of units of family housing that is more affordable might, in the end, be more beneficial than fewer, and more expensive, larger family homes that only a very few will be able to afford.

Nevertheless, the combination of the desire among local people in East London, expressed during consultation, for recognisable family housing such as already exists in East London in the form of terraced houses with gardens, and the move towards a more upmarket housing scheme, as a result of the possible change in ideology and business plan, appears to be leading to a reduction in housing densities, from 10,000 homes to 8000, with significantly less apartments and more recognisable family homes. This chimes with the desire in the host boroughs for a scheme that provides 'aspirational housing', and a radical uplift in the perception of what East London has to offer, but it is not yet clear how this will fit with a land decontamination process that did not envisage the cost of providing homes with gardens that have soil safe for growing things that might be eaten.

In the first draft of the OPLC Corporate Plan, which has just been produced, the evolution of the vision for the housing of the Olympic Park produced by the LMF review process is described as follows:

> A 21st C garden city with family housing neighbourhoods that build on the best of London's exceptional Georgian, and Victorian housing tradition. This type of housing is a response to a real need for family housing within the city's residential market, and the aspirations of East London's residents. For the Olympic park to succeed it must, therefore, supply a product that is not currently on the market, and that responds to the needs of East London, and London as a whole—i.e. not dense high rise apartments. The great estates of London, from private landowners, like The Grosvenor, and Howard de Walden estates, to charities like the Guinness Trust have delivered distinctive, and high quality neighbourhoods of sustained value by intense attention to management, and by undertaking development in a way that allows for successful, and flexible evolution, while retaining control over quality, for example by retaining freehold interests.

6 The Doldrums   149

Whilst this gives the company a new story to tell, and the focus on family houses, rather than apartments, is widely welcomed, there is concern too, for example, in the EDCST Committee of the London Assembly that this kind of scheme will promise gentrification, and not regeneration. Dee Doocey, Chair of the Committee, expressed her concerns:

> I would certainly welcome more family accommodation—I cannot imagine that anyone would not. My only concern is to make sure that it does not become an oasis for yuppies, because I guess with a park of that nature, which is really going to be a very nice place to live served by ten train lines etc., I can just imagine family accommodation being for very, very, wealthy families.
> Olympic Park Legacy Company. Transcript of Item 6. Economic Development, Culture, Sport and Tourism Committee, 21 October 2009.[4]

Walking back to Stratford station one evening, with one of the planners, I empathise with what I know the team must be going through, tolerating the behind-the-scenes hiatus and exclusion of the old Legacy Directorate team from the design-review process, whilst watching the company desperately trying to craft a new and credible set of lines and messages about a significant transformation of the legacy vision. The team is anticipating the appointment of the new Director of Planning, and, tongue in cheek, it has been said more than once, 'Bring back Gareth Blacker!' Taking the opportunity to let off steam, the planner expresses the feeling of ongoing frustration, and genuine concern:

> The last six months have been so demoralizing, with nothing happening, and then suddenly new designers brought in, led by a 'consultant' rather than by us, as clients, and we don't know what our role is anymore, now that they have 20 new designers sitting round a table. I think this is just about people trying to put their stamp on things. The problem now is that the programme [trying to get a planning application in before The Games] is going to be so tight. The Olympics are already under the spotlight for wasting money, and you just hope that everything is going to be OK, but

---
[4] Olympic Park Legacy Company. Transcript of Item 6. Economic Development, Culture, Sport and Tourism Committee, 21 October 2009. https://www.london.gov.uk/sites/default/files/archives/assembly-edcst-2009-oct21-minutes-transcript.pdf. Accessed 10 May 2015.

you look at the processes through which things are being done, and you wonder—there has to be some sense in which we are accountable to the public. At least things are happening now, so we'll just have to wait and see.

Suggested Reading

Barker, K. (2014). *Housing: Where's the plan?* London: London Publishing Partnership.

Carlo Palermo, P., & Ponzini, D. (2015). *Place making and urban development: New challenges for contemporary planning and design.* New York: Routledge.

Dorling, D. (2014). *All that is solid: How the great housing disaster defines our times and what we can do about it.* London: Penguin.

Healey, P. (2010). *Making better places: The planning project in the 21st century.* New York: Palgrave Macmillan.

Keil, R., & Brenner, N. (Eds.). (2005). *The global cities reader.* New York: Routledge.

Longstaffe-Gowan, T. (2012). *The London Square: Gardens in the midst of town.* New Haven: Yale University Press.

Low, S., & Smith, N. (Eds.). (2005). *The politics of public space.* New York: Routledge.

Low, S., & Lawrence Zuniga, D. (Eds.). (2003). *The anthropology of space and place: Locating culture.* Malden, MA: Blackwell.

Sassens, S. (2001). *The Global City: London, New York, Tokyo.* New Jersey: Princeton University Press.

Tonkiss, F. (2013). *Cities by design: The social life of urban form.* Cambridge: Polity Press.

7

Unruly Suitors

February 2011

All hell has broken loose. No one has time anymore to complain that nothing is happening. Everything is happening: all at once. An increasingly bitter and acrimonious battle between the two rival bidders for the legacy use of the Olympic stadium has been unfolding in the press for the last few months, and that conflict is about to come to head with the announcement, next week, of the decision of the Board of the OPLC, about who is to be chosen as the preferred bidder. Vying for supremacy, playing out their rivalry, and recruiting allies to their causes very publically in the press are Premier League football teams, West Ham United, and Tottenham Hotspur.

The West Ham bid, backed by Olympic host borough Newham Council, promises to keep the athletics track inside the stadium, and has the backing, not surprisingly, of UK Athletics. Chairman of UK Athletics, Ed Warner, gave the West Ham bid his formal backing last year, in October, just before OPLC was about to announce which two parties it would enter into negotiations with, out of those that had expressed their interest in the stadium (including Tottenham Hotspur, who submitted, at the last minute, a joint bid with AEG the American owners/operators of the O^2 entertainment complex south of the river, in Greenwich) during last August's process of formal procurement. Ed Warner explained to the BBC why UK Athletics was coming out strongly in support of the West Ham bid:

> We are supporting the joint bid from West Ham United and Newham Council, and the reason we are doing that is that this bid has fully embraced the needs of athletics in all the discussion we've had with them in recent months. We've been really interested to ensure that there's a stadium here, which has an athletics track that can support the needs of the athletics community, grassroots, youngsters, veteran athletes, local clubs, and everything in the bid they've submitted embraces athletics, and we're very excited about that.
> We've taken our time to work with all the bidders over the course of the last few months… this is the bid that stands out for us, so we now want to work with West Ham, and Newham Council to get that bid over the finish line. Last week, Tottenham, and AEG, made clear that they didn't want an athletics track in the stadium in legacy. For us, that was something of an insult to the promise that was made by Seb Coe when he won the Olympics for London in 2005. Ever since then it's been about embracing an athletics legacy in the stadium, making sure the Olympics leave something behind for athletics in the UK. This will be the home of British Athletics. I would urge the Legacy Company to take any bid that doesn't put athletics at the heart of the stadium, and kick it out swiftly, so we can get an early solution to the process, which has gone on for a few months now. I hope it comes to a conclusion quite swiftly from here.
> We are the national governing body for the world's premier Olympic sport, which doesn't have a home that really passes muster in the UK. West Ham has worked with us on the calendar for use of the stadium, the split between football, and athletics, and other usages—community usage, maybe some concerts [Live Nation, the concert promoters are also part of the bid consortium], and we get a full run at the athletics calendar, so we get the things we need in that stadium every year. We get marketing support—we can market athletics to football supporters, and vice versa, and the community is supported at the stadium. The warm up track is re-laid right up next to the Olympic stadium, so that local clubs, schools, universities can

use it, and it really is a home for athletics at all levels. Newham Council really wants to ensure that the stadium works for the community, and so do we—for the community in athletics.

Ed Warner speaking to BBC Olympics Correspondent, Adrian Warner, 11th October 2011.[1]

In November, OPLC formally announced that West Ham and Spurs were the two contending bidders for the stadium, and negotiations began about how to progress the details and business plans around those bids. Both bids propose a 60,000-seat stadium, but Tottenham's proposal is to demolish the upper part of the existing Olympic stadium (because it was only ever designed for temporary use), and to build a new purpose-built stadium around the base structure, but without an athletics track. The aim is to replace the stadium that Spurs have outgrown at White Hart Lane in the north London borough of Haringey. Spurs' idea to tear out the athletics track, and not to keep the Olympic form of the stadium, is bold and irreverent; they make no attempt to pay lip service either to the iconic status of the Olympic stadium or the emotive symbolism of an athletics-focused Games, and their bid demonstrates a refusal to be restricted by a political landscape, in which the reputation of key government, and Olympic figures, depends on the delivery of an athletics-focused legacy for the stadium. Theirs is a hardnosed business proposal in which the only viable legacy for the stadium is to be derived from a Premier League football club tenant, in a stadium built to last, without an athletics track getting in the way of fans' enjoyment. To compensate for the loss of an athletics legacy in the stadium, Spurs have proposed to redevelop the old national athletics stadium at Crystal Palace, suggesting that a 360 days-a-year athletics legacy there is better than having to share the Olympics stadium with a football club that would give athletics access only for a fraction of the year.

In response to this, at the end of December, continuing to lobby hard for the cause of UK Athletics, and hoping to damage the chances of Spurs winning the bid against West Ham, 16 British Olympic and Paralympic

---

[1] UK Athletics Boost for West Ham's 2012 Bid. http://www.bbc.co.uk/blogs/adrianwarner/2010/10 Accessed 2 May 2015.

athletes weighted into the bidding war, putting their support firmly behind West Ham and Newham Council. The Olympians, including Daley Thompson, Steve Cram, Steve Backley, Tanni Grey Thompson, and Dame Kelly Holmes, wrote an open letter to the Board of the OPLC, urging them not to choose a bid that would eliminate the athletics legacy from the heart of the Olympic stadium:

> We are all proud Olympians, and Paralympians, who have competed under the Union flag, and without exception we were all passionate supporters of the bid to bring the world's greatest sporting event to London. A home Games in 2012 gives our country a once in a lifetime opportunity to inspire future generations with a love of sport, be they future Olympians, or the supporters that play such a crucial role in our success.
>
> One of the most compelling aspects of our bid, back in 2005, was the promise of an athletics legacy in the form of a world-class stadium. This promise made the idea of legacy real. It showed that the Games would continue to touch the wider community long after the Olympic, and Paralympic, spectacular had left town. What made the legacy more persuasive was the fact that this wasn't just about the top end of the sport, and giving our top athletes a 'home' stadium to be proud of. This was about the community, about making a facility work as hard as possible, and be as accessible as possible to a wide range of people from a wide range of sports. Here was a stadium that would see young athletes competing for an English Schools title run on the same track as Usain Bolt, where Premiership footballers could play whilst club athletes train. Here was somewhere that could play host to Twenty20 cricket one week, and a pop concert the next.
>
> As Olympians, we are all ardent sports fans, and that is why we believe the Olympic legacy HAS to be the Olympic Stadium complete with track. It would be unacceptable for the stadium to lose the track, and effectively become an Olympic Stadium with no Olympic connection or legacy. We urge the decision makers in this process to ensure the track remains post-2012, and bring to life a sporting promise made to a whole community for generations to come.

The letter from the Olympians makes clear the continued dissatisfaction of UK Athletics with the Spurs bid, and in particular, the idea that the removal of the athletics track from the Olympic stadium could be compensated for by providing an athletics legacy elsewhere. The athletes' letter is unequivocal—it explains the emotive value of the Olympic stadium, illustrates what it is that makes the stadium an iconic venue, and how it is that for them, the stadium is to become a potent, irreplaceable, symbol of Britain's moment in sporting, and in particular, athletics history. Hence, their passionate defence of West Ham's bid which embodies the promise of the original Olympic bid about which the Olympians feel fiercely protective.

A Defining Moment

This is an important moment for Margaret Ford. As soon as she was appointed at the beginning of last year, she staked her reputation on a reassessment of the stadium situation and on exploring again the possibility of keeping the stadium as an important part of the Olympic legacy. Her idea was to retain the stadium as one of the main focus points of a strategy to rethink the vision of the future Olympic Park in terms of the immediate post-Games visitor experience, rather than simply in terms of the long-term return to the treasury of receipts from the housing developments. Uncertainty over the fate of the stadium, and its athletics track, has already jeopardised the UK's chances to bid for the 2015 World Championships, which is a further embarrassment to UK Athletics after the never-ending saga of the failure to provide a respectable home to UK Athletics, and now, only a month away from the time when the UK will have to decide again whether to express its interest in bidding for the 2017 Athletics World Championships, it is time for the OPLC to prove its worth, or lose its credibility.

For other reasons too, the focus on the legacy uses of the sporting venues is intense at the moment. This is partly because of the success of the ODA, which has shown the world how to prepare for an Olympic Games, and is certain to deliver all of the sporting venues a year ahead of time, which puts pressure on OPLC to deliver on its side of the bargain, and find tenants for those venues before the Games begin next year. And, it is also partly because it is beginning to come clear that the hardest legacy promise of all to deliver is going to be the increase in sporting participation that Tessa Jowell was certain would be one of the gains of Olympic legacy. This means that where plans for increases in participation might fail across London, and in the nation more generally, in the

Olympic Park at least, there is going to be no excuse for sporting venues that do not inspire people to take part. It also means that Tessa Jowell is more determined than ever that the Olympic stadium should realise what she promised, which is a legacy for athletics.

Even with a new Conservative-led coalition government now in power and Tessa Jowell no longer the Olympic Minister, her political reputation stills depends on the Olympics delivering to UK Athletics the track in the Olympic Park that was promised in the Olympic bid. No surprise then, that as Shadow Olympics Minister, Tessa Jowell has also just joined in the stadium bidding war. Rather sheepishly, because, of course, she has in fact lost control of the Olympic legacy to her great rival, Boris Johnson, she speaks out in the media, in favour of West Ham:

> It is right and proper that the views of Labour are known, and the point of view of Labour MPs are known, and some 21 Labour MPs across London have come out in support of the Newham Council/West Ham bid, and I think it is important that that is made public, but there is a second point—there are two bids, one from Tottenham Hotspur, and one from Newham Council/West Ham United, and certainly it is the case that the West Ham bid, which keeps the athletics track, will meet the commitment to an athletics legacy, will keep the commitment on the level of community engagement.
>
> We made a very clear commitment at the time of the Olympic bid, as Olympic Minister at the time I set out the broad criteria, which should guide the OPLC decision, and it's pretty clear that only the West Ham bid meets those tests. My understanding, having spoken to the Mayor of Newham is they have tested even the scenario that West Ham might suffer relegation, and, therefore, be a club with less money to spend. They are satisfied that the budget stacks up. Obviously, the final judge of that will be The Board of the OPLC. The fact is we made a commitment to athletics, it was a factor in our winning the bid, and, therefore, it is a commitment that we've got to honour, not just to the communities of the East End, but to our athletes, and to the International Olympic Committee.
>
> Tessa Jowell, 20th January 2011[2]

---

[2] Tessa Jowell Backs West Ham Bid for Stadium to Keep Athletics Promises http://www.telegraph.co.uk/sport/olympics/8270181/London-2012-Olympics-Tessa-Jowell-backs-West-Ham-Bid-for-stadium-to-keep-athletics-legacy-promises.html. Accessed 2 May 2015.

It is ironic that Tessa Jowell should now be supporting West Ham so wholeheartedly, given that she obstructed the original interest of West Ham, back in 2001, to become the legacy tenants of the stadium. At the time, Tessa had put Premier League football clubs off, fiercely defending the athletics-only legacy, by warning that the conversion costs to keep the stadium as a permanent larger capacity football venue would be prohibitive. Now, as a result of that original well meaning, but short sighted decision, the issue is having to be revisited by West Ham, which means that the club now has to find an estimated £95 million to convert the stadium from an 80,000 Olympic capacity venue to a 60,000-seat capacity football stadium with a roof, reconfigured seating to accommodate the athletics track and hospitality facilities. Spurs, in contrast, are proposing to spend about £300 million to build their new stadium on the site, which represents a saving of £150 million compared to the £450 million it would have cost them to rebuild at their current grounds.

Money Matters

Because the Board of OPLC cannot choose to support a bid whose business plan does not stack up, the question of finance complicates matters. West Ham appears to be the natural choice of tenant, because it is the local Premiership team with East London backing, a strong commitment to athletics and local community usage, but financial insecurity means that serious question marks hang over West Ham's proposal. The club is currently at the very bottom of the Premier League and in serious danger of relegation, which means an imminent loss of income. In addition, the cost of West Ham's bid for the stadium, and the likelihood of relegation, means that there is nervousness about whether, or not the side would still have sufficient funds to purchase new players and to up its game in the way that it is envisaged a move to the Olympic stadium would make possible. Spurs are also adamant that the combination of football, and athletics, is not commercially viable, and that West Ham's proposal cannot, therefore, be a sustainable use of the stadium. Daniel Levy, Spurs Chairman, joined in the war of words in the press, going to war with Karren Brady, West Ham's Vice Chair, over what he describes as an emotive campaign, which conceals the facts about what is going to be financially viable, and best value for the taxpayer:

> Let's not deal with emotion. I mean what we've got to make sure for London is that there's something that's there for decades that's going to be financially viable, and if you look at any of the Olympic stadiums around Europe that currently exist, where you try to put football, and athletics, together, it doesn't work, so putting emotion to one side, we have to have a solution that will stand the test of time, and will not involve any form of public subsidy. The easiest solution for us would have been, you know, we'll take the stadium with the running track, but I would not, and, in my opinion, neither would virtually any other club within England, certainly any of the big clubs, support the notion of merging athletics, and soccer, it will not work, and it will end in tears.
>
> What's the point of having a great legacy if, in five years, it's derelict, and the company operating it is bankrupt? What you need is something that's going to be there, that's going to stand the test of time. I believe common sense will prevail, and when one looks at the detail, and the true facts of the matter then the right decision will be made.
>
> Daniel Levy, 8 February, 2011.[3]

In response, Karren Brady is adamant that the retention of the athletics track will not affect the atmosphere in the Olympic stadium. She insists that even the seat that is going to be furthest away from the pitch in their bid, which reconfigures some of the post-Games seating, will still be 10 yards closer than the furthest seat from the pitch at Wembley stadium. This war of words in the press finally reached fever pitch, this month, at the point when there appeared to have been a leak to the BBC from inside the OPLC, suggesting that the bid is going to go in West Ham's favour. This immediately prompted Tottenham to threaten legal action, which sent a shockwave through OPLC, and increased the atmosphere of nervous anxiety, because the prospect of legal action would not only be costly, it could also mean having to stall the whole process, which would create further uncertainty about the stadium's future.

---

[3] Daniel Levy Hits Back at Karren Brady Over the Olympic Stadium http://news.bbc.co.uk/sport1/hi/football/teams/t/tottenham_hotspur/9391299.stm Accessed 2 May 2015.

Contrary to the idea that Spurs have only entered the bidding war to put pressure on City Hall, and Haringey Council to remove the obstacles to their original proposals for a new stadium close to their current home ground, Spurs seem to be increasingly serious about the move to East London, and are insistent that the West Ham business case does not stand up; they are prepared to suggest that a decision in West Ham's favour smacks of an unfair process of decision-making about the stadium's future.

West Ham certainly do not currently have the reputation of Spurs, as a serious contender in the Premier League, and they stand next to no chance, at least for now, of gaining a spot in the top four of the league, which is where the money is to be made in Europe, in the Champions League. Also, because West Ham is less secure in the Premiership, and on the border between Championship and Premier League status, their fan base is not equal to that of Tottenham. The accusation from Tottenham is that West Ham fans are going to be rattling around in a stadium too large for their club, and, to cap it all, having to cope with an atmosphere diminished by an athletics track that will remove the audience from pitch-side action. Tottenham, in contrast, boasts of a waiting list of 30,000 people for its season ticket places, which proves that the club has outgrown its White Hart Lane Stadium in Tottenham, in North London, and it can guarantee, therefore, a filled-to-capacity match day experience for its fans, profit for the club, and a financially viable partnership with OPLC, and, therefore, a good deal for taxpayers.

West Ham's response to this is to explain that their legacy business plan allows for subsidised ticket prices, which would not only lead to a stadium filled to capacity with home fans, but also the growth in their fan base among people who cannot ordinarily afford to attend football matches in Premier League stadiums. However, there are other reasons to question the financial viability of West Ham's ambitions. Firstly, their bid relies on financial support from Newham Council, which at first seems like a good idea, because Newham is one of the Olympic host boroughs, dedicated to delivering Olympic legacy to its residents, and determined to support West Ham as one of its local businesses, but there is a danger that support from the local government in the form of a Newham Council loan to West Ham, to cover the cost of transformation costs, in return for a half-owner share of the deal, smacks of state support.

The problem is that in a fiercely competitive football marketplace, unfair advantages will not be tolerated, and this could backfire down the line both for West Ham, Newham Council, and OPLC.

Secondly, the advent of a Conservative-led national government has, as predicted, led to savage local government cuts, and Newham, despite desperately trying to raise its game to meet the challenge of Olympic uplift (and to contribute to the Convergence agenda), has not been spared. It is being forced to find savings of £43 million. Sir Robin Wales has reassured OPLC that Newham's financial contribution to the stadium bid is unaffected by these cuts, and that the £80 million loan that it is taking from the government to contribute to the stadium transformation costs will be ring-fenced money, not to be used for any other purpose, but even so, the prospect is strange of one of London's poorest boroughs being in a position to lend £40 million to a Premier League football club that ought to be able to stand on its own feet.

Thirdly, there is doubt about the financial strength of West Ham's negotiating position, and long-term financial sustainability, because, despite a £100 million annual turnover, the club is still heavily in debt as a result of the £100 million liabilities that came with the club when new owners, local businessmen—David Gold and David Sullivan—bought the majority share in the club in 2010, after the club had been left in complete financial meltdown by its Icelandic former owner, Bjorgolfur Guomundsson, who lost his fortune in the 2008 financial crisis.

The club's current case is not helped by the fact that when they took over the club, Sullivan and Gold described the business case for West Ham United, just last year [2010], as 'making no commercial sense'. In their statement to the press they made clear that this was an emotional purchase made because they were fans of the club and West Ham supporters from childhood. These statements mean that Karren Brady, who is famous for having turned around the fortunes of Birmingham City football club (also for David Sullivan), has her work cut out to downplay the significance of the debt, and to reassure OPLC that the club's liabilities will be significantly reduced by the time West Ham would be due to occupy the stadium in 2014.

Nevertheless, the financial odds stack up against West Ham, and the more the club has to reassure OPLC about its financial viability, the more

Tottenham looks like the safer bet from a purely business perspective. At a time when OPLC is trying hard to prove its commercial credibility, this is a difficult call to make. Weighing into the fracas, Lord Alan Sugar, former Chair of Spurs, suggests that were the bid to go in West Ham's favour, it would be evidence of the cowardice of OPLC, and a sign that because of political interference, they did not have the guts to support the bid that makes the best business case.

The backstage drama of this intervention is only intensified by the fact that Spurs' rival in this matter is Karren Brady, who is the formidable Vice Chair of West Ham, but also the henchwoman who, on Lord Sugar's hit reality television show, *The Apprentice*, scrutinises, on Lord Sugar's behalf, the candidates who dare to demonstrate their business credentials in a series of weekly competitions that lead the victor to a prestigious place in Lord's Sugar business empire.

The stronger Tottenham makes its own claims, the more vociferous West Ham becomes. In the end, Karren Brady resorts to the kind of traditional territorial claims associated with the passion of football fandom in London, suggesting that Tottenham is never going to be welcome in East London and Newham will not tolerate Haringey 'muscling in where it is not wanted'. This kind of claim is complicated by the fact that on the ground, neither the fans of Spurs or West Ham are keen to move to the Olympic stadium, because it is an unavoidable fact of football that the territorial association of each club with their home ground is passionately felt by the fans. The symbolic value to fans of the more than 100-year histories of their clubs in their home stadiums is priceless, and to be protected at all costs.

Leyton Orient

As if matters were not complicated enough, another local football team, Leyton Orient, who were also involved in the early discussions about occupying the reduced 25,000 seat stadium, but were put off by the retention of the athletics track, have now reentered the fray. Barry Hearn, the club's Chairman, is incensed. His argument is that a move by West Ham to the Olympic stadium would put Leyton Orient out of business, and this is especially the case, because of the promise of cut-price tickets. According to the rules of the Premier League, Hearn insists that it is illegal for a football club to build its stadium within close vicinity of another club. The move of West Ham to the Olympic stadium would break this rule, and, Hearn argues, destroy Leyton Orient's fan base, seriously undermining the club, which also has a long history of fierce fandom in East London. Hearn too has now come out fighting and is also threatening legal action.

This situation is intensified by the fact that Leyton Orient is a long-term stakeholder in the evolution of legacy plans. The club was just one of the thirty-eight stakeholder organisations who made a detailed, and considered, formal response to Output C in 2009, and who were ignored, like the other stakeholders, when OPLC was formed, and plans were put on hold for the LMF. In their consultation response, Leyton Orient reminded OPLC that (having been put off by the athletics track at the original Olympic stadium) they had proposed building a new stadium in the north of the Olympic Park, on land owned by the Lea Valley Regional Park Authority. Leyton Orient reminded OPLC that West Ham too had, at one point, designs on that land for a site for its new stadium, and that plan had been put paid to when Leyton Orient launched a legal challenge. In February 2009, the club wrote to OPLC as follows:

> It is good to hear that the Legacy Masterplan Framework is not yet fixed as we are of the opinion that we have a substantial input to make in the shaping of the Park in legacy, and therefore intend to take an active part in the Consultation process. We sincerely hope that the consultation exercise will be undertaken in a completely open handed and unbiased manner. We appreciate, although we do not agree with, your comments and thoughts on our proposals especially in relation to duplication, balance, lack of appetite for two large stadiums, and the desire to maintain open parkland. We know well the history of the Lea Valley Regional Park Authority's custody of the site, the background of which might well emerge as the consultations progress, but it is interesting to note at this stage that it wasn't that long ago that the LVRPA had decided (prior to Judicial Review proceedings commenced by the Club) to sell the site to West Ham United FC!

Extract of a letter from Steve Dawson, Director of Leyton Orient, to OPLC.

Eventually, exasperated by the lack of progress of the LMF, and infuriated by a lack of response from OPLC, Leyton Orient bypassed the formal channels for stakeholder communication, and wrote, last year [2010], directly to central government. This was a source of great regret to Emma's Consultation and Engagement team, whose hands were tied, but knew that it was disastrous for their relationships with stakeholders that no letters of response had been sent out to those who made a formal response to Output C. No wonder, then, that by now, in February 2011, when the review of the LMF has yielded nothing to Leyton Orient, and Margaret Ford has told the London Assembly categorically that there is not a 'chance in hell' of there being two football stadiums in the Olympic Park, that Barry Hearn is furious that the formal process for the procurement of legacy uses for the Olympic stadium looks like it is going to deliver success to West Ham.

All Change

After the land deal, the stadium deal is the second serious test for OPLC. There is momentum in legacy planning again, at last, but it has been a nail-biting year. Margaret Ford ended 2010 with a message, sent through internal communications, thanking everyone for their perseverance, and urging people to dig a little deeper, because the challenges of the New Year were going to be intense as the transition was made from planning to delivery. This was a reference not just to the stadium process, but also the formal process of procurement going live for operators for the Aquatics Centre, The Multi-Use Arena, and Estates and Facilities Management for the park. The closing date was also imminent, for the Expressions of Interest process for operating The Orbit, which is the mayor's Art in the Park project that won planning permission in the summer of last year. The project, designed by Anish Kapoor, with engineer Cecil Balmond, is a twisting red, steel sculpture, reaching 115 metres high with a viewing platform overlooking the park. Billionaire steel magnate, Lakshmi Mittal, has provided the steel, and a £16 million contribution towards the total £19.1 million budget. Construction began in November of last year, and Boris boldly imagines that the tower might generate 1 million visitors a year to the park, and become one of London's famous attractions, like the popular London Eye, on the Southbank.

Even though the terms of the land deal had been agreed before the General Election, in 2010, the deal itself was not actually done. No money changed hands, and everything was then up in the air, and on hold again until the election was over. On top of this, as soon as the election was won, Boris Johnson, as predicted, made a major play for control over the Olympic legacy, announcing his plans to abolish the LDA in 2012 (subject to new government legislation that will devolve power, abolish all Regional Development Associations [RDAs] in the interests of 'localism', and the decentralisation of government) and to establish a Mayoral Development Corporation (MDC) to take over from OPLC in the same year. This would mean that planners of legacy would be answerable solely to Boris Johnson, not central government any longer, and Boris' Olympic legacy takeover bid would finally come to fruition.

This all means that before OPLC has even got on its feet, a change in the political climate is yet again threatening the organisational structure through which Olympic legacy will be planned and delivered. Rather than watching people pushing a boulder up the mountain, studying the Olympic legacy is suddenly beginning to feel a bit like watching a surreal game, in which serious-minded people are trying desperately to construct a new piece of city on top of a merry-go-round that turns violently with each change in the political landscape. As usual, there is nothing to do but for those planning the legacy to keep their heads down and keep their minds on what it is they are trying to bring to fruition before they run out of time.

To make matters worse, the new Conservative-led coalition government immediately insisted on reviewing the land deal, which caused a further delay, throughout the summer of 2010, so that the final deal was not actually agreed until the end of September. During this whole period the fate of OPLC was in question, and it was becoming increasingly difficult to maintain morale in the company, even at the highest levels. Under these conditions, it was excruciating to have to continue to put out a public facing message of commercial confidence. On top of this, there was nervousness that OPLC might not survive 'the bonfire of the quangos' in which all 901 of the non-government organisations, many of which had proliferated under New Labour, were placed under scrutiny.

What saved the day, finally, was a land deal that worked entirely in OPLC's favour, and proved the backing of the new government for the Olympic legacy project. This and the appointment of a new Executive Director of Comms. who had the wherewithal to go ahead, last summer, even in the face of all the uncertainty, and plan an ambitious official launch of OPLC, in October 2010, to announce to the world that the company was open for business, meant that in October 2010, just as things were beginning to also heat up around the stadium (and an 'expressions of interest' process had been started for the legacy use of the Press and Broadcast Centres), the company was finally beginning to pick up some momentum.

The conclusion of the land deal involved the transfer to OPLC of the lands assembled for the Olympic Park by the LDA, as well as other LDA land not far from the park, called the Three Mills Estate (a conservation area hosting a film studio complex). The cost to OPLC of acquiring this land was £138 million (subsequent to an independent valuation by Jones Lang LaSalle), plus £5.5 million in stamp duty, which was paid to the LDA by central government, from the Department of Communities and Local Government. In return, the LDA was relieved of £300 million of the £550 million contribution it had committed to the Olympic project as a result of the negotiations contained in the 2007 Memorandum of Understanding about the reorganised Public Sector Funding for the Olympic project. The LDA is also to continue, until 2012, with funding the running costs of OPLC for the year 2011/2012, to the tune of £173 million, with a further £14 million coming from the Department of Communities and Local Government (DCLG). Successful in its application to government as part of last autumn's Comprehensive Spending Review, OPLC can rely now on 4 years of central government funding from April 2011, which stabilises the situation somewhat.

The future abolition of the LDA means that its remaining debts of £387 million owed to government on the loan taken out for the land assembly process are to be picked up by City Hall. This, and the likely transfer of OPLC's assets to a new MDC in 2012, means that another game is about to begin of following the assets, and the debts that go with them. Yet again, the London Assembly is going to have to watch like a hawk, while the mayor manoeuvres his way towards increasing powers over the legacy project. At the moment, under the new land deal with the OPLC, the arrangement is that of the first £650 million of receipts on legacy land, and property deals, 85 % will go to central government, and 15 % to the GLA, and of the next £1300 million (if there is any), the GLA will receive 15 %, the Lottery 50 %, and the remaining 35 % will go to central government. The problem is that no consideration has been given to the timing of these payments, and the likelihood of a return to the Lottery diminishes in this deal compared to the previous one.

It is significant too that the mayor is proposing an Urban Development Corporation, rather than an URC, as the legacy way forward. The development corporation is the model for delivering regeneration associated with previous Conservative governments, and, most infamously, with the Docklands Development Corporation, whose way of doing things is not fondly remembered in East London. The URC model, associated with New Labour, is to be superseded, and not surprisingly, this raises concerns about what the fate is to be of the socio-economic aspect of the legacy agenda. Thanks to the persistence of the London Assembly, the responsibility for the employment, and skills part of the legacy, has once again been incorporated back into OPLC, but it remains to be seen how this will play out in a new MDC. Another point of concern is to ensure that all the work that is being done, through the Fringe Master plan strategies, to also develop the areas surrounding the Olympic Park, does not become disintegrated from regeneration plans for a park that is well connected with surrounding neighbourhoods.

The Pink Brochure

Karen Webb, the new Executive Director of Communications and Marketing, arrived not a moment too soon. In March of last year, when morale in the Comms. Team was at an all time low, she took up her post, and, like Mary Poppins, immediately swept everyone up in the whirlwind of her no nonsense, let-us-take-this-up-a-gear, professional enthusiasm. Karen realised that the company had no story to tell about itself, and was at risk of creating a neutral, if not negative impression. Immediately, she set about transforming the interior spaces of the office, literally designing new surfaces for all the reception spaces, and rooms where meetings with outsiders are hosted. Before long, the walls were covered with striking images from planning documents, and photographs from company brochures, which energised the space of the office with the emerging story of the company's work. Its priorities, expressed in lines and messages, were also featured, to illustrate a sense of clear focus, direction, and gathering momentum across the legacy work streams.

Karen had a senior role on the IOC, consulted on the London 2012 Games to the mayor, Olympic sponsors, and London & Partners, and was on the board of UK Sport. She knew how to put on a world-class show, but had no background in urban regeneration. This meant that like the other new Executive Directors, it took her time to get up to speed with project knowledge, and this led to the forging, across the board, of a productive articulation between the high-level newcomers and the stalwarts of the old world, who had much less status, but all the project knowledge to know how to manage their managers and guide them carefully into the labyrinth. This, and the final formal transfer of the LDA staff who had been seconded to OPLC, but whose fates had been up in the air pending the land deal, meant that a new sense of security, greater purpose, and better morale was created in the Comms. Team.

Over the summer, once it was clear that the company stood half a chance, after the General Election, of securing the land deal, Karen rallied the team to the task of planning a high-profile official launch of the company, and its revised vision. The intention was to send out a strong message to the world that the OPLC was open, and ready for business. Signalling the extent of her ambition, and making the most of the coincidence of the Games with the Queen's Golden Jubilee, in 2012, Karen successfully negotiated for the renaming of the park in legacy, and secured royal approval for it to become The Queen Elizabeth Olympic Park.

Fiercely protecting her marketing patch from the overspilling influence of the Design-led Review team that was gaining in power and influence in the company at that time, Karen rejected the idea to hold the launch event at the Tate Modern, and insisted instead on the top of the BT Tower, at the heart of the city, from where all of London could be seen, and the sightline was good, on a clear day, towards East London.

The invite list included key political stakeholders, the media, and the Who's Who of London's investment and property world. Going against the grain of cautious Comms. work, Karen worked with the team to design a public facing document that would demand attention, make a clear impression about the company's newfound confidence, and lend a bit of pizzazz to proceedings.

At a time of increasing masculinity in the company, when several 'heavy hitters' had been brought in to occupy the Executive Director positions, the new company brochure had Karen's distinctly feminine touch. Much more architectural practice than not-for-profit public sector, the oversize, magenta brochure was passionately pink, and strong, with bold graphics and striking photographs. The opening pages positioned the park in relation to its proximity to the City of London, and showed the first image of the newly conceived, as-if-real, Masterplan Framework vision of what the park might look like in 2030, with a 'crescent' of Georgian-style housing, and garden squares, running the length of the North Park on the western, Hackney side of the development.[4]

For anyone in the know, there was not much detail in the brochure, which could have betrayed either a lack of progress, or a need for caution, but at that stage in the company's development, when the scheme for the Master Plan Framework had still not yet been fixed, the brochure could do no more than deliver top-line messages. Nevertheless, this was done in a spectacular way, designed to attract developers with a clear statement about the significance of the park as a new kind of London development opportunity. The offer was described, in the context of a vibrant East London atmosphere, as a new piece of city, a visitor destination, and a place where sustainable lifestyles could be cultivated in aspirational family housing close to green space, waterways, sporting venues, and employment space in proximity to great transport connections.

Like an estate agent's sales brochure, the park's assets were put on display in the brochure (2.4 km^2 site area; 250 acres of open space; 5 new neighbourhoods with a focus on traditional London family housing; 6.5 km

---

[4] See www.gillianevans.co.uk for the 2011 Illustrative Masterplan produced by AECOM showing the cycle circuit before revisions, and the Georgian Crescent in the Northwest of the park.

of waterways; 5 London 2012 Olympic and Paralympic Venues; amazing transport connections, and only 15 minutes from the City of London), and talked up by quotes from the company's leaders and owners.

Most significant about The Pink Brochure, and the vision launch, from the perspective of the Comms. Team, was that Karen completely trusted them to design, plan for, and pull off the event. Gone were the paranoid days of not trusting the old LDA staff, and her confidence in them meant that they rose to the occasion, rallied round, and supported Karen all the way. Miraculously, the sun shone on the evening of the launch, at the beginning of last October, 2010, and the views from the BT Tower were spectacular. Margaret Ford and Andrew Altman confidently guided a packed audience of 120 carefully selected people, through the company's offer, and the ambitions of the revised vision for the long-term future of the park.

The atmosphere afterwards, among the mingling crowd, was buoyant; it felt like a take-off moment, not just for OPLC, but also for the Comms. Team, which was back in business at last. This did not mean that there were not still uphill battles to fight, for example, in Emma's Consultation and Engagement team, whose dedicated members of staff protested strongly about the segregation of stakeholders and community groups, from the vision launch. At a time when it was still the case that no one was talking to consultees about what was happening with the Master Plan Framework, they felt it was wrong to focus exclusively on a 'high-profile' guest list, because it risked a backlash among the people whom they had to encounter on the frontline of their day-to-day work. Emma's team were placated only by the promise that a programme of follow-on consultation and engagement was to follow, but they continued to remind Karen of the risk posed by jeopardising the good relations that have been built up with the long-standing network of organisations, groups, and individuals who had a right to know about the evolution of legacy plans.

Press was mostly positive about the vision launch, and the success of the event was reason for a newfound confidence in, and respect for the Comms. Team at a time when all of the action of the previous year had been about venues.

The LMF

Gritting his teeth at the vision launch, and putting on a brave smile, was Adam Williams of the EDAW (now AECOM, UK) Master Planning team. He and I both knew the significance of the hijack that had taken place of the master-planning process, and were well aware that it was premature to launch a vision that had not yet been fixed. At a time of land deals and bids for central government funding under the Comprehensive Spending Review (CSR), which promised cuts to funding, this was a tense time for OPLC, and it was clear that with the change of government, the launch event was as much about political band standing, winning allies, and favours for the company in government, as it was about declaring to the market that OPLC was a real estate company, open for business, with development opportunities for sale.

Backstage, meanwhile, furious battles were still raging about the master-planning process, and this was the reason for cautious top-line messages and aspirational representations of the park in legacy mode that concealed the truth of the turmoil about some of the changes that had been proposed by the Design-led Review team. For example, the elegant crescent of Georgian-style houses down the western length of the North Park, had been planned, as part of the review, on MOL that was promised to Olympic host borough, Hackney, as part of the restoration of its 10 hectares of green space that were given up for the Games. Charlie Forman, Hackney's formidable 2012 spokesperson, was having regular shouting matches about this with the OPLC's new Executive Director of Urban Planning and Design, Niaill McNevin, and Jules Pipe, Hackney's elected mayor, and member of the OPLC Board, was threatening to refuse to get on board with the new plans if the open space was not restored to Hackney.

Similarly, the plans for the open space, in Hackney, had a knock on effect on plans for the Velodrome's outdoor cycle circuit. The Pink Brochure for the vision launch clearly shows, in the North of the Park, the looping cycle track that winds over, and back across the River Lea to the Velodrome, and there was no sense at the event that this is a second source of heated controversy behind the scenes. The cyclist stakeholder groups have always been some of the most vocal, most passionate consultee groups, determined that the displacement they have experienced as a result of the Games should lead in legacy to exactly what has been promised to them. Emma and her team have worked hard with the cycle-user groups at consultation meetings, and over the last 2 years have built up trusting relations. All this is compromised by last-minute changes to the master plan, proposed by the review team, which take no account of the political landscape of the plans that went before. The cycle users are furious and, like Leyton Orient, frustrated about the lack of information and engagement subsequent to the failure of the company to respond to the Output C responses, in 2009. Finally, in exasperation, this prompted the Eastway Users Group to write a letter of protest directly to Hugh Robertson, the new Minister for Sport and the Olympics:

> We are committee members of the Eastway Users' Group, which has campaigned since 2003 to secure a legacy from the loss of the Eastway Cycle Circuit [to construct the Olympic Park]. This important amenity was enjoyed, from 1975 to 2006, by many thousands of sport, and recreational cyclists. Its 24 hectares of MOL [Metropolitan Open Land] for cycle sport is now in the Olympic Park Lands. Riders enjoy the relocation [to Hog Hill, in Redbridge] we eventually secured after a period of time with no amenity, and look forward to a legacy return to the site of our Olympic sport.
> We have real worries about the late changes that OPLC seeks to bring to the transformation. The consented scheme was carefully consulted over two years, and comes with secure funding from the legacy transformation budget. It is self-contained, and can be delivered by May 2013, independently of the works all around. It manages the many through routes to make a sustainable, and operable sport facility in the shared public realm open space that has rightly been protected through the legacy planning process. It can be used intensively during organised events, and casually for everyday use.
> This was not easy to achieve, but in two years of design we agreed on principal features:—bridges over the River Lea, a road circuit visible from the Velodrome's plinth level, off road trails around the outside of the whole site, all set within a pleasant parkland.
> We first learned, in August 2010 that the OPLC is seeking to build on nearby legacy transformation public realm open space to the west of the river lea [in Hackney]. It seeks to push the Velopark east, off its centre of

gravity around the Velodrome. Moving the cycle circuit east also entails removal of a road, and the loss of development land further east, which already has outline [planning] consent.

We have grave, and informed doubts, about the possible suitability of any revised layout. The OPLC's wish to push the cycle circuit, and whole Velopark aside, puts the future of our sport, and the legacy return at risk. In providing just another development platform it denies the London wide value of reproviding Eastway for cycle sport on exactly the site where Olympic sports had a past, and deserve a future as promised, and paid for.

The consented scheme was truly consulted and agreed. The permissions set out very clearly open space commitments together with a red line plan to show public realm. The OPLC wants to build on the parkland, and is actually attempting to portray these lands as being improved by its development. We wonder if OPLC can meet its open space commitments, and how it will improve MOL [Metropolitan Open Land] by building on it?

I would be grateful if you could let me know whether you agree that a meeting on this matter would be helpful, and appropriate. I am very happy to coordinate, and to bring the relevant parties together for a full discussion of this very important topic relating to legacy open space, and public realm in the Olympic Park.

Yours sincerely
Michael Humphreys, Chair, Eastway Users Group
February 2011

The controversies about MOL, and the cycle circuit, speak of the serious risks of having given a group of architect-led designers a free reign, during the LMF process, to do 'blue sky thinking' about the legacy scheme as if there were no restrictions. Those restrictions, about which the existing EDAW Master Planning team and Emma's Consultation and Engagement team were all too well aware, are now smacking OPLC in the face. Not surprisingly, the proposal for the date of submission of the LMF planning applications is now having to be put forward, again, until June 2011, and the planning team is not surprised, but frustrated about having been excluded from the process, and still, having to pick up the pieces of the Design-led Review. Irene Man is pleased that a new Director is being appointed, but she is frustrated that nothing seems to be coordinated anymore, as if the LMF were somehow separate from the evolution of the stadium work, and so on.

Meanwhile, Adam William's ongoing frustration has been increased by reports in the trade press, following OPLC's vision launch, which, not surprisingly, have swallowed hook, line and sinker, and regurgitated the new lines and messages created by the Design-led Review team, which has claimed ownership of the legacy vision, by trashing, and, therefore, making invisible, and incomprehensible the work of the EDAW Consortium which preceded it:

Legacy company slams original masterplan, and unveils changes to post-2012 housing.
A nine-strong team of practices, including Maccreanor Lavington, Caruso St. John and Panter Hudspith, has drawn up a radically revised masterplan for the Olympic Park after the 2012 games, replacing a forest of 'bland' contemporary residential blocks with designs inspired by traditional London terraces.

Unveiling the legacy scheme on Thursday, Olympics chiefs were openly critical of the original masterplan created by Edaw (now Aecom), Allies & Morrison and Dutch practice KCAP.

Andrew Altman, Chief Executive of the Olympic Park Legacy Company, said it was choked with blocks of small flats, while Chair Margaret Ford said it lacked character. "When we looked at the first masterplan there was nothing that said to me: This is London", she said. "It could have been anywhere. It was all high-rise and fairly bland."

The density of the original masterplan has been slashed by 20 %, from around 10,000 homes to 8000, reflecting a greater emphasis on larger family houses with private gardens. The legacy phase of the 2012 games will now comprise five distinct districts, planned around squares and Nash-inspired crescents. Only a handful of buildings will exceed five storeys.

The proposals will be submitted to the Olympic Delivery Authority for planning consent next summer, and it is hoped that the first tranche of work—houses sited close to the Olympic Village—will go on site in 2014.

The design U-turn has been backed by London mayor Boris Johnson, who has railed against the proliferation of 'hobbit homes' across the capital, and voiced his support for an architecture that builds on the traditional London vernacular. It also mirrors the redesign of the contentious Chelsea

Barracks site, where Richard Rogers' proposed slab blocks have been replaced by a highly traditional "garden square" design.
Bloomfield R. 'Olympic Park Legacy Design is Radically Revised' Building Online[5], October 8, 2010

Socio-economics

Also still fighting against its marginalisation from the legacy planning process is Michelle May, and her small Socio-economics Team. Even though the team has now been incorporated into OPLC, it is having to fight to make its presence known, and have its agenda taken seriously at the highest levels of company operations. This seems to be more than ever the case at a time, under conditions of high pressure, when the company is beginning to move, in 2011, from planning towards delivery mode. Not to be put off, Michelle refuses to be deterred and keeps the pressure on the executive levels of management at OPLC.

In December, the socio-economic policy that Michelle and her team have drafted was endorsed by the OPLC Communities Committee, and Michelle is now trying to get this seen by Andrew Altman, so that the agenda and the work can be understood, and, ideally, properly integrated into the understanding and promotion of company priorities. Even at a time when Andrew Altman has his mind mainly on the big questions of the review of the LMF, the stadium procurement process, and the soft market testing for the Broadcast Centre, Michelle continues to push the socio-economic agenda, referring to the Host Borough's Convergence ambition, and insisting in the policy draft that currently, given the impending abolition of the LDA 'There is a risk [at OPLC] of not having a clear socio-economic policy position to influence key activity across the company.'

Michelle has at least been successful in making sure that the question of what the opportunity for local people, and local businesses will be, is

---

[5] Bloomfield R. 'Olympic Park Legacy Design is Radically Revised'. http://www.bdonline.co.uk/olympic-park-legacy-design-is-radically-revised/5006896.article Accessed 6 May 2015.

embedded into the thinking around how the park, and its facilities, and events will be managed, and its venues operated in post-Games legacy mode. This means that any company bidding for these contracts will have to compete, in part, on the basis of a Community Benefit Clause, which will assess how the bids take into account the provision of training and employment for people living locally to the park. Part of the ambition is also to ensure that OPLC becomes a Living Wage employer.

Michelle has the support of the Real Estate Team, which is helping her to get the socio-economic policy on Andrew Altman's radar. The policy describes a number of small projects that Michelle, and her team, is working to develop with partner organisations, to develop an employment and skills programme for the park. These include a labour market forecasting project to generate the right information, at the right time, about what kinds of jobs will be required by contractors and park employers at different periods of time during the transition to post-Games, legacy use of the park. The idea is to disseminate this information to partners who fund, and/or deliver training, and employment support to young people, so that school leavers can usefully craft their career paths in relation to available opportunities.

Another initiative is the work with the Retail Academy, which is to open later this year, working with the Westfield Stratford shopping mall, to expand the number of training courses available to people living locally, so that they can also access career opportunities in hospitality, and leisure that will be available in the Olympic Park. And, the third idea is for a social enterprise hub, which is to provide access to resources from businesses, the public sector, and voluntary organisations, to grow the capacity of the 600 social enterprises that currently exist in the Olympic host boroughs.

Meanwhile, despite the change of government, the commitment to devolution, and the abolition of the RDAs, as well as many quangos, including the imminent closure of the LTGDC, Roger Taylor, and the Olympic Host Boroughs Unit has hung in there; it has bought time for itself, yet again, and is planning to publish, this year, its Convergence Action Plan for the consideration of central government and the mayor. Despite rumours inside OPLC that the proposals for the transformation of OPLC into a MDC will mean the end of the Host Boroughs Unit, and a still birth for the SRF, there is time yet for Roger Taylor to keep strategising against the odds, making the presence of the Host Boroughs Unit felt, and to stand a chance of having its action plan adopted as the rhetorical, if not, practical and effectual force for the socio-economic transformation of East London.

Tech City

Desperate, at first, to find the solution to its primary employment offer in the Olympic Park, OPLC is finally feeling more hopeful about going to market to soft-test the potential interest for legacy use of the Press and Broadcast Centres. The end of last year brought a greater sense of hopefulness in the form of government support for the idea of investment in an East London 'Tech City' with incubator style workspaces spreading from Shoreditch to the Olympic Park in an entrepreneur-friendly technology-focused business zone. The ambitious idea is based on the Silicon Valley model in which research and development leads to quick business start-ups and phenomenal profits. The idea could complement Boris Johnson's determination to bring a world-class higher educational facility, or set of facilities to the park, and there is some suggestion that US technology giants like Google and Facebook might be lured to host their UK outposts here. Interest from Cisco and Intel has been sufficient to excite central government, and an Internet economy in the UK that is now worth £100 billion per annum suggests that a move towards an IT, and digital economy solution, might be a viable option to the never-ending headache of how to find a viable legacy use for the Press and Broadcast Centres.

It is too soon to say what the Expressions of Interest process will bring to the table, but it is not impossible to imagine that the East London Tech City idea might just work alongside the determination of Olympic host borough Hackney, for the Press and Broadcast Centres to become, in legacy, a hub for the creative and media industries. Lobbying hard for its vision to be sustained, and proving that legacy planning still can be stakeholder-driven and influenced, Hackney has been successful in having its understanding of what it desires to come to fruition included, in the Expression of Interest documentation, as an appendix:

> Hackney's Legacy Vision for the Olympic Media Centres, and the Wick Neighbourhood.
> Our vision is for a modern media centre as the magnet, and economic driver for the creation of a new mixed-use living, and working neighbourhood on the western Olympic fringe. The media centre itself will offer state of the art communications, and infrastructure for future digital, broadcast, and media industry requirements. Our media centre will be home to major media, and new technology companies, and small and medium sized businesses recognising the commercial advantages of being clustered together. The area will be enlivened by shops, cafes, bars, and restaurants, alongside high quality office, and studio workspaces.
> Our vision is of a legacy that creates several thousand sustainable jobs, and job opportunities, including high value, and entry level jobs that can be accessed by local people supported by the high quality local, and regional, training providers already in place, and eager to unearth untapped talent.
> The energetic and talented entrepreneurs in the creative, and cultural sector want to be in Hackney. The creative explosion that led to Shoreditch, and Hoxton becoming a major hub for the new digital media, arts, and design sectors is now being repeated in Hackney Wick. The interest of the media sector is not a new phenomenon. New Media businesses dominated the vision under [Hackney's] pre-Olympic masterplan based on considerable research, and hard evidence that emerged from it.
> There is a significant opportunity to put London—and specifically East London—at the epicentre of the revolution in broadcast, and digital media when the UK switches to digital in 2012. This high level communications site in Hackney Wick can be one of the major European homes for digital broadcasting.
> Press Centre, Broadcast Centre
> Memorandum of Information
> September 2010

Harder to imagine, sitting right alongside this new East London Tech City is the old-fashioned, classicist vision of The Crescent, the Georgian-style town houses promised for this area of the park by the Design-led Review. I cannot imagine the kind of people who might be able to afford to live in these houses, being happy to live right alongside a vibrant high-tech media and digital hub, housed in buildings that are effectively like enormous airplane hangars, and neither can I foresee that the kinds of tech-head entrepreneurs who are going to work in this new employment space would want to live in Georgian-style housing. Surely, they would have preferred the Continental, Amsterdam style of water-side urban sustainability promised by the Dutch-influenced earlier master plan. Or, maybe, in time, this part of the park will prove what the EDAW master planners have been trying to argue all along, which is that the master plan is supposed to be understood as a flexible framework, able to adapt to the long-term changes in ideas about kinds of housing, and development opportunities, that will emerge over time for the different development platforms of the site.

For now, the vision, to entice developers to market, is Georgian-style gentrification, but who knows, down the line, it may emerge that what Hackney sees, next to its realised media, and perhaps tech, and higher education hub, is an entirely different understanding of the kind of homes new kinds of workers want to inhabit. Only time will tell.

Suggested Reading

Bale, J. (2001). *Sport, space and the city*. New Jersey: The Blackburn Press.
Davies, L. (2012). Beyond the games: Regeneration legacies and London 2012. *Leisure Studies, 31*(3), 307–337.
Davies, L. (2010). Sport and economic regeneration: A winning combination? *Sport in Society, 13*(10), 1438–1457.
Davies, L. (2011). Using sports infrastructure to deliver economic and social change: Lessons for London beyond 2012. *Local Economy, 26*(4), 227–231.
Figart, D. (Ed.). (2012). *Living wage movements: Global perspectives*. New York: Routledge.
Frank, S., & Steets, S. (Eds.). (2010). *Stadium worlds: Football, space and the built environment*. New York: Routledge.

Piol, A., & Cometto, M. (2013). *Tech and the city: The making of New York's start up community.* Mirandola Press.

Newenham, P. (Ed.). (2015). *Silicon docks: The rise of Dublin as a global tech hub.* Dublin: Liberties Press.

Rawnsley, A. (2010). *The end of the Party: The rise and fall of New Labour.* London: Penguin.

Smith, D., & Wistrich, E. (2014). *Devolution and localism in England.* Surrey: Ashgate.

8

An Interminable Saga

June 2012

The casualties are mounting up in the heart of the legacy labyrinth. Margaret Ford has gone. Andrew Altman followed not long after. The stadium process has become a farce. Like Tom Russell before them, Margaret Ford and Andrew Altman have paid the price for not delivering on a legacy use for the Olympic stadium. Worse than this, the story of the failure to find a tenant for the stadium has become, in this last year, an embarrassment—an interminable saga worthy of the worst television soap operas.

Pushed out, just like Tom Russell, as a new Legacy Delivery Vehicle (the mayor's new MDC) comes into being, Margaret Ford and Andrew Altman have escaped from the drama of the Olympic legacy with their reputations intact, because of significant achievements made, but the shadow of the stadium saga has cast an inescapable gloom over their triumph. The real winner is Boris Johnson. He has just been elected as Mayor of London for a second term (defeating Ken Livingstone, again, who stood this time as the Labour candidate). Boris has stolen a steady march on the Olympic legacy, and is victorious; he has gained control not only over its spoils, but also (against the wishes of the Olympic host boroughs) local planning powers, and an expansion of the legacy domain to include more lands in the fringe areas of the surrounding host boroughs. At the same time, Boris Johnson has been able to use the new Conservative policies of localism, and devolution, to win himself new powers over policing, housing, and transport in London, making him one of the most powerful mayors in the world. Still, he clowns around and masks his growing authority, but he is increasingly canny; in a country where to wield power over London is to wield power over the nation, he is beginning to look like a contender for the future leadership of the Conservative Party.

David Cameron, meanwhile, is making the most of the fact that London has shown the world how to prepare for an Olympic Games: he hosted his first Cabinet meeting of the year in the Multi-Use Arena (now fondly described as the Copper Box because of its cladding), and told the nation in his New Year's speech that this is the year that Britain must 'go for it'. In defiance of doom mongering about security (after last summer's riots) and concerns about the chaos of Games-time transport in London, David Cameron is adamant, with Boris Johnson, that this will be 'the best Games ever'. Mid-term, Cameron is relying on a 'feel-good' Olympics, and the Queen's Jubilee, to boost the nation, distract it from the endless Conservative cuts to public spending, and to provide the uplift that will see the country through to the turning point, at which the economy might stabilise and begin to move out of recession. This is a tall order, which relies not only on there being no disasters in the staging of the Games, but also on Britain, against the odds, bringing in a healthy haul of medals. Not to be outdone, Tessa Jowell is, not surprisingly, vocal, but from the shadows; there is a limit to what she can do, except to repeatedly remind the nation about her role, and, therefore, Labour's contribution in winning the Games for London, and, for 8 years, steering the project to its successful conclusion.

The Stadium Saga

More or less immediately after the Board of the OPLC voted unanimously, last February, to choose the joint West Ham, and Newham Council bid, as the preferred option for the legacy use of the Olympic stadium, Tottenham Hotspur and Leyton Orient stalled the process by launching separate legal protests, in the form of applications for Judicial Reviews. A Judicial Review is a procedure that allows for the challenge, in the High Court, of decisions made by public bodies in England, and Wales. If a person feels that the powers of a public body have been used to make an unlawful decision, that person can apply for a review in the Administrative Court, which may lead to a decision being overturned, or to damages being awarded.

The threat of Judicial Review was an open challenge to the authority of the OPLC, as a public body, to make lawful and reasonable decisions, and it was a threat, therefore, to the legitimacy of the OPLC Board and its leadership under Margaret Ford. This is disastrous for legacy planning. I remember, at the time, thinking about the contrast between this situation and the extremely difficult position of the master planners at EDAW, who could also easily have protected their own reputation and scuppered the advancement of legacy planning, by making a huge scene and creating a public controversy over the handling of the Design-led Review of the master-planning process. Right or wrong, the fact that EDAW very self-consciously did not create a drama (and instead, grinned and bore it, as they were silenced by their usurpers, and caused to suffer a long and unbearable humiliation), spoke volumes about their political commitment to the project of Olympic legacy. The master planners risked their own reputations for the sake of the higher ideals of the project, and this taught me a lot about the real power of political idealism. Against this background, to see Leyton Orient and Spurs, ready to go to war with West Ham, Newham Council, and OPLC over the legacy use of the Olympic stadium is dispiriting. It is narrow-minded and loses sight of the bigger picture, which is to do with advancing, at all costs, the regeneration of the Lower Lea Valley.

This does not mean that the Legacy Company was not naïve, or that it, the central government, and the mayor who signed off on the Board of OPLC could not have exercised more caution about the process through which they went about agreeing on the decision to award the legacy use of the stadium to West Ham. Aware of the controversy that was already unfolding prior to their decision, they could have covered their backs, for example, by waiting until they were in a position to apply to the European Commission for permission to award the bid to West Ham. This is important because, under current regulations, it is prohibited to confer a competitive advantage on a company through government support, or what is called state aid, unless that support is justified for reasons of economic development.

The problem for Leyton Orient, and Spurs, was that the success of West Ham's bid was going to lead to its ownership of the stadium, which could only have been possible because of the financial support of the £40 million loan from Newham Council that Newham itself planned to borrow from central government. This raised questions about state aid, because it could be said that a competitive advantage had been conferred on West Ham's bid for the stadium, by the loan from Newham Council. Even though West Ham was, in the end, relegated last year, there was still an argument to be made that if West Ham's fortunes were to improve, and, in future, they rose up the ranks of the Premier League, it could lead retrospectively, to claims that the club was benefitting from an unfair advantage. This would be a nightmare scenario, whose terror would be given by the fact that the controversy about the stadium decision was never going to be laid to rest, and would be resurrected, again and again, to haunt all those involved in it.

Newham's argument, in defence, was that the money was not to be loaned directly to West Ham, but to a joint venture company, formed between Newham and OPLC, which would lease the stadium, on a long lease, to West Ham. This was to be yet another SPV—an organisation whose purpose, I now understand, is to isolate particular projects from a parent company with a broader remit, the benefit of which, in part, is to be able to distribute risk, often in the form of significant debts, and to reduce, thereby, the liability of the parent company and others with a vested interest in the side project.

OPLC's defence has been that the preferred bidder status was awarded to West Ham and Newham Council, subject to ongoing negotiations to iron out the exact financial terms of the deal. The position was always that once those terms had been ironed out to everybody's satisfaction an application would have been made to the European Union (EU), if necessary, to ensure that the deal was within EU regulations about state aid. It could be said that OPLC was ill-advised to award preferred bidder status before the terms of the deal had been fully ironed out, and both the mayor and central government could, for this reason, have requested a delay to proceedings, but the pressure was on to secure a deal, and to put at rest the minds of the International Athletics Federation (IAAF) who had accepted London's bid for hosting the 2017 World Athletics Championships.

Margaret Ford, by her own admission, knew nothing about sport when she took up her role as Chair of OPLC. By the end of last year, she was clearly shocked by the extent of footballing rivalry in London, and she had become demoralised by the damaging effects of the unfolding drama of the stadium process on legacy planning. Speaking to a very challenging meeting of the Economy, Culture and Sport Committee of the London Assembly last November, Margaret was justifiably angry; she admitted her bemusement about the whole affair, and made controversial accusations against Spurs, suggesting that they had paid private commercial investigators to tap the phones of the OPLC Board:

> MF: 'The thing that I have learned over the last 12 months is there have been all kinds of behaviour, legal challenge, people who have stood behind an anonymous legal challenge, and all kinds of things have happened. My board were put under surveillance by Tottenham Hotspur… The Metropolitan Police Service is now conducting an investigation into that surveillance. There have been all kinds of behaviour here that I never anticipated—believe me—which has not been pleasant over the last 12 months. I am expecting the unexpected, because that is what the last 12 months has taught me.
>
> Our job now is to narrow as far as we possibly can the scope for legitimate legal challenge in this next process. That is all we can do. If people want then, to be vexatious, and vindictive, whatever they want, they will do that. We will try to narrow the scope as much as we can.

Dee Doocey (Chair): Could I say that I personally find it appalling—and I am sure I speak for the rest of the Committee—at the very idea of your board being put under surveillance. It is reprehensible. It almost beggars belief that this thing can happen. The idea that any board is put under surveillance is absolutely disgraceful.
Economy, Culture, and Sport Committee
London Assembly, 8th November 2011.[1]

Despite denying the accusations and threatening legal action, the claims against Spurs that they had placed the OPLC Board and Karren Brady, Vice Chair of West Ham, under surveillance, were eventually proved to be true, and, in response, Karren Brady initiated legal proceedings. This scandal was in addition to accusations made against OPLC that the stadium process could not have been impartial, because a senior employee of the company had personal ties to a member of senior management at West Ham, which raised a question about whether or not this person had had access to privileged information about the stadium process. Fortunately, as a precaution, those members of staff working on the stadium project had been asked to work in isolation, and secrecy, away from OPLC's everyday business, at the company's legal firm, Eversheds. In this way, the confidentiality of the process had been guaranteed, and the member of staff in question had not had access to, or contact with the stadium team's work process. OPLC had not known about their staff member's contract to also work for West Ham, and so, to play safe, OPLC had suspended that member of staff, and commissioned an independent forensic audit of its stadium process, which found in OPLC's favour, because their caution about the internal handling of the stadium work process had paid off.

Meanwhile, the rumoured £1.3 million spent by OPLC on legal fees has been an onerous burden to the company, and a horrendous waste of taxpayers' money. Alongside the legal fees also paid by Leyton Orient, and Spurs, the lawyers' rewards have been an unexpected Olympic legacy boon for London's legal firms. This in itself is scandalous. I cannot

---

[1] Appendix 1 Economy Culture and Sport Committee 8 November 2011 Transcript of Item 5. http://www.london.gov.uk/moderngov/documents/s6202/Olympic%20Stadium%20Legacy.pdf. Accessed 5 May 2015.

help, but imagine what else could have been done with that money, how many local apprenticeships it could have financed, or, indeed how many law degrees it might have financed for young people living in the host boroughs.

Although the applications by Spurs, and Leyton Orient for processes of Judicial Review were granted in August of last year, the reviews were never seen to fruition, because in October, at the time when the reviews were due to be heard in court, an anonymous complaint to the EU, about state aid in the stadium bid from West Ham, and Newham, led to the threat of an EU investigation. This would have further delayed the stadium process by up to 18 months, and in frustration, West Ham and Newham Council were forced to admit that because of the delays they would be unable to meet one of the conditions of their bid, which was the promise to occupy the stadium for the new football season of 2014. Fearing a fiasco, the government decided to cancel the deal, which amounted to a defeat for West Ham and a victory for Spurs and Leyton Orient, because their resistance had led, eventually, to the collapse of West Ham's bid. Barry Hearn said, in response to this news, that West Ham's defeat in the stadium bid was, 'better [for Leyton Orient] than beating them in a cup final'.

This all meant, in effect, that OPLC was back to square one, and the company then had to start the whole process of stadium procurement again (this time not for ownership, but for rent, with the venue remaining in public ownership, and transformation costs now to be met by the LLDC [the new Mayoral Development Corporation], and the public purse). At a time when the legacy uses of all the other Olympic venues were in place, bar the Press and Broadcast Centres, this was a major blow to the company and, in particular, to Margaret Ford. Spurs, satisfied by the collapse of the West Ham deal, and bolstered by ongoing offers of financial support from the Mayor for its plans in Haringey, withdrew its legal challenge and any claim to the Olympic stadium. Spurs then continued with plans for the development of a new stadium in its home turf, of Tottenham, which had been rocked by the London riots, last summer, and now more than ever wanted Spurs to stay where the club was most needed. Not to be deterred, Leyton Orient continued to rail against unfair treatment when it announced that it would now formally bid for legacy use of the stadium in the new round of procurement, and, at the same time, Boris Johnson said publically that West Ham would inevitably still be the beneficiaries of the new stadium process.

In the end, four bids have now been shortlisted with proposals to rent the stadium, rather than own it. These bids include what has been reported in the press as the outlandish proposal for a Formula One racing track winding its way in and outside of the venue. Out of the running again, is the University of East London, with its joint/Essex Country Cricket Club bid, and the remaining three bids are from West Ham, Leyton Orient, and a new arrival on the scene—Buckinghamshire New University, which has a business college specialising in football and commerce. With West Ham likely, as Boris suggested, to win the bidding process again, there was no way, under these circumstances, that either Margaret Ford or Andrew Altman could survive the transition, in March of this year, of OPLC into the mayor's new SPV, the London Legacy Development Corporation (LLDC). On the eve of the London Games, both company leaders have bowed out gracefully, leaving those left behind in their new, and significantly more expensive, offices in the complex of the now busy and bustling Westfield Shopping Mall.

Raised eyebrows, and disbelief, have been the reaction of legacy staff to the appointment of Daniel Moylan as Margaret's replacement, because it smacks of political manoeuvring. There is no other way to explain why Boris would have brought in a West London Conservative colleague, with a reputation for being to the Conservatives what Peter Mandelson was to New Labour—a political fixer—and who is without experience in the world of sport, or urban regeneration. How this appointment is going to be good for London's Olympic legacy, at a critical point in its evolution, is hard to say. Sealing her own legacy, Margaret Ford summarised OPLC's achievement, at the point of her departure, in the company report for this last year:

> On the eve of the London 2012 Olympic, and Paralympic Games, London can be proud of its legacy plans. Owing to the foresight of the Mayor of London, and Government, we are further ahead than any other host city has been at this stage, with legacy arrangements settled for six of the eight Olympic Park venues, and a powerful legacy plan in place for what will become the Queen Elizabeth Olympic Park.

The last year saw the closing stages of planning, and procurement for legacy, and a shift of focus to the practicalities of delivery. The Legacy Company has put operators in place for these key venues; Balfour Beatty Workplace will operate the ArcelorMittal Orbit, and provide Estates and Facilities Management for the park as a whole, while Greenwich Leisure Limited—a social enterprise based in one of the host boroughs—will take on the [management of] the Aquatics Centre, and the Multi-Use Arena.

These operators have a great track record, and have demonstrated their commitment to Convergence, and local regeneration by agreeing to peg prices to the local average, and by making commitments to deliver 75 per cent of jobs to local people.

The Legacy Communities Scheme [the renamed Legacy Master Plan Framework] planning application has been submitted, paving the way for the delivery of nearly 7000 homes, and alongside this, the Company has launched its first phase of development—up to 800 homes at Chobham Manor, to the north of the Athletes Village. We hope that planning permission will be in place this summer, so that the Legacy Corporation can finalise a development agreement with a preferred partner.

The competition to find legacy users for the Press and Broadcast centres includes two proposals that will make these facilities a hub for employment, enterprise and growth, featuring two of East London's strongest sectors—fashion and design, and digital industries.

The Legacy Company also made progress in securing legacy uses for the stadium. Following a legacy challenge to our original process, we decided to retain the venue in public ownership, and actively manage it by putting in place a successful mix of sports, and events throughout the year, while making sure that the stadium could be available for major events such as the 2017 World Athletic Championship.

Finally, the Legacy Company took over transformation works from the ODA, and has procured contractors to undertake the several hundred million pound Clear, Connect and Complete programme that will follow the end of the games enabling the park reopening to begin in July 2013, one year after the opening ceremony of the Olympic Games.

At the end of the financial year the Legacy Company's assets, and programmes, were transferred to the new body, the London Legacy Development Corporation (LLDC). While the new body will be accountable to the Mayor of London, and will have a wider remit than the Legacy Company, it has been set up with minimal disruption to an intense programme of work. As I hand over Chairmanship to Daniel Moylan I am proud of what we have achieved, and have every confidence that the board, and staff that he inherits will help make legacy a lasting success story for London.

I would also wish to pay tribute to the dedication and commitment Andy Altman, the Chief Executive, has given to the Olympic Park Legacy Company over the last three years. As he moves on to new challenges, I wish him well in his career.

Baroness Margaret Ford
Company Report 2011/2012[2]

Margaret Ford's tidy summation papers over the cracks of what has been an impossibly difficult year. She may well have regretted refusing to pursue the proposal that was made last year [2011], by the Wellcome Trust, to buy the whole park for a billion pounds, which would have spelt an early end to the Legacy Company, and passed its headaches on to become someone else's problems. She, Boris Johnson, and central government were certainly infuriated with the BBC, who stalled and stalled, refusing to formalise their interest, and holding up the process for the Expression of Interest in the Media Centre. The proposal was to move their film set for their mainstay soap opera, East Enders, to the Olympic Park facilities, which would have been a fabulous coup for OPLC, but at the last minute The Corporation pulled out, prompting Boris Johnson to accuse the BBC of dinosaur-like out datedness. I imagine, the BBC will pay for this politically, under an advancing Tory government.

The Legacy Communities Scheme

With Margaret gone, it was inevitable that Andrew Altman would not last long. He too was a victim of the new regime and tarnished by the absolute failure of the stadium negotiations. Andrew was, however, successful in his primary goal of submitting a planning application for the

---

[2] Annual Report and Accounts 2011–2012 Olympic Park Legacy Company. http://queenelizabetholympicpark.co.uk/~/media/lldc/accounts/oplc_annual_report_2012_260712.pdf Accessed 5 May 2015.

Master Plan Framework, renamed the Legacy Communities Scheme,[3] which was finally submitted last October. The scheme might also secure planning permission on target, just in time, before the Games. The 5000-page planning application marked the end of another endless saga, and was submitted without an internal fanfare in the company. For Irene Man, and her small team of planners, as well as for Emma, and her Consultation and Engagement team, it was a milestone in a period of their lives that was consumed by the dramas of the planning and design process.

In essence, the outline application was for up to 6800 homes, 40 % of which is to be family housing (35 % affordable), and employment space for 4400 by 2031. Social infrastructure was to include 9 nurseries, 3 health centres, 3 schools, and 12 community buildings. Submission of the planning application meant that Andrew Altman could also achieve his second ambition, to go to market before the Games, with the park's first development plot and neighbourhood area, between the Olympic Village and the Velodrome which used to be called Stratford Village in the LMF, but was renamed Chobham Manor last year in the 'Your Park, Your Place' competition, designed to encourage a sense of public 'ownership' over the park. The name, Chobham Manor alludes romantically to the fourteenth century, 100-acre estate of Thomas de Chobham, and gives a nod to the Manor Garden Allotments displaced from the park, but, not surprisingly, the reference to ancient history eliminates any trace of the more recent and controversial history of this land, to do with the displacement of Travellers, and the Clays Lane Housing Cooperative for the construction of the Olympic Park.

The process of procurement created a sense of optimism in the Real Estate team, led by Executive Director, Duncan Innes, because there was no shortage of interest, in the property market, in the first of the developments on the Olympic Park site. OPLC was also able to secure a good deal, last year, on the sale of its lands at Sugarhouse Lane to IKEA for a residential development, and by January, of this year, a shortlist of six bidders had been drawn up to develop the Chobham Manor site.

---
[3] Legacy Communities Scheme http://queenelizabetholympicpark.co.uk/our-story/transforming-east-london/legacy-communities-scheme Accessed 5 May 2015.

The potential is still there, too, for a Community Land Trust at Chobham Manor. This had always been an ambition of London Citizens, the community organisation in East London, which campaigned for the Living Wage for Olympic workers. The Land Trust would mean that a portion of land would be set aside for the development of housing at permanently affordable prices for the long-term benefit of local residents who would form a cooperative to manage the trust. Less clear is how OPLC might fulfil the commitment to deliver 35 % 'affordable' housing, when the largest of the family housing units at Chobham Manor—five bedrooms with a garden—is rumoured to be going to cost almost one million pounds.

The Cycle Circuit

In a move that signified the cost to OPLC of having abandoned the process of consultation during the Design-led Review of the LMF, the company was finally forced, in August of last year, to abandon its plans to make significant changes to the layout of the mile-long cycle circuit. Continued pressure from the Eastway Users Group and British Cycling led to OPLC having to reach a compromise with the cycling consultees and to submit new planning applications with the circuit once again crossing over the River Lea, onto the green space on the Hackney, western side of the park.

In the context of a long history of best practice consultation process, the success of the cyclists' pressure group sent a strong message to the Design-led Review team about the importance of consultation; loud and clear, the victory of the cyclists declared that OPLC was not going to be allowed to simply do as it pleased. The argument that had developed between the cyclists and Hackney Council, who would have always preferred the cycle circuit not to cross the River Lea into their green space, was finally resolved to everyone's satisfaction, in a new scheme, which has restored a coherent park space with riverside access to Hackney, reassured cyclists with a slightly reconfigured cycle track that still crosses the river, and satisfied the OPLC designers about the new signature piece of the Legacy Communities Scheme, which is the crescent of Georgian-style housing in the northwest of the park.

The Regeneration Team

Vindicated by lessons learned about maintaining good relations with stakeholders, Emma Wheelhouse was promoted earlier last year to Head of Communities and Business, and is now situated with her small team, not in Comms. any longer, but with Michelle May, and the Socio-economics staff, in the newly created Regeneration Team. This has meant, for Emma, the expansion of her role away from the focus on Comms. and master planning-related consultation work, and towards the development of a series of regeneration projects, such as Art in the Park. Part of this is a collaborative project on the fringes of the Olympic Park, to work with resident groups in the areas of the host boroughs immediate to the park boundaries to understand how they use the space they currently inhabit and how signage linking that space could be developed to also lead people towards the Olympic Park. This project, like the Legacy Youth Panel, and others in the series, was about the creation of long-standing relationships that were followed up on after 6 months, and a year, to see whether the signage was working, and whether or not people living locally to the Park were beginning to develop a meaningful relationship with the new space on their doorstep.

Emma and Michelle have now joined forces, and have continued to fight this year to get the message heard inside OPLC about the importance of community engagement, local interests, socio-economics, and regeneration proper. In a company utterly distracted by other apparently more pressing priorities, Emma and Michelle have both found this battle to be an infuriating and a thankless task.

By the time I had started to conduct formal interviews with individual members of OPLC, last October, Emma was demoralised, and we postponed our appointment for her interview; Emma asked if we could just go to the pub instead, for lunch, and to let off steam. We made our way to Stratford High Street, to the King Edward VII pub, which is the office 'local', and over lunch, Emma explained how she was getting worn down, because she felt like the fight for regeneration had to be fought by stealth, from below, rather than where she felt it should be fought—at the very top as the organising mission of the company. Knowing how hard she has fought over the last 2 years, it was hard to see Emma, disheartened like this again.

Michelle May, who is now Senior Manager of the Regeneration Team, was also demoralised at that time; she shared her frustrations with me and explained, in exasperation, that she had hit a brick wall: she felt that she could not go any further and emphasised that the only good news has been the appointment of Paul Brickell—the popular East End strategist—as the Executive Director of Regeneration. 'He has arrived just in time', Michelle emphasised, 'because there is nothing more I can do, I feel defeated. It's like people [in this company] still don't understand regeneration, and if they don't understand it now, they never will.'

The problem that Emma and Michelle were both struggling with was the feeling that the company had been taken over by particular priorities, the stadium certainly, the venues more generally, real estate, but also the transfer to the company, from the ODA of the management of the £350 million pound process for the transformation of the park after the Games. This brought into the company an 'ODA way of doing things', which was good from one perspective, in terms of the completely ruthless 'on time, on budget' attitude, but completely alienating in other respects, because it was impossible to get that team to slow down, and to take time to listen to ideas about the socio-economic and community engagement agenda, and how that could be incorporated into the process of transformation.

When I spoke to Paul, earlier this year, he explained that it had taken him 3 months, from October to December, to work out what was going on in the company, 3 months after that to build relationships internally, and now it was about getting the story of regeneration straight at the Executive Director level, so that it sat side by side with park transformation and park reopening as a company priority. Paul stressed that his fight on the inside of the company has been the same as it was when he was fighting for community engagement from the outside. Whereas before he fought, and to a certain extent was proved right by the success of the View Tube, about the need to bring people to the park with community hubs that work to create excitement and engagement on the perimeter of the park, so too now, he has fought for community hubs to be included in the plans for the transformation of the park, so that early on, right from the start, when the park opens, people have somewhere to go, something they can relate to, and a visitor centre that can also function as a place to plan community events.

Not to be put off by the argument that the budget for community hubs was bound to be unaffordable and therefore impossible to deliver, Paul, drawing on his experience of the View Tube was irrepressible; he muscled in, put his weight behind, fought for, and won what he knows to be achievable, which is a social enterprise model for innovation in community facilities that meets the highest quality of design standards. Working with the newly formed Design Team, two landscape design competitions were launched last year for the design of North and South Park areas of the post-Games park. These would determine the 'look and feel' of the visitor experience to the park, so it mattered that the details of the design process were right, and that the community interest was considered to draw local people into a relationship with the park.

Also still fighting valiantly for the socio-economic agenda, but from the outside of the company, Roger Taylor, last year, produced the 2011–2015 SRF Action Plan, reporting that the principle of Convergence had been incorporated into the Mayor's new London Plan, and that areas of improvement against specific targets were already beginning to be felt, for example, in educational attainment, employment rates, male life expectancy, children's sporting participation, additional housing, and reduction in levels of violent crime.

The Action Plan recognised that cuts to local government funding had been a serious setback, but it was possible to offset this by focusing efforts on articulating socio-economic strategy with the significant amount of inward investment initiatives taking place in the areas surrounding the Olympic Park, and in East London more generally. The seven themes of the original SRF, published in 2009, were reduced now to three encompassing themes—creating wealth and reducing poverty, supporting healthier lifestyles, and developing successful neighbourhoods. The plan spells out what action needs to be taken in the 'developing successful neighbourhoods' theme, and explains how work in the host boroughs needs to be articulated with the public realm initiatives of OPLC:

> Progress towards Convergence in terms of crime, housing and the public realm is variable. Significant activity has resulted in over thirteen thousand new homes being built including over four thousand affordable homes, but social housing waiting lists have grown. The number of violent crimes

recorded decreased between 2007/8 and 2008/09, but increased slightly in 2009/10. Public realm improvements have taken place around the Olympic Park fringes, but as the park itself is still in development, the improvements in connection between the communities around the park are yet to take place.

Reducing levels of violent crime, and gang related violence remains a high priority and we aim to re-energise joint work in this area in a partnership between the Host Boroughs, the GLA and the metropolitan police.

The Host Boroughs and the GLA will also explore the potential for developing joint work to address violence against women and girls, and how this may help impact on the target of reducing violent crime levels, with the potential of adding actions into the Developing Successful Neighbourhoods plan as it develops over the next 12–24 months.

A programme of public realm improvements around the fringes of the park began in earnest last year, but this needs completing to ensure that fringe communities blend with the new communities of the park in 2014, and beyond. Likewise we are gaining momentum in bringing forward legislative changes that will enable more effective environmental enforcement action. We hope to streamline current arrangements to ensure quick effective action can be taken before, during, and after games time.

Overcrowding is still a problem in the host boroughs area, and we will look again at options for joint work that could alleviate this while increasing the range of homes on offer. The new HCA [Homes and Communities Agency] Affordable Rent model, and changes to welfare benefits will have significant impacts on work in this area, and will be kept under review. Funding responsibility for the Affordable Homes programme 2011–2015 passes to the Mayor, when the HCA's powers in London are transferred in April 2012. Olympic Host Boroughs are keen to be properly involved in ongoing negotiations over scheme grant approvals, and efforts to ensure that rent levels for new family sized homes can be held below maximum benefit levels, even after the full extent of proposed welfare reforms are introduced. This is of particular importance in continuing to help alleviate overcrowding. The Mayor's new pan-London mobility scheme *housingmoves* will be launched in 2012. It will give social housing tenants access to a range of properties across London, in particular promoting moves related to employment, providing care to relatives, and downsizing from underoccupied homes. Greater mobility should be shaped to support achievement of key Convergence outcomes such as reduced overcrowding, improved health, and increased employment opportunity.

The Olympic Park Legacy Company has submitted its Legacy Communities Scheme (LCS) planning application in which it is seeking to create successful neighbourhoods in the Olympic Park, with up to 8000 new homes (including 40 per cent family homes). It is also well advanced in securing tenants, and operators for legacy venues, and in planning the programme of events and activities that will make the Queen Elizabeth Olympic Park an amenity for local people, a magnet for visitors, and a driver of local economic development. The Company, which the Mayor of London proposes to remodel as a Mayoral Development Corporation with an expanded remit from 2012, continues to work closely with the Host Boroughs to ensure that the Olympic Park can fulfil its potential as a catalyst for regeneration, helping local people gain skills, and jobs, and helping businesses win work and grow, as well as providing a legacy of sports infrastructure and participation.

The success of the new city district being built in, and around the Olympic Park is crucial in demonstrating success in the Host Boroughs. Convergence Action Plan 2011–2015.[4]

Ghost in the Machine

Focusing on the articulation of the 'look and feel' of the legacy Olympic Park, with public realm improvements in the fringe areas of the Olympic Park, Eleanor Fawcett is part of the new Design Team at OPLC. Fighting her own battle inside the Legacy Company, to have her work understood and incorporated into the considerations of other work streams, Eleanor is another champion of regeneration proper. As a designer, Eleanor at least has the support of Andrew Altman, who has promoted the cause of better design in legacy planning, but still, Eleanor cannot understand why she has to fight so hard to be heard, and for the value of her work to be recognised. After all, she has been involved with the project from the very beginning, on the conceptualisation of regeneration embodied in the early planning documents of the Lower Lea Valley Opportunity

---

[4] Convergence Framework and Action Plan 2011–2015 https://www.london.gov.uk/sites/default/files/Convergence%20action%20plan%202011-2015.pdf Accessed 5 May 2015

Area Planning Framework (OAPDF 2007),[5] and is one of the very few people with a profound, in-depth project knowledge that has, at its foundations, an understanding of the Olympic Park development in terms of the broader ambitions for the Lower Lea Valley.

One of Eleanor's remits at OPLC is to do with what the SRF Action Plan describes, which is the integration of the Olympic Park with its surrounding areas via a focus on a programme of multi-million pound public realm improvement projects in the fringe areas. Eleanor explains how this has involved working in partnership with the host boroughs, and other public bodies, to deliver what the Opportunity Area Framework imagined, which, in part, was to do with the animation, and connection of the valley in various ways. One of these was the creation of new town centres, which would normally be 'pie in the sky' ideas for planners, but which have become possible as a result of the Olympic catalyst, and clever coordination of strategy towards a regeneration agenda:

> I think that what we were able to do in the Lea Valley, because change was happening, change in private investment was coming forward in such an accelerated way compared with the normal kind of slow processes of change, and because of the deadline of the Olympics, it created the circumstances where it was actually viable, that you could be confident that some of the strategies that you were coming up with about how much change is likely to happen here, were credible.... Like creating three new town centres, was a big part of the strategy at Bromley by Bow [in Tower Hamlets], West Ham [in Newham], and Hackney Wick, and usually that would be pie in the sky. But here that's actually now what's happening. The public sector bought a lot of land around where these new centres were going to go, we've massively changed what all the private sector land owners are doing in that area, we've got Tesco's to deliver a primary school in the park at Bromley by Bow, so with a combination of bits of public sector money, bits of public sector influence like TfL [Transport for London] persuading Tesco to deliver a whole new junction for the Blackwall Approach Road, so that people could cross from one side to the other.
>
> So, I often think of it as being a conductor, or being a choreographer. It's not all about the public sector putting money in, in a heavy handed,

---

[5] The Lower Lea Valley Opportunity Area Planning Framework http://legacy.london.gov.uk/mayor/planning/docs/lowerleavalley-pt1.pdf Accessed 2 May 2015.

Development Corporation way, it's much more about being a choreographer where you can try, and coordinate all the bits of the jigsaw puzzle so that all the players in this process of change are pulling together.

Another example is delivering a new park connecting the Olympic Park down to the Thames, five different organisations to deliver different bits of it, and, because there was a big idea we can deliver it in lots of bits over time. But without that big idea then everybody's just doing their own thing, and it's all a bit of a shambles. And you end up thinking in ten years' time, "oh what a shame, if we'd actually got ourselves organised something really good could have happened there." I do think that's a new role for the public sector that's a lot more subtle than the classic coming in with your big boots on and CPO-ing [compulsory purchase order-ing] land. And actually the Olympics is more of an old fashioned way for the public sector, more top down in the traditional way rather than going with the grain [existing urban form], and understanding your grain, and figuring out how you can manipulate it.

Describing the difference that place-making design can make, and describing herself as 'a ghost in the machine', Eleanor describes what a difference it has made to her work, and the evolution of the public realm projects in the fringe areas bordering the Olympic Park, that she has had an overall strategic sense of how the whole valley has to work (through the connections that are being created between the park and the host boroughs, and through the park from one host borough to another), and had the opportunity and funding to quietly bring these projects to fruition:

> Waltham Forest, and the Leyton project, is a really good example where I don't think the project would have happened if we hadn't been there suggesting things, supporting them [Waltham Forest] egging them on, because this wasn't on their radar at all, because they are not really that much part of the Olympics, and this was the last of the Fringe Master Plans to start. It's a really terrific scheme. The biggest bit is the major rebuilding of the big connection from the London Underground, which will take people up and through to the Olympic Park, and eventually will anticipate the redevelopment of this site, and the delivery of a new bridge. We've put in these really nice granite curbs, where we've made carvings into them that relate to the names of the streets—Walnut Tree Avenue, Draper's Field with a cotton spool and a needle. We've done a whole load of lighting, replaced all the

lights, lit up their historic buildings, lit up these key moments where they've got these beautiful trees, and repaved this street that connects an existing park to another existing park. So, it's all these quite small interventions, which celebrate the place, and the local people really love it. It feels like the whole place is really proud again.

Another lovely project is the White Building, in Hackney Wick. There's all these artists, and soon they're going to get priced out of the area if we don't create the circumstances for them to stay, and for people to start to value them. And so, the White Building project was something we developed specifically to respond to that, it's like a cultural centre, giving a public face to the artists. It's got a hire space, a gallery, little office spaces for creative organisations to be based in, a space for talks, and shows. So, for example we are running an international residency programme there, and the National Portrait Gallery are interested in doing a show there, the Tate are interested. Probably the most important thing is, it's a facility where the community can actually engage with the fact that they've got this amazing resource on their doorstep—of all these committed, interested, dynamic entrepreneurial people. So, one of the big things is about running educational programmes, and apprenticeships, and working with local schools, so we've started a summer school with a local youth club, and it was so successful that it is being funded for a further three years.

Space Studios are going to run it, and we've got loads of really interesting firms signed up to take some of the office spaces. And it's got a café with a micro-brewery, which relates to the whole industrial history of the area, it's going to be just brilliant.

It is impossible not to be excited by the work that Eleanor is doing, inspired as she is by the possibilities of the public realm design work for genuine regeneration. Her passion for the Lower Lea Valley is palpable, and she is another person who has clearly given a whole portion of her life, and career in devotion to the realisation of the original vision of change for the area. When I ask her what East London means to her, on a personal level, she explains:

> It's such a big part of my life that it's sort of more than just a job, you know, I've been working here since 2003, and spend my weekends trudging around the area, and photographing, [mapping], and I genuinely love it, you know. I really feel quite passionate about it.

Eleanor then laughs, and tells me that someone had asked everyone at a dinner party she was at recently, where they would like to have their ashes scattered, and without hesitation, Eleanor had said, 'the Lower Lea Valley', which caused a bit of an awkward silence, because no one at the table could understand what she was talking about, or why she was quite so passionate about the place. Eleanor has the same experience at OPLC; she is frustrated, like Emma and Michelle, by how hard she has to work to get her agenda understood and incorporated into the project briefs of other teams at OPLC. I ask Eleanor to explain why this might be, and she tries to make sense of what is going wrong at OPLC:

> The thing I have found incredibly challenging has been the organisation, and the culture of the organisation. It's a very curiously dysfunctional organisation given how many fantastic people are working here, and what a clear mission we have, and how passionately the majority of people believe in that mission. There's almost no sense of all pulling together in the same direction. And on a day to day basis I've found that really awful, really terrible.

I ask Eleanor what she understands about the organisational culture of OPLC, what has it become, as it has evolved, and she describes an overly hierarchical organisation, with competitive, 'very macho', non-collaborative work stream silos. This perception, among staff members at all levels of OPLC, of the top-heavy dysfunction in the organisation is a repeating refrain in virtually every interview that I conduct. It is driving everyone crazy, and leads me to conclude that the mistake that has been made is in not having appointed a Chief Operating Officer, someone whose sole business is to attend to the efficient functioning of the organisation, leaving Andrew Altman to focus not just on salesmanship relating to Olympic assets, and crisis management, but also on what Eleanor is inspired by in him, which is the focus on, and prioritisation of the value of urban design.

Without this overarching directorial stewardship, there has been a sense in OPLC this last year, of an atmosphere expressed in hushed tones, and frustrated silences, of a failure of leadership, an inability to get the organisation to cohere, as a collective, around a set of shared ambitions.

No surprise, then, that there was a sense of relief expressed in the interviews I conducted, about the end of OPLC, and the beginning of the MDC, the mayor's new Development Corporation, and what it might bring, which is the hope of a change for the better.

I have to say that I could not bring myself to share that sense of optimism, because having already witnessed the transition from one delivery vehicle to another, I feel sure that it will simply be a case of swapping one set of problems for another, and having to endure again, all that comes with a change of leadership, and the struggle to imprint on all that has gone before, the false confidence of a fresh pair of eyes.

Andrew Altman, on his departure, also had the opportunity of the Company Report, to sum up his legacy in a similar way to Margaret Ford, but with more emphasis on regeneration, which was finally, firmly embedded, at the heart of the legacy story:

> While the eyes of the world have been on 27 July 2012, the date of the Olympic and Paralympic Games opening ceremony, the Company has been ensuring that the principal building blocks are in place to allow the London Legacy Development Corporation to meet its target of July 2013, the date when the Queen Elizabeth Olympic Park will begin re-opening to the public.
>
> Over the past year the Company has confirmed legacy plans for key venues, submitted planning applications, and begun the search for development partners. We have let contracts that will enable the London Legacy Development Corporation to deliver a significant programme of works—to clear the Park of Games-time structures, to connect it with surrounding areas, and to complete construction of permanent venues, parkland and infrastructure.
>
> This transformation programme, which has been formulated by the Company, forms a critical part of the London Legacy Corporation's Park Opening Plan and will see the Park opening in phases from July 2013. In addition to physical works valued at several million pounds, the Company has made significant progress in paving the way for mobilising venue operators and estates managers, planning for events and activity within the Park, putting security arrangements in place and strengthening relations with local communities.

At the heart of the programme is a determination to create a Park that is not only a magnet for national and international visitors but also the local park for residents of the Olympic host boroughs; a place not only for relaxation and fun but also for local people to find jobs, apprenticeships and business opportunities that they so greatly need; a place that will inspire people to take part in sport and to live healthily and that celebrates the artistic and cultural vigour of east London. The company is delighted to have been able to engage construction contractors, venue operators and estate managers who not only share our ambitions but are also committed with the London Legacy Development Corporation to address deep-seated social and economic disadvantage in the host boroughs.

Alongside this, the Company has continued to develop the regeneration plans for the Park, which include putting tenants in place for the press and broadcast centres, finalising planning negotiations on the Legacy Communities Scheme, delivering a first phase of housing, as well as leading and supporting projects outside the Park itself. We can now hand the baton over to the Development Corporation satisfied with the progress made towards one of our key objectives—convergence as described in the statement from Baroness Ford.

The objectives the Company set for itself are connected: regeneration and convergence are essential to making a successful place. As we hand over to the Development Corporation we can be proud of the progress we have made and I look forward to seeing a great Park that people want to visit time and again, one that supports local economic growth and new residential neighbourhoods.

The shift—from planning to delivery—sets a challenge for the whole organisation, as do the new responsibilities that accompany the metamorphosis from Legacy Company to Development Corporation. The assets include significant projects in Hackney Wick and Bromley by Bow, two important locations which are on the edge of the Olympic Park, but will be at the heart of the Development Corporation's remit. In October 2012, as work commences on the Park further organisational transformation will take place when planning powers are transferred to the Development Corporation.

The Company has been part of one of London's most impressive success stories, a success that has been made possible only by political commitment and leadership, and dedicated partnership working from Government, the

Mayor of London and the host boroughs. As the Development Corporation enters the next phase of delivery, this partnership should stand it in good stead.

In closing, and as I hand over the reins, as Chief Executive, I would like to pay personal tribute to the leadership and commitment shown by Margaret Ford as Chair of the Legacy Company. Margaret's inspirational approach, political skill, and deep seated commitment to regeneration have enabled the Company to achieve all that it has over the past three years, and have established the firmest of foundations on which future success will be built.
Andrew Altman,
Company Report 2011/12[6]

In their mutually reassuring summations of genuinely significant Legacy Company achievements, Margaret Ford and Andrew Altman distract from the stadium debacle that has been their downfall. It is a good time to bow out gracefully, and I imagine it is with some relief that they have handed over the reins to their successors. Raising a final question in the last OPLC Company Report, and a slight reality check to the rhetorical flourish of Andrew Altman's parting précis, Jonathan Dutton, the steadfast Director of Finance, and Corporate Services at OPLC, manages to have the last word. Working quietly, within the parameters of what public accountability allows, he faithfully reports, in his accounts (as he has done from one company report to another, from 2010 to 2012), a debt owed by Andrew Altman to OPLC that was taken out in 2009, and which by March 2012, despite a yearly salary of £195,000, had still not been repaid.

In the period ended 31 March 2010 an interest free loan of £9000 was made to Andrew Altman, a Director of the Company, as part of the arrangements for his relocation to the UK from the United States. As at 31 March 2012 £9000 was [still] owed to the Company.
Jonathan Dutton, Director of Finance, and Corporate Services
Company Report 2011/2012[7]

---

[6] Annual Report and Accounts 2011–2012 Olympic Park Legacy Company. http://queenelizabetholympicpark.co.uk/~/media/lldc/accounts/oplc_annual_report_2012_260712.pdf. Accessed 5 May 2015.
[7] Annual Report and Accounts 2011–2012 Olympic Park Legacy Company. http://queenelizabetholympicpark.co.uk/~/media/lldc/accounts/oplc_annual_report_2012_260712.pdf. Accessed 5 May 2015.

The question of the debt, relatively small as it is, highlights the greater importance, going forward, not just of keeping an eye on all the other much more significant debts that have been accumulated, and moved around, during the process of legacy planning in London, but also of maintaining a constant vigilance about the potential for publically funded projects worldwide to become devices for a highly paid, constantly circulating elite to extract private value from the public purse.

Suggested Reading

Allies, B., & Haigh, D. (2014). *The fabric of place: Allies and Morrison*. Artifice Books on Architecture.
Barber, B. (2014). *If mayors ruled the world: Dysfunctional nations, rising cities*. New Haven: Yale University Press.
Cawthorne, N. (2015). *Blonde ambition: The rise and rise of Boris Johnson*. Endeavour Press Ltd.
Cefkin, M. (2010). *Ethnography and the corporate encounter: Reflections on research in and of corporations*. New York: Berghahn Books.
Harvey, D. (2013). *Rebel cities: From the rights to the city to the urban revolution*. New York: Verso Books.
Massey, D. (2007). *World city*. London: Polity Press.
Pierre, J. (2011). *The politics of urban governance*. New York: Palgrave Macmillan.
Pillay, S., & Bilney, C. (2015). *Public sector organisations and cultural change*. New York: Palgrave Macmillan.
Garsten, C., & Nykvist, A. (Eds.). (2013). *Organisational anthropology: Doing ethnography in and among complex organisations*. London: Pluto Press.
Smith, A. (2012). *Events and urban regeneration: The strategic use of events to revitalise cities*. New York: Routledge.

Afterword: Summer 2015

Have you been to the Olympic Park? It was the best day out we had in London this summer. The Aquatics Centre is incredible, and only £3.50 for a ticket. The kids swam, and then played outside all afternoon. We had a nice dinner before getting on the train, and the kids slept all the way home.
   July 2015
   A woman speaking to her friends in the café of Stafford station, in the Midlands, England.

I could hardly believe my ears when I overheard this comment about the Olympic Park made by a woman in the café of Stafford train station, talking to her friends about days out she had enjoyed with her grandchildren this summer. I could not help but remember what Margaret Ford had said, at the legacy dinner in the summer of 2009, when she explained her legacy vision of a visitor economy for the park in which families visiting London from out of town would eventually come to think of the Olympic Park as one of their favourite destinations to take the kids for a memorable time. Obviously, Margaret Ford was right about that vision; notwithstanding the miserable British summer, the park has become a place that is being used to host prestigious international sporting competitions, and it is also regularly frequented, at weekends, by families enjoying the open space and sporting amenities.

Against all the odds London hosted a fabulously successful Olympic Games in 2012, and the unprecedented haul of medals for Britain's athletes, as well as an opening ceremony that defied almost all critics, delivering a cultural spectacle that the nation could be proud of, led to exactly the sense of cohesion, and uplift that the government was desperately praying for. No surprise, then, that Tessa Jowell was rewarded in 2012 in the Queen's birthday honours list; her political courage in backing London's bid for the Games paid off, and her political legacy is secure. She is now Dame Tessa Jowell, and hoping to be selected as the Labour candidate to run for London Mayor in 2016, which, were she to be successful, would see her, and Labour, steal the Olympic legacy back out of Boris' hands.

Loudly, and proudly, on the back of the Games, the mantra of a more confident Conservative-led central government, in 2012, became 'Britain can Deliver', and whilst the fortunes of the UK economy slowly began to turn around, the terrible price of this was that cuts to public sector spending were intensified with renewed determination. So far, this has not affected the planning and delivery of Olympic legacy in the park itself, but this might change in future under a new Conservative government, now no longer in coalition. This is especially true if, after Boris Johnson steps down as mayor in 2016 to pursue his political career in Westminster, a Labour candidate wins control of the city again.

Since the Olympic Park began to reopen in July 2013, it has attracted an estimated 3 million visitors. Testament to Karen West's determination, many of those people have been drawn to the Aquatics Centre, which is used by elite swimmers, and because of the affordable access price, local residents too, including 2000 local school children, who are now able to boast of the Aquatics Centre as the location for their weekly swimming lessons. The same is true of the Multi-Use Arena and the Velodrome (which is part of the Lea Valley Regional Park), which are also popular and well-used destinations for a number of different sports enthusiasts, both professional and casual. This is quite a feat bearing in mind the catastrophic situation more generally, in which rapidly declining sports participation statistics are an embarrassment to the original promise of a national Olympic legacy of increased sporting participation. Less popular is the ArcelorMittal Orbit, whose visitor numbers have been disappointing, but surprise, surprise, there are plans to do something about this by adding a giant slide, bringing to fruition Boris Johnson's original vision for a giant helter-skelter in the park.

The Olympic stadium fiasco looks, on the surface, as if it has finally reached a more settled conclusion, with West Ham, as predicted, the main joint beneficiaries, with UK Athletics, of the stadium rental deal. West Ham will start their 2016 season in the stadium, but it will not be a completely clean start for the club, because the issue of state aid still hangs in the air. Even Freedom of Information requests have failed to reveal the actual financial terms of the stadium settlement, and the final costs of conversion are controversial, at three times the original estimate, reaching nearly £300 million. This amount of investment in a stadium for a Premier League club whose fortunes in the league are now looking much brighter could still prove problematic when the rental deal makes it possible for West Ham to inhabit the stadium at a rate thought to be just £2.5 million a year, and European clubs, and potential rivals are beginning to get twitchy about whether or not West Ham's increased good fortunes could be said to be the result of unfair competition. Meanwhile, the tenacity of Leyton Orient finally paid off—the club dropped its legal action against West Ham's move to the stadium, settling instead, for an undisclosed compensation payment from the Premier League.

The future of the Press and Broadcast Centres is looking much brighter, with BT Sport as the new anchor tenant of the successfully realised creative industries and digital media hub, which is now called Here East. To compliment this, Boris Johnson has continued in his determination to see a world-class university take up tenancy in the park, but this idea has grown exponentially, so that there are now plans in place not just for University College London, which is developing a new campus on the park, to the south of The Orbit, but to include this as part of the ambitious Olympicopolis scheme, which is an Education and Cultural Quarter comprising a new museum and arts institution complex to rival Kensington in West London. The Victoria and Albert Museum, Sadlers Wells, The University of the Arts (London College of Fashion), and perhaps even The Smithsonian will form a cluster for the development of a new creative knowledge economy in East London.

On the one hand, the replacement of a housing neighbourhood—Stratford Waterfront (in front of the Aquatics Centre)—with an Education and Cultural Sector is good news, because of the increase in training and employment opportunities, and the crafting of a future-oriented education offer for East London. This compliments well the demographic of the wider area in which a young population is coming of age, and finding more opportunities on its doorstep without having to travel to West London. Overall, the sense of the park and its future is changing, which might be good news relative to the questionable Design-led Review proposal to turn the park into the Notting Hill of London. This shift in focus is proof of how flexible the LMF had to be. Its job was to set out the spaces where development could happen, and to give a sense of what might be envisaged there in future, not to fix in advance exactly what kinds of developments could happen.

On the other hand, even though the mayor has promised that housing lost on the Stratford Waterfront site to make way for the new Education and Cultural Quarter will be reallocated elsewhere in the park, it remains controversial that a scheme, which promised a certain amount of housing in line with the requirements of the London Plan, should now be further reducing its housing offer. The promise of a focus on family housing can no longer be said to be set in stone, and already, the housing development deals done, first at Chobham Manor, and now at the development platforms in the west and south-west of the park, at Sweet Water, and East Wick, have seen a compromise in the amount of housing designated as 'affordable' when the pledge from the beginning was for a site wide 35 % allocation.

The increasing value of residential and commercial property in the park, and its surroundings is good news from the point of view of the stated aim to attract investment to East London, but it has had the knock-on effect of making housing less affordable to those local residents who might now like to stay in the area, but who could not now ever imagine being able to purchase the property they aspire to. The discrepancy between the kind of housing the park is now able to provide, and the extreme levels of housing need in the surrounding boroughs of the Olympic Park continues to be a source of tension. Related to this, the celebrated move of the new University College of London campus to the park is not a neutral achievement, because it comes following a long and controversial battle by the residents of the Carpenters Estate to the south of the park, who fought in 2011 against their displacement and won, which is part of the reason, which led the University College to withdraw their offer to Newham Council to redevelop that land for their campus. Since then, some of the abandoned housing on the estate has been squatted as an act of resistance by young mothers who were displaced from the hostel they were staying in, and have now started a campaign—Focus E15—to highlight the chronic lack of social housing in East London boroughs still affected by drastic government cuts to public spending.

Other ongoing scandals include the fate of the 'diggers' displaced from the site of the Manor Garden Allotments, who were to be relocated to the park after the Games. So far, they have been given only half of their promised land, in the south of the park at Pudding Mill, and, despite the heroic battle of the Club Secretary, Mark Harton, and the other society members, it seems that they have finally been forced to accept that the promise will not be honoured to reinstate the entirety of their lands inside the boundaries of the Olympic Park; they have had to let go of the other land that was promised to them in the north-east of the park, and reluctantly accept that the temporary site they have been occupying outside the park is now to be made permanent.

Not surprisingly, the London Assembly is still pestering about the socio-economic legacy of the plans for the Olympic Park, and holding Boris Johnson to account, determined that he should come up with a coherent training and skills strategy to accompany his Olympicopolis development. Although the mayor did not mention his Regeneration Team in front of the assembly, and appeared to have no knowledge of any socio-economic plan that might be in place, there is no doubt that under Paul Brickell's ongoing leadership, the Regeneration Team will ensure that the Olympicopolis development will provide another opportunity for the development of best practice models of how to incorporate socio-economic outcomes into plans for major urban development in London.[1]

---

[1] The Regeneration Team has initiated a successful apprenticeship scheme, case studies of which can be seen in these films: https://www.youtube.com/watch?v=boDh8Xjz-4M https://www.youtube.com/watch?v=h2KLhhIUHIw

The SRF is reported this year to be on course on 12 out of 21 indicators of progress, but falling short on nine others. When asked by the London Assembly, in March this year, about his commitment to the Convergence agenda, Boris dared to be dismissive. He had finally gained complete control of the legacy project, taking over, in 2012, as Chair of the LLDC after Daniel Moylan, his predecessor, lasted just 3 months in the job.[2] At the March Plenary of the London Assembly, on the matter of Olympic legacy, Boris Johnson was bullish. Clearly, what matters to him is that the trajectory is set for an exciting range of residential, and other developments in the Olympic Park, and when called to account for himself on the topic of convergence, Boris was typically blunt: revealing his hand, he replied sarcastically to the question of ongoing concerns in the assembly about the articulation of legacy planning to the Convergence agenda. His response was revealing, because it signified the difference between a Conservative Development Corporation way of thinking about regeneration, focusing exclusively on development deals, and the previous, Tom Russell-style, URC in which the strength and purpose of the SRF is supposed to be a major part of the project's success. This is because the SRF is the experimental means for integrating new development into its surrounding areas. Clearly, for those people in East London who beg to differ with what the mayor had to say about convergence, the fight for regeneration proper goes on.

> If I may say so, the word 'convergence' though we all use it freely is something of a term of art. I am not sure that it actually means an awful lot to most people in this city.
> Boris Johnson
> March 2015, Plenary of the London Assembly.[3]

---

[2] Boris Johnson stood down as Chair of the Legacy Corporation in May of 2015, and Neale Coleman, who has gradually moved from a behind-the-scenes advisory role—as a 'fixer'—to a front-stage leadership position, succeeded Boris as Chair.

[3] Appendix. March 2015. Plenary of the London Assembly. https://www.london.gov.uk/modern-gov/documents/b12230/Minutes%20-%20Appendix%201%20-%20Transcript%20Wednesday%2011-Mar-2015%2010.00%20London%20Assembly%20Plenary.pdf?T=9 Accessed 10 July 2015.

Lessons from London: a few thoughts for discussion on how things might have been done better.

1. The OPLC ought to have been formed earlier than 2009, and preferably 4 years earlier, immediately on London winning the bid in 2005. This would have meant that the process could have been started much earlier to ensure that tenants were found for the sporting venues, and Press and Broadcast Centres, and the tenants' requirements designed in at the earliest possible stages. The earlier formation of the Legacy Company would have also ensured that legacy champions were on hand straight away to fight for the legacy future of each venue as the design process, and associated contracts evolved over time.
2. The possibility of the failure of private investment in the development, for example, of the Press and Broadcast Centres, ought to have also been accounted for in the provision of contingency budgets, so that damaging processes of 'value engineering' did not have to be applied to the venues retrospectively.
3. The SRF ought to have been produced very early on in the planning process, preferably alongside the development of the bid itself, so that when the bid was won, the Regeneration Framework would have already been there, not just as a legacy of the bidding process, but also to form the policy context for articulation of Olympic-specific site plans, with the immediate social and economic context of the region bordering the future Olympic Park. This would have also meant that once the Legacy Master Planning Team was appointed, it would have been working immediately to articulate its park-specific plans to the ambitions of the wider aims of the Regeneration Framework. The early formation of the SRF would then also have immediately informed the establishment of the OPLC, with regeneration established right from the beginning as the overall aim of the company, towards which the other objectives of the company would have been geared. This would have also meant that an Executive Director of Regeneration would have been in place straightaway, directing the socio-economic agenda right from the beginning. Every aspect of the

company's work, and related contracts with private companies would then have been informed by the regeneration agenda instead of it having to be fought for constantly as an add-on item.
4. The socio-economic agenda of legacy planning ought to have also included a focus on the socio-economics of the planning operation itself, with a more transparent focus on the economic and social organisation of the tripartite (OPLC, LOCOG, and ODA) Olympic planning operation, and the dense network of private contracts associated with that. Part of the commitment of the SRF ought to have been to do with the articulation of the private contracts associated with Olympic and Legacy planning, with the provision of employment and skills training, apprenticeship, and job opportunities in the Olympic host boroughs. To be clear, this would have meant that for every single private contract awarded, some kind of employment and skills legacy ought to have been involved for the residents of the host Olympic boroughs. For example, Eversheds, just one of the legal firms profiting from the legal legacy of the Games, ought to have had to contribute to the development of the SRF Convergence agenda in proportion to the degree to which the company profited from its involvement in the legacy process. This programme of providing opportunities in private companies relating to the behind-the-scenes legacy-planning operations could also have included, for example, the chance for young people from the host Olympic boroughs to learn more about the political process involved in the legacy-planning operation, across central, London, and local government.
5. The by-now clear understanding that a model of 'trickle down' economics does not work in urban regeneration means that a lot more financial emphasis ought to have been placed on supporting those exact mechanisms through which the planning and delivery of urban change was 'stitched in' to the process of transformation in the areas surrounding any one development. These were stitches to do not just with tying in development to local training and employment frameworks, locally based supply chains, or social enterprises, and small businesses, but also stitches in the spatial fabric of the city related to planning for regeneration, as spelled out by the LMF, and the Fringe Master Plans. It may turn out to be the case, for example, that the

significant reductions in the proposed housing densities, which was one outcome of the Design-led Review programme, will not be in the best interests of the host boroughs whose residents might have been better served by the earlier scheme, which would have provided family housing in higher numbers, yielding greater returns in terms of number of affordable units. In addition, in the light of an increasingly valuable property market in East London, it is difficult to justify the compromises that have been made to the promise of 35 % affordable housing across the scheme, especially against the background of a history of London Plans that have suggested a need in the city for a 50 % proportion of affordable homes in new housing developments.

6. The economic and spatial focus of regeneration planning could also have been powerfully strengthened by an Olympic Opportunities programme more specifically focused on 'the social stitches' required to properly integrate the 11 immediately neighbouring political wards into the Olympic Park. This would have led to a localised, in-depth process of targeted transformation, leading to a set of sustainable, ongoing relationships with local housing estates, voluntary sector organisations, and individual families and young people against whose life chances legacy promises could have been intimately measured over at least a 10-year period, from Olympic bid to park opening (2003–2013). This localised experiment in 'stitching in' a new development, articulating its future possibilities to the contextual challenges facing existing neighbourhood areas, would have led to the possibility of a rigorous analysis of what it takes to deliver radical change in life opportunities at the level of the housing estate, and from there, to the broader neighbourhood, and city area. The failure, for example, of Tessa Jowell's 'Social Connectors' project, which cost a great deal of money, and was to do with her determination to feel more closely connected to the people of East London, could have been avoided, by spending the money instead, on supporting those voluntary sector organisations that already have a track record in East London. This would have made possible an arrangement in which such organisation could have mediated between the Olympic planning organisations and the people on the ground, to address the

problems people in East London felt were most in need of attention.

7. The story of the evolution of the Olympic legacy Community Consultation and Engagement programme reveals just how important to the momentum of the legacy project it was to build and maintain relations of trust, and open dialogue with local stakeholders, community organisations, and residents. The breakdown of this trust, and momentum, during the Design-led Review of the masterplanning process was risky and controversial. Rather than undermining the process of consultation and engagement during the period of planning hiatus, communication with stakeholders and consultees ought to have been increased to provide reassurance during a process of uncertain change.

8. The best practice models of Consultation and Engagement in the legacy-planning programme could have been developed much earlier along the lines of the projects Emma Wheelhouse was eventually able to develop when she joined the Regeneration Team. Only then, was she able to use the case study of the Legacy Youth Panel, as an example of consultation-as-education/life opportunity to develop a more general programme of community education about urban planning.

9. In the case of the Manor Garden Allotment Society, the long battle faced by the society's current secretary, Mark Harton, for the society not to be dispossessed of the other half of the land it was promised in the north-east of the Olympic Park, suggests strongly that community organisations that are having to face up to the juggernaut of the Olympic planning operation ought to have special mentoring relationships in place to equip them for their unexpected involvement in bureaucratic/urban planning battles to secure their position in the face of unprecedented and fast-moving processes of urban change.

10. There is room for extreme caution about the effects of regime change on the momentum of legacy planning and delivery. The expectation that new leaders will want, and need to claim ownership of projects, and work achieved so far, or, indeed, to start all over again whole processes of planning after years of work have already been put in, poses an extreme risk to legacy planning, and costs a fortune. So too, does any significant shift in the political landscape of the city or the

nation. Somehow, the Olympic legacy-planning project ought to have been better protected from the disruption and insecurity created by the constantly shifting political landscape in London and in the UK.
11. There was perhaps a need on the Board of OPLC for greater planning expertise, so that proper oversight of the process of master planning could have been given. There was a need too, in retrospect, for greater expertise in high-level sports business management, especially in football, which could potentially have prevented the prolonged saga of the stadium tenancy, especially because neither Margaret Ford, nor Andrew Altman had any expertise in the world of sport. Instead of a disproportionate focus on 'the entrepreneurial' credentials of the board, a useful balance could have been struck with greater expertise about 'operational' matters, so that more guidance and stewardship could have been given on how to create a new organisation that can function effectively in a sustainable way. Part of the challenge of all directorial boards is that their members are too far removed from the realities of the day-to-day business of the companies, or organisations they are supposed to be responsible for overseeing. It would be an exceptional board member who took the time to overcome these barriers, and to find out what was really going on—on the ground.
12. The political coordination in London, of the local, city, and central government has been a triumph of the legacy-planning process. In part this has been to do with the determination of the Olympic host boroughs to come together to secure a regeneration legacy for the areas local to the Olympic Park. The pre-existing work of local strategists, and change-makers in East London, has also been an important part of the process through which the ambitions of the Olympic planning operation have been harnessed to the desires, and ambitions of what those who know and best understand East London have been determined to realise as legacy. Rather than ignore these strategists, Olympic planners could have done more to incorporate locally generated ideas for legacy of the host Olympic boroughs, and, in the case of the Press and Broadcast Centres in Hackney, for example, or the Olympic stadium in Newham, the precedent of the fight for a locally informed agenda has been impossible to ignore. The case of the Press

and Broadcast Centres also reveals how far in advance it needs to be considered that provision of government subsidy for employment uses might be a necessary expense, rather than assuming that the market can be relied on to provide the solution to the search for tenants for Olympic venues.
13. Greater efforts could have been made to ensure that the industrial and manufacturing history of the Lower Lea Valley was embodied in the design of the Olympic Park, so that any visitor either from London, Britain, or abroad, could not help but have to engage with, and make sense of the history of the place that this future looking park is the transformation of. This greater focus on history could have also incorporated more of a focus on the Olympic inheritance itself, perhaps with an Olympic museum in the park (which could yet be an important addition to the new Education and Cultural Quarter). The focus on the industrial and manufacturing heritage of the area would have made possible an interesting point of engagement for those residents living locally who feel keenly the loss of industry and manufacture in East London even as a new service sector economy begins to take shape. Similarly, greater focus could have been placed on measures for providing continuing support for existing industrial and manufacturing uses alongside the development of new service sector land uses as post-industrial schemes for urban transformation take hold.
14. The best practice model of land assembly for the Olympic Park, whereby those displaced from the park were relocated to new premises outside the park could have been followed up with a long-term analysis of the future fate of those people and community groups and businesses that were forced to move to new premises. The loss of the LDA made this difficult, but in future, the lessons learned from the land assembly process could be made more pertinent by an ongoing analysis of the implications of displacement for those involved at the rough end of urban transformation.
15. A greater focus could have been placed, in general, on developing a live archive of the processes through which the legacy-planning operation came about. For example, it is very difficult online to now access any of the planning documents, diagrams, maps, and so on,

relating to the earlier master-planning process, which makes it seem as if a process of erasure has been taking place as each new phase of legacy planning supersedes what preceded it.

16. Those in charge of the Olympic legacy-planning operation are to be praised for allowing and supporting the research, and critical commentary on their world of a social anthropologist. Arguably, this is another example of urban planning best practice that ought to be replicated for every Olympic Games, and, indeed, every major project of urban transformation in Britain and elsewhere. This could become part of the process of how host cities and urban development projects learn from each other over time, so that the wheel does not have to be reinvented with each planning cycle.

17. The controversy around the transfer of land and debt, or not, from the Legacy Directorate to the OPLC, means that a best-case scenario business model ought to be developed in future, in advance of the land assembly process that provides for the freeing of any future host city legacy company from the burden of that debt, especially where it means that freehold of the land can remain in public ownership. Similarly the legacy business modelling must take into account sufficient provision for post-Games planning including capital funding for the transformation of the park to legacy uses and operational costs for legacy venues and parkland management.

18. The kinds of initiatives that Paul Brickell developed (such as the View Tube and its innovative model of social enterprise development, to make sure that local populations were not overly alienated by the security fences surrounding the development of the Olympic Park) ought to have been more widely implemented around the fringe areas of the Olympic Park. This, and the model of the community hubs in the post-Games park, ought to provide the template for how to increase community engagement with the park in advance of, and immediately after the Games. This model could also be more widely replicated for other major projects of urban transformation.

19. The importance cannot be underestimated of the presence in the Legacy Company of key members of staff who have a deep understanding of, and are in sympathy with the local dynamics of the area immediate to the Olympic Park. The more usual scenario in which

urban transformation happens through the imposition on the local area of outsiders who live elsewhere, and have nothing to lose, is less than helpful and does nothing to change the stereotype of urban regeneration as a top-down process of forced change that is bound to fail. The recruitment and retention of locally embedded actors have been vital to the success of the Olympic legacy project, and this precedent ought to be replicated elsewhere.

Bibliography

Abram, S. (2011). *Culture and planning*. Surrey: Ashgate.
Abram, S., & Weszkalnys, G. (Eds.). (2013). *Elusive promises: Planning in the contemporary world*. New York: Berghahn Books.
Allies, B., & Haigh, D. (2014). *The fabric of place: Allies and Morrison* (Artifice Books on Architecture). Annual Report and Accounts 2011–2012 Olympic Park Legacy Company. Accessed May 5, 2015, from http://queenelizabetholympicpark.co.uk/-/media/lldc/accounts/oplc_annual_report_2012_260712.pdf
Appendix 1 Economy Culture and Sport Committee 8 November 2011 Transcript of Item 5. Accessed May 5, 2015, from http://www.london.gov.uk/moderngov/documents/s6202/Olympic%20Stadium%20Legacy.pdf
Bale, J. (2001). *Sport, space and the city*. New Jersey: The Blackburn Press.
Barber, B. (2014). *If mayors ruled the world: Dysfunctional nations, rising cities*. New Haven: Yale University Press.
Barker, K. (2014). *Housing: Where's the plan?* London: London Publishing Partnership.
Bernstock, P. (2014). *Olympic housing: A critical review of London 2012's legacy*. Surrey: Ashgate.
Blakely, G., & Evans, B. (2013). *The regeneration of East Manchester: A political analysis*. Manchester: Manchester University Press.

Bloomfield, R. *Olympic park legacy design is radically revised.* Accessed May 6, 2015, from http://www.bdonline.co.uk/olympic-park-legacy-design-is-radically-revised/5006896.article

Brenner, N., & Theodore, N. (2003). *Spaces of neoliberalism: Urban restructuring in North America and Western Europe.* New York: Wiley.

Bridge, G., Lees, L., & Butler, T. (2012). *Mixed communities: Gentrification by stealth?* Bristol: Policy Press.

Bullivant, L. (2012). *Masterplanning futures.* New York: Routledge.

Carlo, P. P., & Ponzini, D. (2015). *Place making and urban development: New challenges for contemporary planning and design.* New York: Routledge.

Carmon, M., & Fainstein, S. (Eds.). (2013). *Policy, planning, and people: Promoting justice in urban development.* Philadelphia: University of Pennsylvania Press.

Cawthorne, N. (2015). *Blonde ambition: The rise and rise of Boris Johnson.* Endeavour Press.

Cefkin, M. (2010). *Ethnography and the corporate encounter: Reflections on research in and of corporations.* New York: Berghahn Books.

Cohen, P. (2013). *On the wrong side of the track? East London and the post-Olympics.* London: Lawrence and Wishart Ltd.

Comfort, N. (2013). *The slow death of British industry: A sixty-year suicide 1952–2012.* London: Biteback Publishing.

Convergence Framework and Action Plan 2011–2015. Accessed May 5, 2015, from https://www.london.gov.uk/sites/default/files/Convergence%20action%20plan%202011-2015.pdf

Daniel Levy Hits Back at Karen Brady Over the Olympic Stadium. Accessed May 2, 2015, from http://news.bbc.co.uk/sport1/hi/football/teams/t/tottenham_hotspur/9391299.stm

Davies, L. (2010). Sport and economic regeneration: A winning combination? *Sport in Society, 13*(10), 1438–1457.

Davies, L. (2011). Using sports infrastructure to deliver economic and social change: Lessons for London beyond 2012. *Local Economy, 26*(4), 227–231.

Davies, L. (2012). Beyond the games: Regeneration legacies and London 2012. *Leisure Studies, 31*(3), 307–337.

Davis, J. (2011). *Urbanising the event: How past processes, present politics, and future plans shape London's Olympic legacy.* Ph.D. Thesis. London School of Economics and Political Science.

Dorling, D. (2014). *All that is solid: How the great housing disaster defines our times and what we can do about it.* London: Penguin.

Evans, G. (2001). *Cultural planning: An urban renaissance?* New York: Routledge.

Evans, G. (2006). *Educational failure and working class white children in Britain.* Basingstoke, Hampshire: Palgrave Macmillan.

Evans, G. (2012). Materializing the vision of a 2012 London Olympics. In V. Girginov (Ed.), *The Routledge 2012 Olympics special issue.* New York: Routledge.

Fainstein, S. (1994). *The city builders: Property development in New York, and London, 1980–2000.* Cambridge, MA: Blackwell.

Figart, D. (Eds.). (2012). *Living wage movements: Global perspectives.* New York: Routledge.

Florida, R. (2004). *Cities and the creative class.* New York: Routledge.

Florida, R. (2014). *The rise of the creative class revisited.* New York: Basic Books.

Foster, J. (1998). *Docklands: cultures in conflict, worlds in collision.* London: UCL Press.

Frank, S., & Steets, S. (Eds.). (2010). *Stadium worlds: Football, space and the built environment.* New York: Routledge.

Garsten, C., & Nykvist, A. (Eds.). (2013). *Organisational anthropology: Doing ethnography in and among complex organisations.* London: Pluto Press.

Grix, J. (Ed.). (2014). *Leveraging legacies from sports mega-events: Concepts and cases.* New York: Palgrave Macmillan.

Harvey, D. (2013). *Rebel cities: From the rights to the city to the urban revolution.* New York: Verso Books.

Healey, P. (2010). *Making better places: The planning project in the 21st century.* New York: Palgrave Macmillan.

Holt, R., & Ruta, D. (Eds.). (2015). *Routledge handbook of sport and legacy: Meeting the challenge of major sports events.* New York: Routledge.

Horne, J., & Whannel, G. (2012). *Understanding the Olympics.* New York: Routledge.

The First Legacy Games: The physical and socioeconomic transformation of East London. Accessed May 10, 2015, from http://www.lse.ac.uk/newsAndMedia/videoAndAudio/channels/publicLecturesAndEvents/player.aspx?id=482

Imrie, R., Lees, L., & Raco, M. (2008). *Regenerating London: Governance, sustainability, and community in a global city.* New York: Routledge.

Imrie, R., & Raco, M. (Eds.). (2003). *Urban Renaissance?: New Labour, community and urban policy.* Bristol: Policy Press.

Jacobs, J. (1993). *The death and life of great American cities.* New York: Random House.

Kavetsos, G., & Szymanski, S. (2011). National well-being and international sports events. *Journal of Economic Psychology, 2010*(31), 158–171.

Keil, R., & Brenner, N. (Eds.). (2005). *The global cities reader*. New York: Routledge.
Lees, L., Slater, T., & Wyly, E. (2007). *Gentrification*. New York: Routledge.
Lees, L., Slater, T., & Wyly, E. (2010). *The gentrification reader*. New York: Routledge.
Lindsey, I. (2014). *Living with London's Olympics: an ethnography*. New York: Palgrave Macmillan.
Longstaffe-Gowan, T. (2012). *The London Square: Gardens in the midst of town*. New Haven: Yale University Press.
Low, S., & Lawrence Zuniga, D. (Eds.). (2003). *The anthropology of space and place: Locating culture*. Malden, MA: Blackwell.
Low, S., & Smith, N. (Eds.). (2005). *The politics of public space*. New York: Routledge.
Mangan, J., & Dyreson, M. (Eds.). (2013). *Olympic legacies intended and unintended: Political, cultural, economic, and educational*. New York: Routledge.
Marshall, P. (2010). *Before the Olympics: The Lea Valley, 1981–2010*. http://www.blurb.co.uk/books/3488533-before-the-olympics
Massey, D. (2007). *World city*. London: Polity Press.
Minton, A. (2012). *Ground control: Fear and happiness in the 21st century city*. London: Penguin.
Newenham, P. (Ed.). (2015). *Silicon docks: The rise of Dublin as a global tech hub*. Dublin: Liberties Press.
Olympic Park Legacy Company. Transcript of item 6. Economic Development, Culture, Sport and Tourism Committee, 21st October 2009. Accessed May 10, 2015, from https://www.london.gov.uk/sites/default/files/archives/assembly-edcst-2009-oct21-minutes-transcript.pdf
Olympic Strategic Regeneration FrameworkItem 3, Appendix A, Economic Development, Culture, Sport and Tourism Committee, 12 January 2010. Accessed May 10, 2015, from http://legacy.london.gov.uk/assembly/edcst/2010/jan12/minutes/transcript.pdf
Paton, K. (2014). *Gentrification: A working class perspective*. Surrey: Ashgate.
Pierre, J. (2011). *The politics of urban governance*. New York: Palgrave Macmillan.
Pillay, S., & Bilney, C. (2015). *Public sector organisations and cultural change*. New York: Palgrave Macmillan.
Piol, A., & Cometto, M. (2013) *Tech and the city: The making of New York's start up community*. Mirandola Press.
Poynter, G., & MacRury, I. (Eds.). (2009). *Olympic cities: 2012 and the remaking of London*. Surrey: Ashgate.
Poynter, G., Viehoff, V., & Li, Y. (Eds.). (2015). *The London Olympics and urban development: The mega-event city*. Surrey: Ashgate.

Preuss, H. (Ed.). (2007). *The impact and evaluation of major sporting events.* New York: Routledge.
Raco, M. (2013). *State led privatisation and the demise of the democratic state: welfare reform and localism in an era of regulatory capitalism.*
Raco, M. (2015, June). Sustainable city building and the new politics of the possible: Reflections on the governance of the London Olympics 2012. *Area, 47*(2), 124–131.
Rawnsley, A. (2010). *The end of the party: The rise and fall of New Labour.* London: Penguin.
Robertson, A. F. (1984). *People and the state: An anthropology of planned development.* Cambridge: Cambridge University Press.
Rogers, R. (1997). *Cities for a small planet: Reith lectures.* London: Faber & Faber.
Rutheiser, C. (1996). *Imagineering Atlanta: The politics of place in the city of dreams.* New York: Verso.
Ryan-Collins, J., & Sander-Jackson, P. (2008). *Fools gold: How the 2012 Olympics is selling East London short, and a 10 point plan for more positive local legacy.* London: New Economics Foundation.
Sassens, S. (2001). *The Global City: London, New York, Tokyo.* New Jersey: Princeton University Press.
Scott, J. (1999). *Seeing like a state: How certain schemes to improve the human condition have failed.* New Haven: Yale University Press.
Sinclair, I. (2010). *Hackney, that Rose Red Empire: A confidential report.* London: Penguin.
Sinclair, I. (2011). *Ghost milk: Calling time on the grand project.* London: Hamish Hamilton.
Smith, A. (2012). *Events and urban regeneration: The strategic use of events to revitalise cities.* New York: Routledge.
Smith, D., & Wistrich, E. (2014). *Devolution and localism in England.* Surrey: Ashgate.
Strategic Regeneration Framework: An Olympic Legacy for the Host Boroughs. Accessed May 10, 2015, from http://www.gamesmonitor.org.uk/files/strategic-regeneration-framework-report.pdf
Tallon, A. (2010). *Urban regeneration in the UK.* New York: Routledge.
Tessa Jowell Backs West Ham Bid for Stadium to Keep Athletics Promises. Accessed May 2, 2015, from http://www.telegraph.co.uk/sport/olympics/8270181/London-2012-Olympics-Tessa-Jowell-backs-West-Ham-bid-for-stadium-to-keep-athletics-legacy-promises.html
The Lower Lea Valley Opportunity Area Planning Framework. Accessed May 2, 2015, from http://legacy.london.gov.uk/mayor/planning/docs/lowerleavalley-pt1.pdf

Tighe, R., & Mueller, E. (2012). *The affordable housing reader*. New York: Routledge.
Tonkiss, F. (2013). *Cities by design: The social life of urban form*. Cambridge: Polity Press.
UK Athletics Boost for West Ham's 2012 Bid. Accessed May 2, 2015, from http://www.bbc.co.uk/blogs/adrianwarner/2010/10
Wagg, S. (2015). *The London Olympics of 2012: Politics, promises and legacy*. New York: Palgrave Macmillan.
Ward, K., & Peck, J. (Eds.). (2010). *City of revolution: Restructuring Manchester*. Manchester: Manchester University Press.
Wates, N. (2014). *The community planning handbook: How people can shape their cities, towns, and villages in any part of the world*. New York: Routledge.
Williams, K., Erturk, I., Froud, J., Johal, S., Leaver, A., & Moran, M. (2011). City state against national settlement: UK economic policy and politics after the financial crisis. Working Paper 101. *CRESC working paper series*.

Index

A

Abercrombie, Sir (Leslie) Patrick, 29
AECOM, 168, 170, 173
AEG, 152
Affordable homes, 67
  See also Social housing
Allen, Charles, 115
Allotments, 43–45
Altman, Andrew, 120, 138, 169, 174–175, 181, 197
  See also Communications Team (Comms.); OPLC
APPG (All Party Parliamentary Group), 139
Aquatics Centre, 120–123, 189
  See also West, Karen
ArcelorMittal Orbit, 163, 189, 209
Architecture, 82, 99, 173
Architecture Crew, 82
Arena Fields, 42
Art in the Park, 113, 163, 193
  See also Orbit, The
Artists, 92, 115, 120
Athletics, 151–157
  Helsinki, 33
  legacy, 35
  Picketts Lock, 33
  track, 34–35, 137, 151–162
  UK Athletics, 33, 151–156, 209
  World Championship 2005, 34
  World Championship 2015, 155
  World Championship 2017, 155

B

Balfour Beatty Workplace, 189
Barclays plc (bank), 6
BBC (British Broadcasting Corporation), 95, 145, 152, 158, 190

Belvedere, The, 71, 113
Bermondsey, 48
Blacker, Gareth, 36, 38–39, 108–110
Blair, Tony, 51
Blake, Geraldine, 115
Blears, Hazel, 85
BNP (British National Party), 13, 55, 114
BOA (British Olympic Authority), 35
Bolt, Usain, 154
'Bonfire of the quangos, the', 164
Brady, Karren, 161, 186
Brickell, Paul, 53, 55, 57–60, 194–195
British Cycling, 192
Broadcasting Centre. *See* Press and Broadcast Centres
Bromley-by-Bow, 53, 70, 198
Brownfield sites, 22
Bryant and May, 40
BT Sport, 209
BT Tower, 165, 169
Buckinghamshire New University, 188
Building heights, 71
Burdett, Ricky, 143–144
Business
  communities, 98, 137
  opportunities, 203

C

Cabinet, The, 8, 10
  Cabinet Office, 114
Caborn, Richard, 34–35
Cameron, David, 13, 182
Canals, 39–41

Canary Wharf, 6, 131
Candidate File, 62
Canning Town, 90
Capitalism, 30
Car parking, 70
Carpenters Estate, 211
Channel Tunnel, 60
Character areas, **70–71,** 75, 88, 97
Childcare, 46
Childrens' play areas, 71–73
Chobham Manor, 189, 191–192, 210
City Airport, 60
City Hall, 159, 165
Class, social, 16
  middle class, 10, 12, 44, 45, 47–48, 145
  working class, 7, 12, 16, 22, 31, 43, 45, 48–49, 56, 62, 90, 93
  working class history, 62
  See also Communities
Clays Lane Housing Cooperative, 191
Coe, Lord Sebastian, 33, 34
Coleman, Neale, 13, 105
Common land, 41–42
Commonwealth Games, 21, 46
Communications Team (Comms.), **134–137,** 142–145, 166–169
Communities, 56, 78, 98, 190–192
  centres, 55, 200
  groups, 38, 169, 218
  organisations, 49, 55, 56, 76, 87, 90, 115, 216
  social, 56
Community Benefit Clause, 175

Community Hubs, 194–195, 219
Community Land Trust, 192
Community-led planning, 52–58
Community Links, 115, 117
Community Planning, 55
Community workshops, 97–101
CompeteFor, 46
Comprehensive Spending Review (CSR), 165, 170
Connectivity, 69
Conservative Party (Tories), 12–13, 15, 182
   coalition government, 156, 164
   See also Cameron, David; Johnson, Boris
Construction, 37, 41, 43, 44, 46–47, 55, 57, 62, 64, 80, 84, 86, 94, 163, 191, 202
Consultation, 81–82
'Convergence', 139–140
   Convergence Action Plan, 175, 197
Coombe, Christopher, 115
'Copper Box', 182
CPO (Compulsory Purchase Order), 38
Creative industries, 63, 189, 200, 209
Crescent, The, 177
   Georgian-style housing, 168, 170, 178, 192
Crime, 41, 142, 195–196
Crossrail, 60
Crystal Palace, 153
Cultural activities, 46, 70, 209
Cultural Olympiad, 46
Cycling, 170–171, 192

D
DCLG (Department of Communities and Local Government), 7, 118, 130, 165
DCMS (Department of Culture, Media and Sport), 10, 33, 118
DDC (Docklands Development Corporation), 166
Debts, 32
   National Lottery, 110, 130–131, 166
   Olympic, 67, 72, 129–131, 166
Democracy, 56, 104, 123
Deprivation, 141
Deregulation, 13
Design Advisor, 144
Design and Planning, 64, 133, 145–147, 191
Design-led Review process, 149, 167, 170, 172–173, 178, 183, 192, 210, 215, 216
Design Team, 146, 195, 197
Developers, 28, 56, 63, 130
Development platforms, 67, 70, 72, 119
Devolution, 182
Digital industries, 189
Dikstra, Richard, 94–97
Displacement, 11, 38, 39, 43, 44, 171, 191, 211, 218
   eviction, 44
Diversity, 76, 91
DLR (Docklands Light Railway), 53, 82
Docklands, 22–23
Docks, 37–39, 58

Doocey, Dee, 149, 186
Draper's Field, 199
Dutton, Jonathan, 204
DWP (Department for Work and Pensions), 140

E
East London, 48, 56, 159, 161–162, 176, 195, 212, 215–218
  East End, 7, 10, 15, 16, 28, 29, 31, 35, 38, 40, 43, 48, 49, 52–53, 57–58, 60, 76, 83, 116, 132, 137, 156
  East Enders, 10, 99, 190
  See also Greenwich, London Borough of; Hackney, London Borough of; Lower Lea valley; Newham, London Borough of; Tech City; Tower Hamlets, London Borough of; Waltham Forest, London Borough of
East London Tech City, 176, 177
Eastway Cycle Circuit, 41, 171
Eastway Users Group, 171–172, 192
Economy
  industry, 13, 93, 117
  knowledge, 12, 31, 209
  post-industrial, 10, 12, 16, 29, 40–41, 59, 72, 92
    community, sense of, 48, 56
  policy, 30–31
  service, 12, 30–31
  social, 46–47
  'trickle down', 23, 214
  urban, 7, 12, 21, 22, 25, 28, 31–32, 41, 53, 56, 61, 85–86, 89, 91, 132, 178, 211, 214, 219–220
EDAW (Eckbo, Dean, Austin and Williams), 51, 60, 63–64, 72, 106, 144–145
Education, 63, 70, 77, 82, 89, 195, 200
Education and Cultural Quarter, 209
  Sadlers Wells, 209
  Smithsonian, The, 209
  University of the Arts (London College of Fashion), 209
  Victoria and Albert Museum, 209
ELBA (East London Business Alliance), 93–95, 115
Electricity pylons, 61, 62
Electronics, 40
Employment, 31, 47, 61, 175, 195, 210
  apprenticeships, 47, 187, 200, 203
  Ford speech, 189
  Legacy Community Scheme, 191
  Output C, 67, 70
  SRF, 140
  Wick Master Plan, 93
  worklessness, 46, 140, 142
EMT (Executive Management Team), 133
Enclosure, of land, 42
Entrepreneurs, 176
Environment, 22, 29, 30, 41, 43, 47, 56, 63, 64, 76, 82, 88, 89, 116, 196
  wildlife, 41, 43
Equality, 59

Essex County Cricket Club, 188
Estates and Facilities Management, 163, 189
Ethnicity, 44, 46, 55, 69
EU (European Union), 136, 185, 187
European Commission, 184
European elections, 114
European Parliament, 114
Events, staging of, 47–48
ExCel Centre, 60
Expressions of Interest, 136, 137, 163, 165, 176
Eyres, Laura, 135–136

F

Faith groups, 69
Faraday, Michael, 40
Fawcett, Eleanor, 197–203
Finance, 157–161
  financial capitalism, 26, 30
Fisher, Graham, 115
Fish Island, 70
Focus E15, 211
Football, 34–35, 157–163, 209
  See also individually named clubs; Olympic Stadium
Ford, Baroness Margaret
  Olympic stadium, 155, 163
  OPLC, 104–107, 129–130, 133, 135–137, 181
  See also OPLC
Forman, Charlie, 170
Freedom of Information, 209
Fringe Masterplans (Master Plans), 70, 105, 166, 199, 214
Fundamental (architectural centre), 82

Funding, 61, 63, 84, 105, 116, 118, 134, 140, 165, 219
  CSR, 170–171
  private sector, 89–91, 109
  project, 46, 53
  public sector, 24, 33, 80, 89–90, 146, 165, 204
  See also Fawcett, Eleanor; Livingstone, Ken; National Lottery (Lottery)

G

Gainsborough Primary School, 42
Games Monitor, 42
Gardeners, 43–45
  See also Allotments; Manor Garden Allotment Society
General Election, 130
Gentrification, 111, 149, 178
Geographical features, 66, 147
Georgian housing, 148
  Georgian-style housing, 168, 170, 178, 192
Germany, 31, 96, 97
GLA (Greater London Authority), 15–16, 105, 130, 140–141, 166, 196
GLC (Greater London Council), 14
GOE (Government Olympic Executive), 10, 115
Gold, David, 160
Government
  central, 10, 13, 23, 27, 32, 41, 93, 129, 130, 132, 140, 163–166, 170, 175, 176, 184, 185, 190, 208, 217

Government (*cont.*)
  local, 9, 27, 30, 52, 56, 65, 85, 108, 118, 130, 132, 144, 159, 160, 165, 195, 214
Gravel supplies, 40
Green Belt, 41
Green spaces, 63
Greenway, The, 84
Greenwich Leisure Limited, 189
Greenwich, London Borough of, 27, 152
  See also Host boroughs

H

Habitats, wildlife, 41
Hackney, London Borough of, 27, 52, 62, 70, 92–97, 125, 170–171, 192, 217
  allotments, 43–45
  See also Host boroughs; Tech City
Hackney Marshes, 41–42
Hackney Wick, 70, 88, 92, 177, 198, 200, 203
Hackney Wick Dog Track, 62
Haringey (London borough of), 153
  Haringey Council, 159, 161, 187
Harton, Mark, 44
Haves, Rebecca, 104
HCA (Homes and Communities Agency), 114, 196
Health, 59, 63, 69, 195–196, 1410
Hearn, Barry, 161–163, 187
'Helter Skelter', 113
  See also Orbit, The
Here East, 209
Heritage, 112, 218
  industrial, 31, 61

Higher education, 119, 142–145, 176
Historical legacy, 117–118
Hog Hill, 41, 171
Hospitality, 175
Host boroughs, 58, 85, 105, 108, 117, 123, 133, 140–141
  housing, 140, 148
  See also Fawcett, Eleanor; Johnson, Boris; Newton, Geoff; Russell, Tom; SRF
Host Boroughs of the Olympic Games, 52
Host Boroughs Unit, 108, 112–113, 196–197
  Convergence Action Plan, 174
  See also Taylor, Roger
Host Cities
  Athens, 4
  Barcelona, 4
  Rio, vii
  Sydney, 4, 42
Housing, 29–30
  Chobham Manor, 191–192
  'churn', 68, 91
  Convergence Action Plan, 195–195
  densities, 29, 111, 112, 148, 215
  EDAW, 147–148
  Georgian style, 168, 178
  high density, 130, 139–140
  Johnson, 182
  overcrowding, 68, 140, 142, 196
  policy, 67, 68
  social, 31, 56–58, 67, 98, 195–196, 210
  Stratford Waterfront, 210–211
Housing estates, 48–49

I

IAAF (International Association of Athletics Federations), 185
ICA (Institute of Contemporary Arts), 8
IKEA retail group, 191
Inclusivity, 46
Industrial sites, 61
Industries, 13, 117
  creative, 63, 200, 209
  digital, 189
  higher education, 93
  historical, 39–40
  Lower Lee Valley (area), 39–41
  See also Higher Education; Tech City
Infrastructure, 63
  social infrastructure, 63, 66, **68–70**, 88, 148, 191
Innes, Duncan, 191
International Rail Line, 60
Investors, 28, 56, 61
IOC (International Olympic Committee), 34, 47, 61–62, 167
IRA (Irish Republican Army), 51
Iron works, 39–40
Isle of Dogs, 125

J

Jasper, Lee, 15
JobCentre Plus, 140
Johnson, Boris, 14, 27–28, 36, 49, 176, 181–182
Joint Planning Advisory Team, 52

Jowell, *Dame* Tessa, 8–12, 17, 155–157, 182, 208
  See also DCMS; SPAD
Jubilee Line, 60
Judicial Reviews, 183–187

K

Kapoor, Anish, 163
KCAP (Kees Christiaanse Architects and Planners), 62, 173
Kennedy, Chris, 92–94

L

Labour Party, 9, 12, 15
  Blairites, 5
  Councillors, 53
  New Labour, 12, 14, 16, 23, 33, 91, 164, 166, 188
  Old Labour, 5
Land acquisition (land assembly), 37–39, 129–130, 137, 218
Land decontamination, 148
Land enclosures, 42
Land Team, 37, 64, 72, 86, 109
Land use, 61–62
Law firms, 136, 186, 214
LCS (Legacy Communities Scheme), 197
LDA (London Development Agency), 6, 45–46, 49, 52, 60
  Blacker, 109–110
  debts, 129–131, 133–134, 165
  land acquisition, 62–64
  Livingstone, 15–17

LDA (London Development Agency) (*cont.*)
  Olympic legacy, 72, 77, 105
  See also May, Michelle; OPLC; Russell, Tom
Lea Bank Square, 42, 94
Lea Navigation Canal, 42
Leaside Regeneration, 55, 81
Legacy Board of Advisors, 36, 49
Legacy Communities Scheme, 190–192
Legacy Directorate, 6, 15–17, 28, 32, 37, 45–47, 49–51, 57, 60, 64, 67, 69, 72, 75, 77, 79, 80, 83, 85, 87–90, 104, 105, 109–111, 113, 120, 123, 131, 133, 135, 139, 141, 147, 149, 219
Legacy Lectures, 142–145
Legacy Master Plan Framework (LMF), **65–70,** 87–89, 91, 110–112, 119, 172–173, 210, 214
  Chobham Manor, 189–191
  consultation process, 81–83
  Haves, 104
  Leyton Orient, 162–163
  review process, cost of, 146–147
  Velodrome, the, 192
  Williams, 119
  See also Altman, Andrew; Blacker, Gareth; Character areas; Ford, Baroness Margaret; Output C; Wheelhouse, Emma
'Legacy Now', 46
Legacy promises, 21, 26, 33, 43, 50, 215
Legacy Youth Panel, 82–83
Legal actions, threats of, 158, 162

Legal costs, 186–187
Legal firms, 136, 186, 214
  legacy, 186–187
Lehman Brothers, 6
Leibowitz, Alan, 115
Leisure, 61, 70, 175
LETF (Local Area Training Framework), 86
Levy, Daniel, 157, 158
Leyton, 62, 125, 199
Leyton Orient FC, 161–163, 171, 188, 209
  Judicial Review, 183–187
  threaten legal action, 158–159
Life Island, 44
Lifetime Homes, 68
Live Nation, 152
Livingstone, Ken, 14–16, 34–36
  See also LDA; Olympic Bid
Living Wage, 56–57
LLDC (London Legacy Development Corporation), 187–190, 202–204, 212
LLV (Lower Lea Valley), 68
LMF (Legacy Master Plan Framework), **65–70,** 87–89, 91, 110–112, 119, 172–173, 210, 214
Local dynamics, 219
Local issues, 122
Local leaders, 57, 88
Local residents, 22, 55, 62, 67, 76, 77, 87, 97, 121, 192, 208, 210
Lock, John, 59–60, 88–91, 119
LOCOG (London Organising Committee of the Olympic Games), 33, 47, 56, 78, 115, 214

London
  development, 168
  Plan, 28–30, 62, 195, 210, 215
  2012, viii, 6, 7, 10, 11, 167, 169, 188
London Assembly, The, 131, 165, 166
London Citizens, 192
London Docklands, 60
London School of Economics (LSE), 143, 144
London Underground, 199
Lower Lea Valley (area), **39–43**, 52, 58, 66, 119, 218
  Fawcett, 197–198, 200–201
  housing, 67–68
  industrial history, 117
  Olympic stadium, 183
  Output C, 112
  regeneration, 72
  SRF, 140
  Water City, 60–63
LSC (Learning and Skills Council), 140
LSE (London School of Economics), 143, 144
  See also Legacy Lectures
LTGDC (London Thames Gateway Development Corporation), 60, 62, 84, 175
LVRPA (Lea Valley Regional Park Authority), 162

M
MAA (Multi Area Agreement), 89
Manchester, 21–23, 33–36, 95
  city centre, 21, 51

East Manchester, 21–23, 31
  See also Commonwealth Games; IRA; Russell, Tom; SRF; Taylor, Roger
Manchester City FC, 21, 94
Man, Irene, 172
Manor Garden Allotment Society, 43–45, 191, 211
Manufacturing, 39–41
Market gardening, 40
Master-planning, 51, 61–66, 69, 72, 81, 83, 109, 146–147, 170, 183, 219
  See also AECOM; EDAW; KCAP
Mawson, Lord Andrew, 53, 58–59
May, Michelle, 85–87, 138, 174–175, 193–194
Mayoral elections. See Johnson, Boris; Livingstone, Ken; Pipe, Jules; Wales, Sir Robin
Mayors
  Hackney, 93, 133, 170
  London, 6, 30, 41, 52, 61, 62, 91, 106, 113, 120, 129, 130–132, 139–141, 163–167, 173, 183–185, 187–189, 195, 196–197, 204, 208, 210–212
  See also Johnson, Boris; Livingstone, Ken
  Newham, 53, 133, 153, 160
McNevin, Niall, 170
MDC (Mayoral Development Corporation), 164–166, 175, 181, 202
Media, 76–77
  media industry, 10, 26, 38, 46, 70, 78, 80, 88, 176–178, 209

Media (*cont.*)
  press, 8, 11, 15, 80, 92, 105, 108, 110, 113, 118, 135, 136, 145, 151, 157, 158, 160, 169, 173, 188, 203
  See also Media Centre; Press and Broadcast Centres
Media Centre, 92–97
Mega-events, 47, 48
Memorandum of Understanding, 130, 165
Millenium Dome, 33, 60
Mittal, Lakshmi, 163
MOL (Metropolitan Open Land), 41–42, 71, 170–172
Money market, 96
Moylan, Daniel, 188
Moynihan, Lord Colin, 35
Multi-Use Arena, 182, 189

N
National Lottery (Lottery), 130–131, 166
National Vocational Qualification (NVQ), 142
Navigant Consulting, 139
Neighbourhoods, 61, 68–71, 195–196
  working class, 12, 22, 31, 48–49, 56, 90
  See also Character areas; Chobham Manor
NEM (New East Manchester), 23
Netherlands, 64
Newham Council, 151–154, 156, 159–160, 183–185, 187, 211
Newham, London Borough of, 27, 52–53, 98, 115, 117, 217

Greenway (cycle route), 84
University College of London, 210–211
West Ham (town centre), 198
  See also Host boroughs; Lock, John; Olympic Stadium
New Labour, 13, 33, 90
  See also Livingstone, Ken
Newton, Geoff, 46, 49, 72, 87, 138
Northern Olympic Fringe, 69–70
NVQ (National Vocational Qualification), 142

O
O^2, 60
OAPDF (Opportunity Area Planning Development Framework), 68, 198
ODA (Olympic Delivery Authority), 37, 45, 47, 62, 83–84, 155
  Kennedy, 94
  Legacy Company, 189
  West, 121
  Wheelhouse, 78
Old Ford, 70
Olympic Broadcast and Press Centre, 62
Olympic debts, 32, 72, 129–131
Olympic Games, 12–14, 26, 33, 34, 40, 42, 45, 47, 52, 57, 59, 78, 94, 104, 155, 182, 189, 208, 219
Olympic Host Boroughs Unit, 173–176
Olympicopolis (scheme), 209, 211
Olympic Opportunities, **45–50**, 85, 87, 138, 215

Olympic Park, 37–39, 71–72, 142
  Park, The, 112, 138, 162, 170, 193, 202, 203
  Queen Elizabeth Olympic Park, 167, 188, 197, 202
Olympic Park Legacy Company. *See* OPLC
Olympic, planning, 6, 25, 47, 57, 62, 214–217
Olympic Planning Permissions, 62
Olympic Quarter, 70
Olympic Stadium, **32–37**, 151–157, 159–161, 181, 183–190
  Communications Team (Comms.), 136–137
  financial matters, 157–161
  LMF, 117
  white elephant, 7, 21, 32, 34
Olympic Village, 109, 173, 191
Open spaces, 68–69, 71–72
OPLC (Olympic Park Legacy Company), 104–106, 109–110, 114, 118, 123, 126, 129–131, **132–134**, 135–149, 151–167, 174–176, 183–188, 190, 191–193, 195, 197–198, 201–202, 204, 213–214, 217, 219
  See also Altman, Andrew; Ford, Baroness Margaret; LMF; West, Karen
OPRSG (Olympic Park Regeneration Steering Group), 87, 142
Orbit, The, 113, 163, 165, 191, 211
  Kapoor, 163
  Mittal, 163

Outline Planning Applications, 52
Output C, 66, 69, **72–73**, 89–90, 165
  See also LMF

P

Paralympians, 154
Parklands, 73–74
Part buy/rent housing, 69
Partnerships, private-public sector, 48
PCT (Primary Care Trust), 61
Personal Best, 48
Pink Brochure, The, 166–169
Pipe, Jules, 93, 133, 170
Place making, 65, 112, 199
Planning
  applications, 51, 52, 60, 61, 64, 65, 106, 110, 172, 192, 202
  'character areas', 69–71
  community-led, 52–58
  early, 61–64
  legacy, 65–68
  LMF, 65–68, 166–169
  Olympic Park, 71–72
  urban, 58–61, 68–70
  See also EDAW
Play spaces, 68–69
Political interest, 80
Poplar HARCA, 53
Population, 69
  growth, 29
Post-industrial Britain, 30
Post-industrial cities, 23
Post-Industrial Economic Policy, 30–31

Poverty, 29, 49, 91, 115–116, 132
  Lock, 91
  political background, 12–13
  SRF, 141–142, 195–196
Power, generation of, 40
Premier League, (football). *See* Football
Press and Broadcast Centres, 62, 92, 134, 165, 176–177, 187, 189, 203, 209, 213, 217
  legacy, 187, 189
Private sector, 27, 46, 81, 92, 93, 114, 198
Private sector funding, 89–91, 109
Procurement process, 174
Property, 22, 23, 47, 67, 134, 166, 168, 191, 210, 215
Public realm, 139, 171–172, 195–200
Public sector funding, 24, 33, 146, 165, 204
Public service, 26, 75, 88, 89, 111
Pudding Mill, 70, 84, 211

Q

Queen Elizabeth Olympic Park, 167, 188, 197, 202

R

Racial tensions, 55
RDA (Regional Development Authority), 164, 175
Real Estate Team, 175
Recession, 182
Recreational areas, 54

Regeneration, 21–22, **84–87**, 149, 200, 202–204, 212–217
  cultural and arts, 46
  early planning, 62–63, 69, 71–72
  EDAW, 147
  Fawcett, 197–205
  fears, 98
  Livingstone, 15
  LMF, 111
  London Assembly, 166–167
  Olympic stadium, 183, 188–189
  OPLC, 131, 149
  Regeneration Team, 193–194
  Russell, 7
  SRF, 139–142
  Sumray, 52–53
  urban development, 55–56
  West, 124
  Wheelhouse, 76–77, 79–81, 137–141
Regeneration Team, 193–197
Religious groups, 69
Relocation, 38
Retail Academy, 175
Retail space, 63, 70
Revitalisation, 59
Rio Games, vii
Rivers
  Channelsea, 43
  Lea, 6, 39, 43, 170, 171, 192
    See also Lower Lea Valley
  Thames, 39, 48, 60, 152
Rogers, Richard, 99, 174
Royal Docks, 60
RSL (Registered Social Landlord), 67
Russell, Tom, 38, 118
  Canary Wharf, 7–8, 17
  Legacy Directorate, 51, 67

Manchester, 21–24
SRF, 27–28, 35–36
Ryner, David, 6, 8–12, 17, 114, 117–118

S

Sand supplies, 40
Scheme Fix, 64, 106
School leavers, 175, 210
Schools, 68–69, 208
Security fences, 44, 78, 219
Select Committees, 137
Service economy, 12, 30–31
Services, procurement of, 146
Shipbuilding, 39–41
Shopping centres, 132
   See also Westfield Shopping Mall
Shoreditch, 176, 177
Silicon Valley, 176
Singapore, 14
Site limitations, 66, 147
Skills and training, 46, 140, 142, 175, 210
Smith, Chris, 33
Social attitudes, 48
Social care, 69
Social enterprise hub, 175
Social housing, 31, 55–58, 67, 98, 195–196, 210
Social infrastructure, 68–70, 191
Socio-economics, 111, 115, **137–139,** 143, 174–176
Southbank, 65–66, 164
Space (organisation), 115
   Space Studios, 200
SPAD (Special Advisor), 8–10, 13, 17, 117

Sport England, 121–122
Sporting participation, 46, 49, 134, 139, 155, 195, 208
Sporting venues, 71–72
   See also Aquatics Centre; 'Copper Box'; Multi-use Arena; Olympic Stadium; Velodrome, The, (cycling circuit
SPV (Special Purpose Vehicle), 90, 104, 110–111, 114, 184, 188
SRB (Single Regeneration Budget), 92
SRF (Strategic Regeneration Framework), 22, 69–71, 84–88, **139–144,** 195, 212–214
   Host Boroughs Unit, 85
   OPLC, 105
   Output C, 88–89, 112
   remit, 21–22, 27, 30
Stakeholders, 63, 79, 115, 216
State aid, 183
Stendall, Chris, 115
Stratford, 59, 69–70, 131
Stratford High Street, 70, 193
Stratford Shopping Centre, 131–132
   See also Westfield Shopping Mall
Stratford Village, 70, 191
Stratford Waterfront, 70, 210
Sugarhouse Lane, 70, 191
Sugar, *Lord* Alan, 161
Sullivan, David, 160
Sumray, Richard, 52
Sustainability, 45–50, 160, 178

T

TAG (Teviot Action Group), 55
Taylor, Roger, 85, 108, 115, 139, 141–144, 175–176
Tech City, 176–178
Technical documents, 63
Technical workshops, 88–92
TELCO (The East London Communities Organisation), 56
Tesco, 198
Teviot Estate, 53
TfL (Transport for London), 198
Thatcher, *Baroness* Margaret, 98
Three Mills, 70
Three Mills Estate, 70, 165
Tottenham Hotspurs FC (Spurs), 34, 151–155
   Judicial Review, 183–187
   threaten legal action, 158–159
   White Hart Lane, 153, 159
Tourism, 70, 113, 119
Tower Hamlets, London Borough of, 27, 52–53, 61–62, 84, 115, 198
   See also Host boroughs; Mawson, Lord Andrew; West, Karen
Townsend, Crissy, 53–55, 57
Toynbee Hall, 115
Transport, 39–41, 55, 63, 182
Treasury, The, 110, 130
Trees, 42

U

UDC (Urban Development Corporation), 22
UEL (University of East London), 59–60, 88–89, 119
UK Athletics, 33, 151–156, 209
United Kingdom Independence Party (UKIP), 114
University College of London, 210–211
University of East London, 188
Urban change, 58–60
Urban development, 30
Urban Development Corporation, 166
Urban fabric, 61, 69
'Urban stitches', 68–70
URC (Urban Regeneration Corporation), 23, 27, 36

V

Velodrome, The, (cycling circuit), 170, 190
View Tube, 83–84
Villiers, Arthur, 43
Vision
   vision launch, 169–170, 173
   vision statement, 61, 108
   See also Olympic Park
Visitors, 111, 119
   experience, 116–117, 134, 155, 195
Volunteers, 46

W

Wales, Sir Robin, 53, 133, 153, 160
Waltham Forest, London Borough of, 27, 52, 61–62, 199
   See also Host boroughs; Taylor, Roger

Warehouse spaces, 92, 115, 200
Warner, Ed, 151–153
Water City, 61–63
Waterways, 63, 66
Webb, Karen, 166–169
Wellcome Trust, 190
Welton, Peter, 115
Wembley, 33, 158
Westfield Shopping Mall, 116, 132, 175, 188
West Ham (town centre), 198
West Ham United FC, 151, 157, 159–162, 209
  first bid, 34
  Judicial Review, 183–187
  UK Athletics, 152–155
West, Karen, 120–125
Westminster, 8–10
Wheelhouse, Emma, **75–83,** 103–108, 137–139, 142, 145, 191
Eastway Users Group, 171–172
Regeneration Team, 193–194
See also Communications Team (Comms.)
White Building, 200
Whitehall, 8–10
White Hart Lane, 153, 159
Wildlife habitats, 41
Williams, Adam, 103, 105–107, 118–120, 146–147, 170, 173
Workshops, 88–92, 97–101
World Athletics Championship, 33, 155

Y

Young people, 175, 210

MIX
Papier aus verantwortungsvollen Quellen
Paper from responsible sources
FSC® C105338

Printed by Books on Demand, Germany